D1665310

East Asia and Eastern Europe in a Globalized Perspective

Ordnungspolitische Dialoge

Herausgegeben von
Bernhard Seliger, Jüri Sepp und Ralph Wrobel

Band 5

Bernhard Seliger / Jüri Sepp / Ralph Wrobel (eds.)

East Asia and Eastern Europe in a Globalized Perspective

Lessons from Korea and Estonia

Bibliographic Information published by the Deutsche Nationalbibliothek
The Deutsche Nationalbibliothek lists this publication in the Deutsche Nationalbibliografie; detailed bibliographic data is available in the internet at http://dnb.d-nb.de.

This book was supported by a grant of the Academy of Korean Studies in Korea.

Cover illustrations: © Ralph Wrobel

Library of Congress Cataloging-in-Publication Data
East Asia and Eastern Europe in a globalized perspective : lessons from Korea and Estonia / Bernhard Seliger, Jüri Sepp, Ralph Wrobel (eds.).
    pages cm. -- (Ordnungspolitische Dialoge ; Band 5)
  Includes index.
  ISBN 978-3-631-66860-3
  1. Economic development–East Asia. 2. Economic development–Europe, Eastern. 3. Economic development–Korea (South–Case studies. 4. Economic development–Estonia–Case studies. 5. Korea (South)–Economic conditions–21st century. 6. Estonia–Economic conditions–21st century. I. Seliger, Bernhard, 1970- editor. II. Sepp, Jüri editor. III. Wrobel, Ralph Michael, editor.
  HC460.5.E235 2015
  338.94798–dc23
                            2015032611

ISSN 1868-7989
ISBN 978-3-631-66860-3 (Print)
E-ISBN 978-3-653-06228-1 (E-Book)
DOI 10.3726/978-3-653-06228-1

© Peter Lang GmbH
Internationaler Verlag der Wissenschaften
Frankfurt am Main 2015
All rights reserved.
PL Academic Research is an Imprint of Peter Lang GmbH.

Peter Lang – Frankfurt am Main · Bern · Bruxelles · New York · Oxford · Warszawa · Wien

This publication has been peer reviewed.

www.peterlang.com

Foreword

"[I]t is necessary to have a strong state—impartial and powerful—standing above the mêlée of economic interests, quite contrary to the widely held opinion that "capitalism" can thrive only where there is a weak government. The state must not only be strong; unmoved by ideologies of whatever brand, it must clearly recognize its task: to defend "capitalism" against the "capitalists" as often as they try to travel a more comfortable road to profit than the one indicated by the sign "principle of service" and to shift their losses onto the shoulders of the community."

Wilhelm Röpke (1936/ 1963), pp. 236–237.

The development experience of states in the 20th century at the first glance offers a bewildering variety and often downright contradicting models, which nevertheless led to catching-up and rapid growth rates, leaving policy-makers in countries trying to emulate such models at a loss. Take, for example, the contradicting cases of West Germany after World War II and South Korea under Park Chung-Hee. West Germany embarked on a path of liberalization of markets under its system of Social Market Economy and "order policy" (*Ordnungspolitik*). South Korea, though studying and sometimes explicitly referring to the West German experience, on the contrary, used a model of state-led development to achieve the goal of rapid development. And both, though using starkly contradicting policy prescriptions, were very successful. In Germany, the unleashing of market forces from decades of intervention brought the "economic miracle", the rapid recovery from war-time scars in less than a decade. In South Korea, state-led development in an authoritarian setting brought a skyrocketing from the bottom into the upper third of countries in terms of GDP. Central and Eastern European states in their development choices after the change from centrally-planned economies certainly first looked West. This had cultural and historical, political and economic reasons. None the least, requirements of the joint rules of the European Communities which these countries wanted to join as soon as possible made such a choice looking natural. However, over time and through various crises on the regional and worldwide level, increasingly the experience of East Asian states became an interesting object of study. This was related as well to the successful long-term growth experience of countries like South Korea, but also the successful models of state transformation there, which, though in a different political setting, achieved high growth rates without the deep transformation recession typical for European transformation states.

Since economists, used at optimizing, are uneasy with such a divergent growth experience, various explanations have been forwarded to reconcile these seemingly contradictory results. One of them is that different stages of economic development need different institutional settings, and in this sense that South Korea in the 1960s were rather comparable to Germany in the late 19th century. Another one is that there is no single institutional optimum, but there are several peaks. This again might be related to institutional embeddedness and informal institutions. Looking at these explanations by "models", one tends to forget that these are themselves not given entities, but in a constant flux. Germany, facing enormous difficulties after its unification, embarked on a long search of a new economic model, which resulted in at least two ousted governments and a comprehensive overhaul of the social sector, before suddenly, helped by external circumstances of the Euro crisis, the reversal of capital flows made the German "model" once again look much better and stronger. Korea itself, though serving since the last decade increasingly as an admired role model for developing states, feels an urgency of the decoupling of growth and the fate of ordinary citizens, leading to strong calls for a new economic model, which was echoed and widely discussed after a McKinsey Report in 2013 (Choi et al. 2013). Ironically, again it chose Germany as a model to emulate, citing its strength in the "creative economy", in particular the role of SME and the sound system of vocational training. But the exact way, how this system works, how it can be understood as a role model, and how it might be used as a prescription in a different institutional setting, is contested.

Most of the papers in this collection were first presented at the *5th Dialogue on Social Market Economy:* East Asia and Eastern Europe in a globalized perspective: Lessons from Korea and Estonia at the University of Tartu, Estonia, on April 24–27, 2013. The South Korean economy lived through very tough times in the past two decades: after the Asian crisis of 1997 and 1998 unraveled the old Korean growth model, a spectacular recovery followed around the turn of the millennium. However, soon the world financial and economic crisis hit Korea hard. Though it could escape from a recession and even grew slightly in 2008, the main crisis year, the Korean economy with its dependence on exports was facing a tremendous challenge. At the same time, South Korea became a leading member of the G20 and hosted the 2009 summit of this powerful organization. All the time, the North Korean threat hung like a Damocles sword over the region, hampering severely South Korean economic stability. This was the background for the conference, which was made possible by a generous grant of the Academy of Korean Studies in Korea. It brought together European, American, Asian and Korean scholars to discuss the potential lessons from economic development of Korea and Estonia.

In the first chapter, Ralph Wrobel discusses economic models for new industrializing countries in comparative perspective. Catching-up has been shaped by internal and external factors, for example the acceptance of a set of rules called "*acquis communautaire*" (joint rules) for states seeking membership of the European Union. This concerns first of all the "big choice" of seeking a more market-oriented or a more authoritarian type of economic development model. Some economists have recently argued that for the poorest countries for former choice might not work. However, even in the set of countries choosing the market-oriented model still there is a need for a more fine-tuned model of economic institutions. There is not one such model, but rather a selection of potential models helping them to find adaptive institutions for their own catching-up process. Sung-Jo Park in the second chapter revisits the experience of the developmental state in South Korea in the 1960s and 1970s. He focuses on the birth of the development state, and in particular the role of economic governance played by state organizations like the Economic Planning Board, and private organizations like the big business Federation of Korean Industry in shaping Korea's model of guided corporatism, but also on the strategic choices balanced versus unbalanced growth and import substation versus export orientation, looking in details into this crucial period of Korea's institutional and industrial development.

In chapter 3, Janno Reiljan and Ingra Paltser take a sectoral look at the implementation of R&D policies in European and Asian countries. They compare national innovation systems of 27 EU members states, Croatia, Turkey, Iceland, Norway, Switzerland, and the East Asian states South Korea, China and Japan. The creation of favorable institutions and organizations promoting R&D is a task of the public sector. Herman W. Hoen in chapter 4 looks at the question if globalization leads to institutional convergence between European and Asian economic models, in particular through the pressure exerted by the financial crises of the late 1990s and the late 2000s, respectively. However, he does not find institutional convergence between the two large blocs of economic systems he labels coordinated vs. liberal market economies. Karmo Kroos in chapter 5 analyses the role of the welfare sector in developmental states in East Asia, in particular Korea. While the welfare regime, which includes the educational sector, in the time of development was rather "suppressed" according to his analysis, this led to an accumulation of challenges and problems which in the case of South Korea might be considered an explosive mixture, in particular in the educational sector.

In chapter 6 Joachim Ahrens and Manuel Stark look at the peculiar role, independent organizations play in authoritarian regimes, which at the first glance might seem as self-contradictory. As well in authoritarian regimes in general as in the developmental-state-type authoritarian regimes they tend to exist and play an important role. This role is, however, fundamentally different. Authoritarian governments of so-called developmental states have effectively used (relatively) independent organizations in order to implement market-oriented reforms, to improve private-sector coordination, and to foster economic growth and development in the long run. In other authoritarian regimes, they may exist to serve the interests of the ruling elites. Chapter 7 by Erik Terk deals with the "practice of catching-up". Terk compares three East Asian states, South Korea, Taiwan and Singapore, and three Central and Eastern European states, Slovenia, the Czech Republic and Estonia, which are all considered relatively successful in their setting as being fast in catching up. He predicts that the capital accumulation achieved in earlier phases of catching up are declining through the expansion of democratic participation which impedes the mobilization of resources. In chapter 8 Jüri Sepp and Uku Varblane decompose the productivity gap between Estonia and South Korea. While both countries try to master the challenge of closing the gap between them and the richest countries in the world, South Korea has not only a head start in terms of a much earlier start of this race, but also exhibits much higher aggregated productivity. As Sepp and Varblane show, this is especially true for the manufacturing industry and the public sector, while in the service industry Korea's performance is considerably weaker. In both countries, financial intermediation and real estate shows a high productivity.

Chapter 9 by Jüri Sepp, Helje Kaldaru and Jürgen Joamets compares the economic structures of Estonia and South Korea vis-à-vis the other OECD countries. Both can be considered as manufacturing states, with a relatively high share of industry, though the specialization of South Korea together with countries like Germany is in high-tech manufacturing, while the Estonian specialization, together with countries like Portugal, is in relatively lower-tech manufacturing. The last chapter (10) by Bernhard Seliger, a reprint from the Handbook of Emerging Economies, once again looks at the South Korean development way, which underwent quite dramatically different evaluations over time: being considered successful until its entry into OECD as its 29th member in 1996, only a year later the East Asian crisis brought critiques of "crony capitalism". However, a few years later South Korea made not only a splendid come-back, but also emerged largely unscarred from the global financial crisis of 2008. In contrast to this outside evaluation, however, South Koreans feel an acute sense of crisis regarding their own economic model.

South Korea and Central and Eastern Europe faced stark choices when starting their respective catching-up process. For other countries, institutional choices were less stark, but still were and are relevant, beyond simple piecemeal engineering of certain microeconomic or macroeconomic variables. The conference, which was the fifth conference in the series "Dialogues on Social Market Economy", organized by Prof. Dr. Jüri Sepp, PD Dr. Bernhard Seliger and Prof. Dr. Ralph Wrobel, showed that the debate about economic systems, though today rather neglected in many economic curricula, still is raging and indeed came to the forefront of economic policy-making again after the world financial crisis, though often disguised in much more limited terms like reform of the financial sector. The cross-regional comparative study of problems, here that of Korea and Estonia, was a very useful approach; not in the meaning of a one-way relationship but as a source of comparative learning.

Many people helped to organize successfully the conference as well as finish this book. We would like to thank Tim Bork, and, in particular, André Gottwald, for producing the manuscript of the book.

The role of the state, as already Röpke pointed out in his book on the Economics of the Free Society, written in the dark years of exile from National Socialism, has to be strong, but strong in the sense of defending the market. "Our economic system is misunderstood by most people probably because they regard certain of its more puzzling phenomena as harmful and senseless outgrowths of "capitalism", as he remarks (Röpke 1963, pp. 232–233). Does this sound familiar? His analysis is today as actual as it was in the late 1930s, and it is important to remember that the public opinion debates of today, but also the academic discourse, tend to disregard and, indeed, forget, the insights of yesterday. We hope, our book is a constructive contribution to the economic debate of today not falling into that pitfall.

References

Choi, Wonsik et al. (2013). Beyond Korean style: Shaping a New Growth Formula, McKinsey Global Institute.

Röpke, Wilhelm (1963). Economics of the Free Society, Chicago: Henry Regnery Company (translation of: Die Lehre von der Wirtschaft 1936).

Contents

Table of Abbreviations

BRIC	Brazil, Russia, India, China
CCP	Child Care Programme / Chinese Communist Party
CEE	Central and Eastern European
CME	Coordinated Market Economies
CSRC	China Securities Regulatory Commission
DPA	Direct Production Activities
EITC	Earned Income Tax Credit
EOI	Export Orientation Industrialisation
EPB	Economic Planning Board
EU	European Union
FDI	Foreign Direct Investment
FKI	Federation of Korean Industries
MNCs	Multi National Companies
FPP	Family Planning Programme
GDP	Gross Domestic Product
GNI	Gross National Income
GNP	Gross National Product
HCI	Heavy and Chemical Industries
IAI	Industrial Accident Insurance
ICCP	Infant- Child Care Programme
IMF	International Monetary Fund
ISI	Import Substitution Industrialisation
KAMCO	Korean Asset Management Company
KWNS	Keynesian Welfare National State
LAO	Limited Access Orders
LDC	Less Developed Countries
LDP	Liberal-Democratic Party
LFPAP	Low Fertility and Population Aging Policy
LG	Lucky-Goldstar Corporation
LME	Liberal Market Economies
LTCI	Long-Term Care Insurance
MCW	Mother-Child Welfare
MFCWP	Mother-Father-Child Welfare Programme
MITI	Ministry of International Trade and Industry
MPF	Market-Preserving Federalism

NBLSS	National Basic Livelihood Security System
NEET	Not in Education, Employment, or Training
NGO	Non-Governmental Organization
NHI	National Health Insurance
NIC	Newly Industrializing Countries
NPS	National Pension Scheme
OAO	Open Access Order
OECD	Organization for Economic Cooperation and Development
ORB	Overall Resource Budget
PAP	Public Assistance Programme
R&D	Research and Development
SEZ	Special Economic Zones
SOC	Social Overhead Capital
SOE	State-owned enterprises
STAN	Database for Structural Analysis
SWPR	Schumpeterian Workfare Post-national Regime
TVE	Township-Village Enterprises
USA	United States of America
USSR	Union of Soviet Socialist Republics
VoC	Varieties of Capitalism
WTO	World Trade Organization
WWII	World War II

Ralph Wrobel

Economic Models for New Industrializing Countries in Comparative Perspective

1. Introduction

The last decades are characterized more and more by the catching-up of former communist and developing countries especially in Central and Eastern Europe as well as in East Asia. Nowadays, most of the Central European countries are members of the European Union. Therefore, their role model was determined by the acquis communautaire of the EU. However, other countries catch up without a clear role model. Especially in East Asia different models are discussed. While Malaysia focuses on Singapore for instance, South Korea is starting to discuss the German model. Furthermore, China defines its Market Socialism as a step on its way to a market economy, but does not clarify its final development goal. But which economic system is able to develop an economic successful catching-up combined with human development and poverty reduction? Does any "Single Peak Economy" exists which can act as a role model for New Industrializing Countries (NICs)?

Economists like Jeffrey Sachs or Paul Collier have argued that free market will not work for the development of the "bottom billion" in the poorest countries of the world. Instead, they offer technocratic, administrative solutions to the poor (e.g. Sachs 2005; Collier 2007). In the author's opinion this solution is wrong. Reality shows that the richest societies in the world are market economies. As we know – contrasting to a socialist central planning system – that every kind of market economy is favourable (see e.g. as classics in this sphere von Mises 1936; Hayek 1982). Market economies are able to attain a higher GDP per capita by functioning market incentives and freedom of entrepreneurs and consumers. Therefore, it is not the question if market systems should be implemented in poor societies but only which kinds, how and by which strategies. A lot of developed market economies are available as role models and can be studied to search for better functioning market economic institutions: Following several varieties of capitalism approaches Liberal Market Economies (Laissez Faire, like in the Anglo-Saxon countries) have to be distinguished from Coordinated Market Economies like the Nordic Welfare State [Scandinavia], Mediterranean Capitalism [France and Southern Europe], or a Social Market Economy [Germany]. Together with the

Asian development model all these economic systems are competing with each other in the current competition of systems in the globalised world.

Therefore, emerging economies can use the experiences of the developed market economies to improve their catching-up strategies, not only in the positive sense. They can also learn from their mistakes. NICs are already quite developed and reached a level of functioning institutions, which allow focussing on developed role models from the Western World or East Asia. Therefore, first catching-up strategies of Less Developed Countries (LDCs) and NICs in the past will be described briefly. Afterwards, common experiences from the Western world and different developed market economies as role models will be discussed. Additionally, the comparative perspective shows the advantages and disadvantages of these models. Of course, when analysing catching-up or transformation processes key attention has also be given to an understanding how institutions of a society change and evolve. For that reason, basic problems like path dependency, cultural constraints, necessity of political entrepreneurs, etc. have to be taken into consideration, too. But to discuss these problems is not purpose of this paper.

2. Catching-up Strategies and Institutions

After independence from the colonial powers in the 20th century a lot of African, Asian and Latin-American countries oriented their institutional framework to socialism and communism. (Besters/Boesch 1966: 1537–1545) Beside all differences common goal was an independence from economic exploitation by the former colonial powers and their remaining enterprises. The socialist models were characterized by central planning of the economy, a high degree of state property and cooperatives in the fields of production, credit and consumption. To refuse market models the specific condition in the LDCs and political-ideological aspects were given as reasons. Especially the assumed lacks of reaction to incentives by the very poor people and functioning enterprises as well as abilities to save and invest money were main arguments. Additionally, weaknesses of the institutional and real infrastructure were emphasized. (Clapham, undated)

Till the beginning of the 1970s, the Western development policy focused on the goal of economic growth, assuming a trickle-down of the welfare to the poorest people in the LDCs. This strategy was characterized by the target of an industrial catching-up with focus on large industrial or infrastructural projects as well as import substitution policy. (Schnabl 2010: 6) This policy also focused on central planning and a lot of state interventions that were seen as indispensable for the industrialization. In several countries the selection of projects, financed by bilateral or multilateral aid, and enforcement of the projects were mainly organized by central governments. In contrast, individual responsibility and initiative were neglected. In the 1970s the focus of developmental aid changed to the fight against mass poverty. Basic needs of the poor had to be satisfied at first. This should lead to better possibilities of the poor people to participate in the economic system by a higher productivity of work. But also during this time the main role of the state was emphasized. The poor people were treated like "objects" and not like "subjects" of the development process. Both, the growth-oriented as well as the basic-needs oriented strategy failed. Underdevelopment and poverty could not be overcome as it was expected. A fundamental change took place in 1987 with the Brundtland report "Our Common Future" which focused primarily on sustainability in connection with development of LDCs and environmental problems. The new conception concentrated predominantly on the domestic institutional framework of the LDCs as well as on the international framework. Both should be changed to improve the conditions for governmental development policy and initiative of the poor themselves. Additionally, the idea of the necessity of a long-term policy establishing a free basic order, which is characterized by human rights, rule of law, democratization, good governance, and efficient market institutions, evolved. At all, it can be emphasized that the importance of institutions for the development of LDCs and NICs came on the top of the agenda. (Clapham undated)

During the 1970s and 80s a few countries – especially in East Asia – were able to catch up by the establishment of market institutions. Therefore, the term "New Industrializing Countries" or "Newly Industrializing Economies" was established to name those countries which did not fit any more all characteristics of LDCs, but were not fully industrialized. First, the term was applied to the "Asian Tigers" (or "Dragons"), South Korea, Taiwan, Singapore and Hong Kong, while nowadays we find a lot of NICs respective tigers in the East Asian region. Malaysia, Thailand, the Philippines, and Indonesia count as Small Tigers since the 1980s. Most of the Asian Tigers followed Japan in its strategy of an anticipatory industrial policy enforced by public controlled banks. Some also speak about a "development dictatorship". When public directed investments failed like in Malaysia or South Korea with respect to heavy industries in the 1970s, mistakes could be retracted quite fast because of a non-ideological pragmatism. (Seliger 2009: 263–265)

Additionally, these countries demonstrated that welfare gains cannot be attained by protectionism and industrial policy. An export based development model is needed instead. (Schnabl 2010: 6) The basic idea of this model is to finance growth of investments and progress in productivity by revenues from exports. Conditions for such a strategy are a rising international trade and the creation of an export position by comparative advantages within the catching-up country.

(Knogler 2010: 10) Likewise, the opening to technology transfer from abroad supported the fast development of the Asian Tigers. In the Asian case, it was mainly an import of know-how from Japan which started by FDIs and production of low-labour-cost-products in the Tiger Countries. The so-called wild geese model was characterised by innovation in Japan, production in the Large Tiger Countries during the growth stage and in the Small Tigers in the maturity stage. Fixed exchange rates – in combination with under-evaluated domestic currencies – and voluntarily high saving ratios in the Small Tiger Economies supported their catching-up massively, too. (Seliger 2009: 265) While Prasad/Rajan/Subramanian (2007) emphasised that LDCs focusing only on external financial sources, consequently, do not grow as fast as those which focus on domestic savings, we know that the importance of international capital flows for NICs are obvious. In contrast to domestic capital accumulation international capital flows improve and defragment capital markets. The degree of liquidity rises while interest rates decrease, provided that political and macroeconomic stability is given. By rising FDIs old structures of production and low marginal productivities can be overcome. Thereby, foreign capital flows improve the efficiency of capital allocation and production. In such a process implemented expectations are self-fulfilling. A rising growth stabilizes economic policy. Public deficits and inflation rates decline. Improved credit ratings attract additional FDIs. But also weaknesses of the export based development model have to be mentioned. The Asian crisis in 1997/98 already showed that strategies of fixed exchange rates lead to speculative capital inflows and excessive monetary expansion while the banking systems were fragile and the political and economic framework questionable. (Schnabl 2010: 6–7) Nowadays, an additional wave of East Asian countries – China and Vietnam – penetrates into the international markets. Especially China is seen as the new challenge of the West. Obviously, all these countries were able to introduce well working institutions supporting entrepreneurship and markets.

Till the end of the 1980s most "Western" economic reform packages were quite neglecting the importance of institutions. The best example to be mentioned is the Washington Consensus. As Stiglitz (2002: 53) pointed out the Washington Consensus was "designed to respond to the very real problems in Latin America and made considerable sense". Later it became a universal formula for transformation problems. The term Washington Consensus was coined in 1989 by Williamson (1989) and describes a set of ten relatively specific economic policy prescriptions, which constituted the "standard" reform package promoted for crisis-wracked developing countries. Origin was the policy of Washington, D.C.-based organizations like the International Monetary Fund or the World Bank. The prescriptions encompassed policies in various areas like macroeconomic stabilization, economic opening with respect to both trade and investment, and the expansion of market forces within the domestic economy. The main problem of the Washington Consensus was the inobservance of institutions. For instance, Sachs (1991: 236), who was mainly responsible for the design of the Polish reform programme, suspected that basic institutions of a market economy could be established in the country within one year. But it has proven to be false: transformation has to be seen as time-taking process with complex necessities of innovation, imitation and adaptation. (Wrobel 2000: 153–155)

Fortunately, when transformation in the Central and East European Countries (CEECs) started most of them focused on European integration, i.e. political and economic integration with the EU, and exports. In this way, an export oriented development strategy was combined with an institutional imitation process. The result of that was a growing trade in both directions, from East to the West but also from West to the East, as well as a rise of international capital flows, first of all as FDIs from Western Europe into the transformation states. In this way, during two decades most of the CEECs were integrated into the European division of labour. Low labour costs, small distances to the West European markets and a qualified working force enabled these countries to attain respectable growth rates. (Knogler 2010: 11) At the same time political as well as economic institutions were stabilized and basically harmonized. The integration strategy of most CEECs was quite successful. Already, the EBRD Transition Report 2009 showed that in the European transformation states a positive relation between FDIs and growth rates could be observed. (EBRD 2009) But growth financed with outside capital led also in this case to macroeconomic imbalances and fragile financial sectors. One result was not only a fast growing current account deficit which was only partly compensated by FDIs, but also a growing foreign indebtedness of the banking sector as well as other enterprises. In this way, the integration and export based strategy development brought a long-term growth and institutional stability as well as a consumption boom, a debt overload and a financial dependence from foreign financial markets. (Mirow 2010: 3–4) The sharp decline of growth rates in a lot of CEECs and in several Asian NICs between 2008 and 2010 illustrate this problem impressively. All these countries suffered from the crisis by two channels mainly: firstly, by a sharp decline of exports and, secondly, by a drop of net capital flows from the industrialised countries. (Gern 2010: 13–14)

Therefore, especially institutional stability characterized by copying and adaptation of West European institutions, has to be emphasized as an anchor of the CEECs catching-up process. (Wrobel 2000; North 2005) West Europe became the leading role model for all transformation states. While some of them focused on more liberal models (like the Czech Republic and Estonia) others preferred more coordinated models of market economies. Finally, all new members of the EU accepted the acquis communautaire and thereby all basic political and economic institutions of the West European countries. This was – for sure – the main reason of their success. In contrast, East Asian countries followed the Large Asian Tigers by adaptive copying of their institutions while most of the LDCs failed in finding adequate institutions for a better development. Therefore, it must be asked which institutions support prosperity and development.

3. Economic Role Models

3.1 Common Experiences from the Western World

While the Geography Hypothesis, the Culture Hypothesis and the Ignorance Hypothesis failed to explain prosperity versus poverty in the world, we can follow Acemoglu/Robinson (2012: 73) that "countries differ in their economic success because of their different institutions, the rules influencing, how the economy works, and the incentives that motivate people." Obviously, especially Western institutions were able to support the development of prospering societies in the past. As Acemoglu/Robinson (2012: 46) already pointed out, also one hundred or one hundred and fifty years ago nearly the same Western countries were characterized by high prosperity like nowadays. But also Japan and most of the Large Tiger Economies were able to copy and adapt these basic principles of prosperity. Insofar, the East Asian Tigers became successful when they adopted the "basic rights" of Western OAOs like corruption-free public administration and market-enhancing instead of market-distorting interventions. (World Bank 1993) But which institutions make the difference? The reason for the developmental gap between developed market economies and LDCs can be described by the new approach of North/Wallis/Weingast (2009), for instance. They distinguish so-called limited access orders (LAOs) and open access orders (OAOs). While the first-mentioned orders are growing slowly and are vulnerable to shocks, the latter ones enjoy a mainly positive political and economic development. LAOs, also called natural states, are characterised by polities without consent of the governed, a relatively small number of organisations and the predominance of social relationship organised along personal lines, including privileges and social hierarchies. As North/Wallis/Weingast (2009: 12) pointed out, most of the societies in the world are LAOs. In contrast, OAOs are characterised by a bigger, but more decentralised government, a rich civil society with lots of organisations and widespread impersonal social relationships including rule of law, secure property rights, fairness and equality. Already Eucken (1952/90) brought these ideas into the scientific discussion, calling them "interdependencies of orders". Also Panther (1997: 111) has to be mentioned, because he characterised the Latin West of Europe by a high degree of "civicness" what he defines as "a set of values and norms requiring actors to treat each other as equals, to be tolerant of each other and encouraging mutual solidarity."

Nevertheless North/Wallis/Weingast (2009) do not limit their analysis to the differentiation of new ideal types of social orders. They also make some detailed investigation into the transformation process from a LAO to an OAO. Concretely, they define two steps for natural states to become an open access order. At first, personal relations within the dominant coalition have to be transformed into impersonal ones. Then, three doorstep conditions have to be fulfilled. These conditions are, first of all, the implementation of the rule of law for the elites. The second condition is the existence of continuously lived forms of public and private elite organisations. This means a civil society where many organisations exist and develop. And the third one describes that the military has to be come under consolidated political control, for instance the Ministry of Defence. However, this process will only occur if the members of the dominant coalition find it advantageous to transform their privileges into general, impersonal rights (North/Wallis/ Weingast 2009: 150–166) While the conditions for a development from a LAO to an OAO are described in detail, the emergence of the monopoly of power during the transition process is hardly dealt with. (Zweynert 2010: 5) Therefore, also the success of a political development is depending on the willingness and success of political entrepreneurs to implement the rules of an OAO. It can only be supposed that globalisation – understood concrete as an institutional competition process (see Hodgeson 2007) – will reinforce these processes.

3.2 Different Role Models in Comparison

3.2.1 Categorizing Economic Systems

After the fall of the Berlin wall market economy and democracy became the main goal for most of the former socialist countries. Japan and the large Asian Tiger Countries introduced market institutions, too. But this is not the "end of history" as Fukuyama (1992) had declared it two decades ago. Nowadays, competition between several types of market economies is strengthening. For instance, Mueller (1996: 33) already wrote: "Human history up to the present day can be seen as a process of wealth creation by individual efforts within given sets of economic and political institutions, and wealth transference (rent seeking). A kind of Darwinian process is at work that selects for survival those institutional structures that are best at creating and protecting wealth." But which institutions are worth to be copied and adapted by the NICs to catch-up successfully, nowadays?

Several models of capitalist variety were established during the last decades. Especially, in the late 1990s, capitalist diversity had become the subject of a broad literature, culminating in a number of widely read books (e.g. Stallings 1995; Crouch/Streeck 1997 or Coates 2000). However, the most influential approach was presented as collective volume edited by Peter Hall and David Soskice (2001): "Varieties of Capitalism: the Institutional Foundations of Comparative Advantage". Especially in the book's introduction both developed a conceptual model of capitalist variety, which distinguishes two different coordination regimes that vary systematically across countries. At one end of the spectrum there are Liberal Market Economies (LMEs) and on the other end Coordinated Market Economies (CMEs). While the LMEs use markets as their main means of coordinating economic activity, CMEs rely more on non-market institutions to solve coordination problems of society. While the LMEs consist of the six Anglo-American countries including Ireland, CMEs include Germany and its smaller neighbours (the Netherlands, Belgium, Switzerland, and Austria) as well as Scandinavia and Japan. Thereby, Germany is the paradigmatic case of CME for Hall/Soskice. But this binary classification of national forms of market systems leaves many countries in an ambiguous position, because they cannot be clearly categorized. For instance, France, Italy, Spain, Portugal and Greece are classified as "ambiguous", or as an alternative they constitute a third "Mediterranean" type. (Streeck 2010: 24) Another one-dimensional approach was presented by the French author Michel Albert. In his "Capitalism against Capitalism" Albert (1993) distinguished Rhineland capitalism, led by Germany and Japan, and the Anglo-American model, with France sitting on the fence. Also in this case the main differentiation between the Anglo-Saxon model and the German Social Market Economy becomes obvious.

However, the dualist approaches are too simple to form concrete groups of countries as role models for NICs. Several "ambiguous" countries in Europe and the neglecting of the East Asian uniqueness don't allow an application to the search for a role model for NICs, nowadays. Therefore, in this paper the author follows the most sophisticated approach by Amable (2003), who is using factor-analytical econometric techniques on a large set of macroeconomic variables to distinguish five types of market economies. As Crouch (2005: 448) emphasises Amable's quantitative data are on a vast range of characteristics, e.g. product and labour markets, financial, social and educational system, etc. The results of his analysis are five groups of countries: Market-Based Economies, Social Democratic Economies, Continental European Capitalism, South European Capitalism and Asian Capitalism. Amable (2003) analysed OECD countries only. But his ideal types can be used to set up the following geo-cultural groups of countries as role models, also taking in consideration the results of other authors:

(1) **Anglo-Saxon Free Market Economy (Market-Based Economies):** This group consists of the six English-speaking countries including Ireland which are characterized by a non-involvement of the state in product markets and coordination through price signals. They are open to foreign investment and competition. Financial markets are highly sophisticated. Here exists only a low employment protection but flexible labour markets. The social protection systems are weak and public expenditures for education are low.

(2) **Nordic Welfare States (Social-Democratic Economies):** To this group belong all Scandinavian countries which are characterized by a high involvement of the state in product markets and a high degree of coordination through channels other than market signals, but also by openness to foreign investment and competition. The financial markets are not sophisticated. Employment protection is moderate and wage bargaining is centralised coordinated. Social protection is on a high level, also public expenditure for education.

(3) **Social Market Economy (Continental European Capitalism):** Germany and its direct neighbours build an additional group. In this case public authorities are involved into the product markets and the non-price coordination is on a high level. A low degree of protectionism against foreign competitors and investors is discriminatory, too. Financial markets are only low sophisticated. High employment protection is combined with low labour market flexibility and active employment policy. Social protection is on a high level, also public expenditure for education.

(4) **Mediterranean Economies (South European Capitalism):** While Amable (2003) describes France as ambiguous others add it to the Mediterranean group which – as a result – consists of the Romance and Greek speaking countries as well as Malta. This model consists of involvement of the state into the product markets and a little non-price coordination. Protectionism against foreign competitors and investors is moderate. Small firms are dominating. Sophistication of financial markets is low. Furthermore, a moderate level of social protection is combined with low public expenditures for education.

(5) **Asian Capitalism:** Amable's group of Asian capitalism consisted of the OECD countries Japan and South Korea, only, but also the other Large East Asian Tiger Countries can be added. This model is characterized by a high involvement

of the state in the product markets and a high degree of non-price coordination. Protectionism against foreign competitors and investors is on a high level. Large firms are dominating. Employment protection is moderate. Sophistication of financial markets is low. Also the level of social protection is low as well as public expenditures for education.

Therefore, five economic systems – four from the Western world and one Asian – are available as role models for NICs to be studied. But what are the advantages respective disadvantages of these economic systems?

3.2.2 Concrete Economic Systems as Role Models

Main role model from the West is the Anglo-Saxon Free Market Economy. Here, the role of the state is traditionally described as "night watchman" implementing only a minimum of regulations and levying only low taxes. In such kind of a market economy, incentives to work are high. Additionally, efficiency is on a high level because the price signals can work without distortions. But on the other hand, a rising social inequality, a monopolization of the product markets and non-internalization of negative externalities characterize such a system. The advantages of a neo-liberal reform can be illustrated by the rise of Thatcherism in the UK, for instance. Since the late 1960s, the British economy had begun to experience unprecedented economic recession. Reasons were the bad incentives caused by an overwhelming welfare system and the results of the Keynesian demand management policy. Britain's economic growth rate fell into one of the lowest among Western nations of that time. Therefore, the major practical foundation of the British consensual ideology was ruined and a new model was presented by the Conservative Party and its new leader, Margaret Thatcher, in the end of the 1970s. The core idea of her conservative and neo-liberal ideology was the return of the free market as the only means to promote economic prosperity through greater efficiency in allocating and using scarce resources. She also emphasized the maintenance of sound money as a critical underpinning of the market system and the rolling back of state intervention that was largely responsible for the economic inefficiencies. To carry through these ideas it was necessary for Thatcher to bring the union's power under her control. As a result of her consequent policy, Britain faced a new decade of prosperity in the 1980s. Growth rates rose while unemployment rates fall consequently. (Hoon 2001: 63–65; see also Brendan 1999) But nowadays, the picture of Britain is mixed. Britain suffers from quite bad social welfare systems, but was not able to rise its economy into a top position in the long run.

For NICs the model of a Free Market Economy is attractive because less state coordination is necessary than in the cases of coordinated market economies.

Therefore, it is quite simple to implement. As the Britain experience has shown high growth rates and less unemployment can be reached, too. But the neo-liberal model did not succeed everywhere. Within the last 20 years, especially transformation economies and emerging societies have been threatened by wrong reform programs neglecting the needs of market regulation. One was the failure of price liberalization and privatization in the Russian Federation due to a lack of market-oriented regulatory framework, a second one was dissatisfaction with economic reforms in South America following the "Washington Consensus" and neglecting the importance of safety nets and social insurance. Further the Asian banking crisis revealed that financial liberalization without prudent regulation can have disastrous consequences. (Ahrens 2009: 114–115) These failures of the free market approach in developing societies have now been followed by the financial and economic crisis caused by a failing regulation of the international financial markets and an inflationary monetary policy in different Western states. But these disparate developments helped reinforce the efforts to put institutions on the reform agenda of policy makers. Today, it is widely recognised that privatization, price liberalisation and macroeconomic stabilization are necessary components of transformation but are insufficient without implementation of adequate economic rules and regulations. (Wrobel 2012: 54)

Therefore, more coordinated market economies may be the better decision. Here, three Western models – the Nordic Welfare State, Social Market Economy and the Mediterranean Capitalism – as well as the Asian Model of Capitalism have to be compared. In the Nordic Welfare State the state acts successfully as a protector and a promoter of economic and social well-being as well as a distributor of income and wealth. So, a high degree of social security and welfare can be attained. For instance, in the Legatum Prosperity Index 2012 all Scandinavian countries hold the first ranks: Norway (1), Denmark (2), Sweden (3) and Finland (7). (Legatum Institute 2012: 1) In this way, the question about the "best economic system" or a "Single Peak Economy" (Gries 2001: 469) seems to be answered. But the social systems are very expensive for citizens who have to pay either high taxes or to suffer from rising public debts. Reduced incentives for all economic actors have to be mentioned, too. This can be illustrated by the Swedish Welfare State model. Traditionally, it was characterised by a high degree of state involvement in the life of all citizens – from the cradle to the grave! Public financed social services were provided for and were used by everyone. A universal pension system was already introduced in 1913. But taxes are among the highest in the world. Consequently, in the early 1990s, when there was a turbulent period for welfare states in general, also Sweden suffered. With its high taxes, the public budget of a welfare state is extremely sensitive to fluctuations in economic activity. When growth in Sweden was negative for three years 1991–1993, the budget deficit rose to an alarming 13% of GDP. Therefore, during the 1990s, the Swedish model has been altered and reformed in several ways. (Bergh 2010: 110–112) For NICs the model seems to be attractive at first sight, but the establishment of a welfare state requires a lot of financial resources and moreover, it is fragile to economic disturbances as the Swedish case shows.

For that reason, the German conception of Social Market Economy may be the right alternative to a Nordic Welfare State on the one hand and a Free Market Economy on the other hand. The idea of the Social Market Economy is based on the principles of economic order by the German economist Walter Eucken and was introduced in West Germany after WW II by Minister of Economic Affairs Ludwig Erhard (Wünsche 2001: 72–84). It combines private enterprise with measures of the state to establish fair competition, low inflation, and social welfare. The basic theoretical approach is the competition order in the sense of Walter Eucken (1952/90). It includes not only a regulatory framework of a functioning price system, monetary stability, freedom of contract and private property, open markets, but also the principle of liability and the principle of constancy and coherence of economic policy. In contrast to a free market economy, the idea of the Social Market Economy accepts the existence of weaknesses and deficits within the market order, which require correction. It should combine the principle of freedom with social security. While the freedom of the individual is manifested in competition, social problems that cannot be mastered through the market are to be solved by an appropriate social security policy. (Tuchtfeldt 1973/82: 65)

Walter Eucken's ideals (including modifications) drove the creation of the post-World War II German Social Market Economy and its attendant economic miracle. Additionally, West Germany implemented an export-oriented strategy supported by an under-evaluated currency within the Bretton-Woods-System. But, it must be emphasized, that Germany developed into direction of a welfare state during the last decades. Also here the social budged exploded. (Wünsche 2001: 108–111) Thereby, even Germany is marked by a too tight network of regulations (especially in the fields of taxes and social measures), equal to other welfare states in Europe. For NICs the approach of Social Market Economy seems to be attractive because it combines openness of development in freedom and responsibility with the peace-making social measures. At the same time, the role of the state includes competency as well as responsibility for the establishment of market economic institutions. Therefore, the Social Market Economy gains a maximum of "welfare for everyone", without neglecting incentives of the market system. On the other hand, an immanent tendency to a Nordic Welfare State has to be emphasized, too.

In contrast to these three models, the South European model of capitalism is ambiguous. Most of these states prefer price coordination as well as low levels of employment protection and public expenditure like free market economies. In contrast, financial markets are not sophisticated and the levels of protectionism and social protection are moderate. The largest of these countries, France, has implemented even a kind of indicative planning in the past. Till the 1990s it had developed the most comprehensive framework for national economic planning in the non-communist world. (Hansen 1964: 11) Later – because of the introduction of the European Single Market – France had to privatize public enterprises and to liberalize its economic structure. Therefore, till nowadays France seems to be capitalism in transition, halfway between two models of regulation. Additionally, its macroeconomic performances continue to be quite poor in terms of growth and unemployment. (Coriat 2006: 95) In contrast to France, especially Greece, Cyprus, Portugal and Spain are characterized by a high importance of tourism instead of industry. Sepp (2010: 172) calls them "tourism countries", therefore. As he points out, these countries suffered from unequal distribution of income and wealth as well as from high public debts already before the current debt crisis. Therefore, the Mediterranean Capitalism seems to be more an ambiguous kind of capitalism, somehow more close to the transformation states in Central and Eastern Europe then to the role models of Western and Northern Europe. As the current debt crisis in Europe shows all these Mediterranean countries – including Italy and partly France – are suffering from the high public debts and its incapability to establish structures supporting growth enormously. Therefore, the Mediterranean Capitalism can be neglected as role model for NICs.

The East Asian model – characterized by developmental dictatorships as well as rise of employment and FDIs – is worthy to discuss. In this case it must be questioned if it is really a challenge to the old industrialized countries. Still ten years ago several European countries focused the Large Tigers and Japan as role models while the Small East Asian Tigers do it nowadays, too. In these countries, the typical overlapping of economy and state was assumed as an advantage in two fields: In the first place, the state can be strengthened because it can confide in the power of its mostly large enterprises. And secondly, the enterprises do not compete as single enterprises in the international markets but as a group, for instance as "Japan Inc.". But nowadays, exactly this overlapping of economic and political system is seen as a disadvantage. Responsibilities are unclear and the liability principle does not work. Therefore, all these states suffer from too much regulation and are recommended to deregulate and to divide economic and political subsystem of society. (Starbatty, undated) Already Krugman (1994) argued that "The Myth of Asia's Miracle" was basing on quantitative rise of production factors only. He emphasized especially the rise of employment and high saving ratios. At that time, the limits of this kind of growth were obvious in Japan as well as in South Korea. But his formula of "perspiration instead of inspiration" did not match the whole reality. Indeed, the quantitative rise of production factors is one main fact describing the East Asian development process, but it is not the only one. Additionally, the high ability to adapt technologies, e.g. by FDIs, has to be mentioned. (Seliger 2009: 268) Therefore, the results of the Asian model are mixed. Not only, the Asian crisis in 1997/98 exposed the weaknesses of this model. Nowadays, Japans looks back to two decades of stagnation and deflation. On the other hand, Asia's growth cannot be set aside as quantitative only. Even in China R&D expenditures are on the rise, topping Japan's expenditures in absolute terms several years ago. (Herrmann-Pillath 2008: 487) Even, especially China and the East Asian Tigers overcame the last crises quite well whereas the Western countries suffered from them massively. But structural distortions in these countries are obvious. (Schnabl 2010: 7) Therefore, at the moment it is quite unclear if the Asian model of development will work as role model for NICs in the future, also.

4. Conclusion

Not only LDCs want to catch-up with the top industrialized states but also NICs, especially in Central and Eastern Europe as well as in East Asia. While the latter combined an export-oriented strategy with some kind of "developmental dictatorship", the CEESs brought together export-orientation with adaptive institutional imitation of Western European institutions. Also LDCs learned the importance of basic institutions as necessary conditions for a successful development process. The rule of law ("good governance"), a civil society of equal individuals and a consolidated control of the military represent the doorstep conditions to become an OAO supporting growth and prosperity. Additionally, as possible role models for NICs (but also LDCs) five country groups were defined: (1) Anglo-Saxon Free Market Economy, (2) Nordic Welfare State, (3) Social Market Economy, (4) Mediterranean Capitalism, and (5) Asian Capitalism.

As a comparison of these models shows most of them have advantages as well as disadvantages, too. Only the Mediterranean Capitalism as an ambiguous form of capitalism cannot fit as role model for NICs. While a Free Market Economy is quite simple to implement and sets strong incentives but leads to social inequality a Welfare State offers a high level of social care for everyone but is fragile and expansive as well. In contrast, the fast developing Asian model – focussing on exports and a "developmental dictatorship" – is threatened by sticking in quantitative growth. Additionally, the overregulation by overlapping public and economic sectors is a disadvantage in the long run, too. Therefore, from the author's point of view, the conception of the Social Market Economy seems to be the right alternative approach of capitalism in our times because it brings together the main advantages of Free Market Economies and the Nordic Welfare State. Especially for transforming and emerging economies the approach seems to be interesting because it allows societies to transform into direction of a market economy without neglecting regulative as well as social aspects. In less developed countries which have to do large efforts in poverty reduction the Social Market Economy may be a superior approach than the Free Market Economy on the one side or the hybrid system of a Socialist Market Economy on the other, too. But at all, this analysis doesn't imply the absolute predominance of one role model. There exists no "Single Peak Economy". Additionally, NICs cannot copy the whole set of institutions from other countries. According to North (2005) the direction of change processes is determined by path dependence. Therefore, role models shall give political deciders an impression which model may be helpful to find adaptive institutions for the own catching-up process.

References

Acemoglu, Daron / Robinson, James (2012) Why Nations Fail – The Origins of Power, Prosperity and Poverty, London.

Ahrens, Joachim (2009) Transition towards a Social Market Economy? – Limits and Opportunities, in: Seliger, B./Sepp, J./Wrobel, R. (eds). Das Konzept der Sozialen Marktwirtschaft und seine Anwendung. Frankfurt/M.: Peter Lang.

Albert, Michel (1993) Capitalism Against Capitalism: How America's Obsession with Individual Achievement and Short-term Profit Has Led It to the Brink of Collapse, New York.

Amable, Bruno (2003) The Diversity of Modern Capitalism, Oxford.

Bergh, Andreas (2010) Towards a new Swedish model?, in: Population ageing – a threat to the welfare state?, pp. 109–119.

Besters, H. / Boesch, E.E. [ed.] (1966) Entwicklungspolitik – Handbuch und Lexikon, Stuttgart.

Brendan, E. (1999) Thatcherism and British politics, 1975–1999, Sutton.

Clapham, Ronald (undated) Entwicklungsländer und Soziale Marktwirtschaft, in: Konrad Adenauer Foundation [ed.]: Lexikon Soziale Marktwirtschaft, online: http://www.kas.de/wf/de/71.11450/.

Coates, David (2000) Models of Capitalism: Growth and Stagnation in the Modern Era, Cambridge.

Collier, Paul (2007) The Bottom Billion: Why the poorest countries are failing and what can we be done about it. Oxford: Oxford University Press.

Coriat, Benjamin (2006) Moves Towards Finance-led Capitalism: the French Case, in: The Hardship of Nations, pp. 69–96.

Crouch, Colin (2005) Models of Capitalism, in: New Political Economy, Vol. 10, No. 4 (Dec.), pp. 439–456.

Crouch, Colin / Streeck, Wolfgang (1997) Political Economy of Modern Capitalism: Mapping Convergence and Diversity, London.

EBRD (2009) Transition in Crisis? – Transition Report. London: European Bank for Reconstruction and Development.

Eucken, Walter (1952/90) Grundsätze der Wirtschaftspolitik. 6th ed., Tübingen.

Fukuyama, F. (1992) The End of History and the Last Man. Free Press.

Gern, Klaus-Jürgen (2010) Die Schwellenländer können auch bei schwachem Wachstum der Industrieländer kräftig expandieren, in: ifo-Schnelldienst 2010/6, pp. 13–17.

Gries, Thomas (2001) Soziales Marktmodell Europa versus liberales Marktmodell Amerika, in: Wirtschaftsdienst 2001/VIII, pp. 462–469.

Hall, Peter / Soskice, David [ed.] (2001) Varieties of Capitalism: The Institutional Foundations of Comparative Advantage, Oxford.

Hansen, Niles (1964) Indicative Planning in France: Model for the Future?, in: The Quarterly Review of Economics and Business, Vol. 4/4, pp. 7–18.

Hayek von, F. A. (1982) Two pages of fiction: the impossibility of socialist calculation. The journal of economic affairs 2.3, pp. 135–142.

Herrmann-Pillath, Carsten (2008) China: Globales Leitbild für Wachstum und Fortschritt?, in: Wirtschaftsdienst, Vol. 88, No. 8, pp. 486–487.

Hodgson, G. (**ed.**) (2007) The evolution of economic institutions: a critical reader. Cheltenham: Elgar.

Hoon Jaung (2001) The Rise of Neo-Liberal Revolution in Britain: Thatcherism in the British Conservative Party, in: Global Economic Review, Vol. 30, No. 1, pp. 57–78.

Knogler, Michael (2010) Die neuen EU-Mitgliedsstaaten in der Wirtschafts- und Finanzkrise: Ende des aufholenden Wachstums, in: ifo-Schnelldienst 2010/6, pp. 9–13.

Krugman, Paul (1994) The Myth of Asia's Miracle. A Cautionary Fable, in: Foreign Affairs, Vol 73, No. 6, pp. 62–78.

Legatum Institute (2012) A Unique Global Inquiry into Wealth and Wellbeing: The 2012 Legatum Prosperity Index, online: www.prosperity.com.

Mirow, Thomas (2010) Osteuropas Entwicklungsmodell im Krisentest: Schwächen, Stärken, Schlussfolgerungen, in: ifo-Schnelldienst 2010/6, pp. 3–6.

Mises von, Ludwig (1936) Socialism: an economic and sociological analysis. London: Cape.

North, Douglas C. (2005) Understanding the Process of Economic Change, Princeton.

North, Douglas C. / Wallis, John J. / Weingast, Barry R. (2009) Violence and social orders: a conceptual framework for interpreting recorded human history. Cambridge: Cambridge University Press.

Panther, Stefan (1997) Cultural Factors in the Transition Process – Latin Center, Orthodox Periphery?, in: Backhaus, J./Krause, G. (eds), Issues in Transformation Theory, pp. 95–122. Marburg.

Prasad, E. / Rajan, R. / Subramanian, A. (2007) Foreign Capital and Economic Growth, Brookings Papers on Economic Activity, Vol. 31, No. 1, pp. 153–230.

Sachs, Jefrey (1991) Poland and Eastern Europe: What Is To Be Done?, in: A. Köves/P. Marer (Hrsg.): Foreign Economic Liberalization. Transformations in Socialist and Market Economies, Boulder, pp. 235–246.

Sachs, Jefrey (2005) The end of poverty. New York: Penguin.

Schnabl, Gunther (2010) Das kapitalmarktbasierte Wachstumsmodell – Wirklichkeit und Illusion, in: ifo-Schnelldienst 2010/6, pp. 6–9.

Seliger, Bernhard (2009) Die zweite Welle – ordnungspolitische Herausforderungen der ostasiatischen Wirtschaftsentwicklung, in: Seliger, B./Sepp, J./Wrobel, R. [ed.]: Das Konzept der Sozialen Marktwirtschaft und seine Anwendung: Deutschland im internationalen Vergleich, Frankfurt, pp. 259–300.

Seliger, Bernhard (2010) Theories of „economic miracles" – a comparative study of the German, Japanese, Korean and Chinese case, in: Seliger, B./Sepp, J./Wrobel, R. [ed.]: Chancen und Risiken für die Soziale Marktwirtschaft im internationalen Wettbewerb der Wirtschaftssysteme, Frankfurt, pp. 43–70.

Sepp, Jüri (2010) Europäische Wirtschaftssysteme durch das Prisma der Branchenstruktur und die Position der Transformationsländer, in: Seliger, B./Sepp, J./Wrobel, R. [ed.]: Chancen und Risiken für die Soziale Marktwirtschaft im internationalen Wettbewerb der Wirtschaftssysteme, Frankfurt, pp. 151–174.

Stallings, Barbara [ed.] (1995) Global Change, Regional Responses: The New International Context of Development, Cambridge.

Starbatty, Joachim (undated) Ausprägungen von Marktwirtschaften, in: Konrad Adenauer Foundation [ed.]: Lexikon Soziale Marktwirtschaft, online: http://www.kas.de/wf/de/71.11488/.

Stiglitz, Joseph (2002) Globalization and its Discontents, New York.

Streeck, Wolfgang (2010) E pluribus unum? Varieties and commonalities of capitalism, MPIfG Discussion Paper No. 10/12, online: http://hdl.handle.net/10419/43292.

Tuchtfeldt, Egon (1973/82) Social Market Economy and Demand Management: Two Experiements in Economic Policy, in: H. Wünsche (ed.): Standard Texts on the Social Market Economy – Two Centuries of Discussion, Stuttgart: Gustav Fischer Verlag, 1982, pp. 65–80.

Williamson, John (1989) What Washington Means by Policy Reform, in: Williamson, John (ed.): Latin American Readjustment: How Much has Happened, Washington.

World Bank [ed.] (1993) The East Asian Miracle – Economic Growth and Public Policy, Oxford.

Wrobel, Ralph (2000) Estland und Europa: Die Bedeutung des Systemwettbewerbs für die Evolution und Transformation von Wirtschaftssystemen, Tartu University Press, Tartu.

Wrobel, Ralph (2012) The social market economy as a model for sustainable growth in developing and emerging economies, in: Economic and Environmental Studies, Vol. 12, No.1 (21/2011), 47–63, March 2012, pp. 47–64.

Wünsche, Horst (2001) Die Verwirklichung der Sozialen Marktwirtschaft nach dem Zweiten Weltkrieg und ihr Verfall in den sechziger und siebziger Jahren, in: Otto Schlecht and Gerhard Stoltenberg (ed.): Soziale Marktwirtschaft: Grundlagen, Entwicklungslinien, Perspektiven, Freiburg: Herder, pp. 61–114.

Zweynert, Joachim (2010) The French Revolution and the Transfer of Open Access Orders to the South-Western German States and Prussia. HWWI Research Paper 5-10.

Sung-Jo Park

Developmental State in Korea (60s–70s) Revisited: Institution-Building for the Making of 'Coordinated Market'

> "The polity and the economy are inextricably linked in any understanding of the performance of an economy and therefore we must develop a true political economy discipline. A set of institutional constraints and consequent organizations defines the exchange relationships between the two and therefore determines the way a political/ economic system works…"
>
> (North 1990: 21–22)

1. Introduction

How can we make capitalism in former colonies and former socialist economies? This question encountered Social Science after the Second World and since the end of the Cold War. The dealing with Third World countries as 'development policy' and with former socialist economies as 'system transformation' has been two challenging tasks for Social Science. It seems that, even though in both cases problem-solving attempts have been in full swing, general remedies seem not to be in sight (Park 2007; Andreff 1993; Merkl 1999; Mackow 2005).

The developmental state of Korea evoked much interest among scholars. What was the most significant factor for the economic performance in Korea in the 60–70s? Experts concerned with economic development of Korea stress the role of the government (Kohli 2004; Sklair/Robbins 2002), government-business relations (corporatism) (Kang 2002, Lin 2001), role of big business groups (Chaebols) (Lombardi 2011; Cho 1990), human resources (Kim 2005), and the charismatic leadership of Park Chung Hee (Kim 2003). The institutional approaches by Choi (1987), Chung (1985) and Lee (1993) focused on the role of bureaucracy in the public administration.

The author leaning on the notion of the Northian institutional economics (North 1993) and VoC (Varieties of Capitalism) by Hall/Soskice (2003) aims to show how the private sector and market in Korea *developed* in the shade of the

World War II and Korean War legacies, and to describe how the Park Chung Hee regime (1961–1979) *guided the private sector* in the 60–70s. Particular attention will be directed at the question how the state built up developmental institutions, big business groups (Chaebols) and how these institutions *worked together* which laid the foundation for development of the Korean type of capitalism.

Hall/Soskice (2003: 8) defined the Korean capitalism as 'coordinated market economy' with the following characteristics: non-market relationships for coordination entailing relational contracting and network; equilibrium is outcome of interplay among market actors., not by supply and demand. Hall/Soskice (2003) dealt with mechanisms of the 'coordinated market economy', *not how it developed.* Until now little consideration was paid to the question, to which extent the development state under the Park Chung Hee regime contributed to the institution-building instrumental for development of the capitalism in Korea.

2. Birth of Developmental State, Planning, and Governance

2.1 Economic Planning Board (EPB), Blue House, and Governance

2.1.1 EPB

The take-over by General Park Chung-Hee of power in 1961 was not only a political coup d'Etat, but also brought about a radical economic change. Knowing that at that time Korea as one of the poorest countries in the world with less than per capita 80 US Dollars – over 60% of the population living still below the absolute poverty level – the highest infant mortality with 90%, and was struggling with devastations of material and social infrastructures caused by the Korean War Park Chung Hee laid the highest priority on precipitated economic recovery and development, and sought to find political legitimacy therein (Adelman 190?). As the first decision he abolished the Ministry of Reconstruction which was in charge of economic affairs in the 50s, because it was caught in inertia and corruption. He instead established a 'super ministry', *Economic Planning Board (EPB)* which was expected to form the core of economic planning in future. Park having served the Japanese Army after the graduation from the Japanese military academy before 1945 had a profound knowledge about the role of the government in the industrialization of Meiji period in Japan.

Park's first priority was extended to the question of how to get a *self-reliant economy* free from foreign aid from the USA, on which the Korean economy under President Syngman Rhee depended to a large extent. Park did not want to continue being recipient of the American aid. That might have been the reason why his first visit to a foreign country is not USA, but Germany which extended the Park Government 'generous credits' for financing the construction of the Seoul-Pusan Highway under the contractual condition that Korean miners and nurses would be dispatched to West Germany suffering shortage of manpower in both fields.

Park tightened government control over the private sector by nationalizing banks, merged the agricultural cooperatives movement with the agricultural bank and announced a seemingly drastic *cleanup of illegally enriched companies*. From now on the Park government was able to exercise economic command through the EPB as "nerve center for Parks' plan to promote economic development". For the set-up of the EPB in the center of the entire executive Park must have had in mind the 'big state' modeled after Japanese MITI (tsusan sho) model (Amsden 1989; Johnson 1982).

Park equipped the head of the EPB with the status of a deputy prime minister, the EPB being staffed by "high intellectual capability and education background in business and economics". (http://country studies.us/south-korea/47.htm)

The super ministry was provided with *threefold function planning, budgeting and foreign capital inducement*. The epoch-making change was that instead of the separated function of planning and budgeting, as it has been the case in Korea, both functions were united under the same roof. Herewith the Park regime signaled a significant yardstick for a *Big State* for pushing ahead economic development (Lee 1993).

2.1.2 Flexibility of Planning Authorities: Power Shift from EPB to Blue House?

The Park regime classified the planning *explicitly* into three categories: *normative, indicative, and imperative* (Park 1977; Park 1980; Lee 1993).

- **under the auspices of the EPB**:
    1) The *normative planning* beginning in 1961 was characterized not merely by indicating development goals, but by binding power to reach the announced development goals *in compliance with financial allocation to a large extent*. The EBP's controlling over planning and budgeting was the very institution of mandatory power to pursue the planned goals for the three five year plans (1962–1976).
    2) The *indicative planning* started in 1977 when the private sector, especially big business groups (Chaebols) reached a certain level of maturity in managerial and financial capability, and were capable of responding allegedly to market mechanisms by means of their diversification strategy (Cho 1990; Song/Cho 1998). This implied that *big business groups were thoroughly in a*

situation to comply their business goals with the goals defined in the national five year plans (1977–1996).

- **under the auspices of the Blue House**
  3) The *Heavy and Chemical Industries* (HCI) Plan (1973–1981) had character of *Imperative Planning*: at the beginning of 70ties the Park regime became increasingly repressive and authoritarian. Instead of stepping down from the presidency, as President Park previously promised, his intention was to continue his dictatorial rule by means of the revision of the constitution in 1972 (the so called Yushin Constitution). Park sought to strengthen his position in dealing with oppositional forces. Since the Carter Administration announced the withdrawal of American troops from Korea and South Vietnam surrendered to the communists he thought the military self-strengthening as of pivotal importance for Korea's security. For this purpose he thought the accelerated development of heavy industries in close connection with establishment of defense industry as absolutely necessary. With this goal in mind he launched in 1973 the HCI Plan (planned investment volume: 9.6 billion US Dollars) with 6 priority fields such as iron & steel, nonferrous metal, machinery, shipbuilding, electronics and petrochemical industries (Kim Hyung-A 2006). Park's actual plan was to combine this HCI Plan distinctly with defense industry in Korea.

The HCI Plan was classified by Park as an *imperative plan,* different from the previous five year plans, being composed of detailed project investment programs with exact time schedule. The government, offering the diversified scope of projects, 'urged' only a handful of big business groups to join implementation of these projects by at the same time granting various incentives to them. The HCI Plan aimed at the *built-in cluster formation* which implies that the related industries of projects in a specific industry were to be forcibly placed in industrial parks such as the machine industry in Changwoon Machinery Industry Park, or the petrochemical industry in Yeochoen Industrial Park (Oh 2011).

President Park with the HCI Plan neglected economic-rationally founded arguments: Korea was in shortage of capital, technology and qualified manpower; the domestic absorptive capacity too small; the gestation period for huge investments too long and negative environmental effect would be immense. Even the EPB was also critical and upholstered a counter-position by pinpointing the Oil Crisis-driven recession of the global business entailing shrinking demand for capital goods. Critical arguments came not only from economists in Korea, but also from the American side, as the Korean investment inducement delegation was on a tour in USA (Lee 1993).

Given this constellation Park, convinced of necessity of the *institutional-backup* for the HCI Plan, strengthened the position of the Blue House Secretary in charge of defense industry and set up under his direct responsibility the HCI Promotion Council attuned to implementing the HCI Plan.

There was another reason for this responsibility shift. The conflict between the EPB focusing on *market orientation,* and other ministries (e.g. Ministry of Commerce and Industry, and Ministry of Finance) abiding by *state intervention* became increasingly virulent so that the governance at ministry level was seen as impossible. Finally the Blue House directly had to arbitrate conflicts. A critical moment was that the EPB failed to solve problems of insolvent companies at the end of 60s. President Park must have thought that the 'autonomy' the EPB enjoyed in planning and policy-making to a large extent should be curbed by the Blue House. This led to considerable weakening of the EPB. In other terms, *the blueprinting and implementation of the HCI Plan hinged less on market rationality than state intervention.* The question how the Park regime 'successfully' managed to solve goal-and implementation-conflicts between market rationality and state intervention has remained unanswered until now.

Even the comprehensive studies by Dr. Lee Man Hee (1993) and Prof. Choi Byung-Sun (1987) do not provide a satisfactory reply.

The HCI Plan was formally overlapping with the ongoing third five year plan, but in reality undermined the Third Five Year Plan. The function of the HCI Council was ranging from handpicking private investors to devising incentives. In line with this the important institution was National Investment Fund which tapped financial resources from public employee pension funds and a substantial portion of private savings at commercial banks. These funds were preferably allocated to those projects favored by the government. Further, banks were urged to finance projects requiring additional investment.

Project-participating firms were granted tax concessions to draw back of customs duties on import of necessary machines and raw materials.[1] Through the decision by President Park in favor of the HCI Plan he ignored market-conform decision-making and created a more powerful institution for this plan than the EPB.

---

1   According to Kim Kyung-A (2003) not the EPB, but the Ministry of Commerce and Industry was believed to implement the HCI Plan, since there was a great number of civil servants specialized in engineering. After the coup d'Etat by General Chun Doo Whan at the end of 70s the new National Committee of Emergency Measures for Protection of Security (Kuk Bo Whi) took over the planning responsibility for Heavy and Chemical Industries (Lee 1993).

2.2 Implicit Knowledge of Planning and the Sogang School's Growth Ideology

After the World War II and the Korean War the ideas about the planning were offered by American experts. Even though in the second half of the 50s the Korean Government frequently made mention about necessity of planning a large ambiguity about the planning knowledge was looming. Nevertheless Park hurried to assemble soon available economists and experts who were willing to contribute to economic development. Most experts (such as Kim Yutek, Park Choonghun, Shin Hyunhak), trained in Korea and/or Japan, strongly inclined towards Keynesianism, were 'patriotism'-disposed enthusiastic bureaucrats instead of relying on profound knowledge about planning.

Korea suffered lack of highly qualified experts in modern economic theories and policies. At the first stage of economic planning experts from the World Bank and USA extended consultancy as regards planning. Later, in the year 1969 Dr. Nam Duck Woo who returned from USA, and teaching at Sogang (Catholic) University was appointed Minister of Finance. With his nomination the expression 'Sogang School' was born. Very soon Dr. Lee Sung Hoon and Dr. Kim Manje also from Sogang University, both trained in USA, joined the Government by achieving high ranking position in economic policy.

This School is not comparable for instance to the Chicago School, or Frankfurter Schule as regards a consistent theoretical and methodological edifice. It stands for the group of economic bureaucrats who were graduated from or teaching at department of economics, Sogang University. The Sogang School[2] supporter of the economic growth has been playing the most decisive role in planning and policy making for economic development in the 70s and 80s. The characteristics of this School in practical politics were and are: *first growth, then distribution, accent on export-orientation and on heavy and chemical industries, chaebol-friendly policies, on expansion of foreign trade and FDI* (Economy Chosun, retrieved February 24, 2013). The Sogang School was of cobsiderable influence for the whole period

---

2   The distribution-oriented economists graduated from Seoul National University were grouped around Prof. Byun Hyung Yoon (Seoul National University), called "Hakhyun School", having influenced the economic and financial policies under the Kim Dae-Jung and Roh Myun Yun president. This School, originating from Dept. of Economics of SNU, consisted of left-wing, progressive economists trained in Korea and also partly in Germany. The most serious criticism which met the Sogang School was that it was made responsible for causing the IMF Financial Crisis of 1997. One can describe the juxtaposition between the Sogang Univ.-centered growth orientation and the SNU-centered distribution orientation as still influential in economic debates.

of development state from president Park to Roh Tae Woo in policy making so that it is associated with the period of high growth and developmentalism in Korea. The debate between the growth-centered *Sogang School* and its counterpart, distribution-centered *Hakyun School* is still continuing. Depending on which political party the president is belonging to the orientation of economic policy toward growth or distribution is decided on. With the new president Park Geun Hye it is likely that the Sogang School – she graduated from this university – gains more influence again.

Compared with practices in economic planning and policy making in other underdeveloped countries Korea under the Park regime was unique in the sense that neither the military nor former bureaucrats have exercised influence on developmental institutions, but instead relied on those experts with profound knowledge and experiences. This entailed strengthening of military-neutral effect so that by entry of the Sogang School's economic elite into the government gave a buoyant momentum to the rationalization of bureaucracy in Korea. Especially the EPB became emblematic of a rationally working institution.

By increasing the planning experiences knowledge and skills of planning-concerned bureaucrats, developmental institutions became increasingly sophisticated. During the 18 years rule by the Park regime the best sophisticated five year plan was said to be the second five year plan based on input-output matrix and a dynamic projection model for the consistency of the overall plan as well as estimating sector-specific investment and import requirements. The plan has stressed further three aspects: implementation machinery, planning machinery and translation of the plan into action programs. Also the plan required other ministries and agencies of the government to participate in the planning.

Based on experiences with the implementation of five year plans the third and fourth plan were more diffused and decentralized, more detailed. This was thanks to the young generation of planners and bureaucrats in cooperation with the Korea Development Institute (founded in 1971) (Oh 2011).

1.3 Korea Institute of Science and Technology (KIST) and Brain Circulation

The industrial policy undertaken, first of all, by the Park regime to accent electricity and electronics went together with shift from import-substitution to export-led strategy mid-60s which implied necessity to localize production of electronic parts. The problem was lack of relevant high tech and engineers. The establishment of KIST was thanks to the support by the American government to Korea. The American government requested President Park to dispatch Korean troops to the

Vietnam War. In compensation for Korea's troops joining the US army in Vietnam President Johnson supported the establishment of KIST. The Report by Donald F. Hornig, special advisor to the President Johnson soon conducted a F/S study in Korea and recommended set-up of KIST.

However, the most difficult problem KIST was faced with was to pursue its *staffing* due to shortage of noteworthy scientists in Korea. The Battelle Institute suggested KIST to *recruit Korean scholars working abroad* which led to scouting young experts at Yutah University, Harvard University, Columbia University, and other universities and research institutes in USA. The next problem was the question whether a *special ministry* in charge of science and technology was needed. Scholars and scientists, in particular, the president Park favored a new ministry of science and technology which was established in 1967, this as the *first ministry of science and technology in the Third World*.

Figure 1: Changes of Science- and Technology-related Institutions (1960–2000).

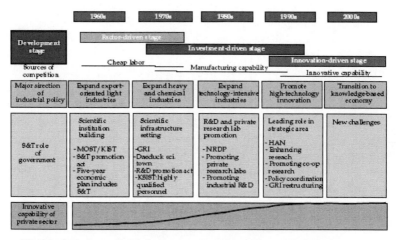

Source: World Bank, Korea as a Knowledge Economy 2006: 20, cited from Mitchell 1997

The mission of KIST was to assume a central role as the first comprehensive research agency for promotion of the nation's modernization of engineering fields. It has since then developed into the foremost R&D organization and the foundation of technological development in Korea, now with four branches, three in Korea and the fourth in Saarbruecken, Germany.

As Figure 1 indicates, the Park Government has shown great interest to get institutions aiming at promoting science and technology. Especially in the 60 ties with the first and second five year plan, above all, the set-up of the Daeduk Science Park was stressed.

2.4 Big Business Groups, Federation of Korean Industries (FKI), and Guided Corporatism

One speaks of the industrialization in Korea as not only government-led, but also Chaebol-led. The new government saw the major role in implementation of the five year plans in close cooperation with Chaebols.

Hall/Soskice (2003) described the capitalism in Korea as *group*-based, 'coordinated market economy', for which the *family-based* Chaebols are of crucial importance. The coordination in Korea functioned formerly in more 'protectionistic' ways than Japanese keiretsu (Hall/ Soskice 2003: 34), but since the Financial Crisis of 1997 the coordination by Chaebols is opener than in the case of Japanese keiretsu. The IMF's bail-out enabled a significant corporate reform which led to foreign companies' joining in intra-company transactions.

At the beginning of the Park regime Korea suffered lack of big companies endowed with financial, managerial capability, and human resources. Park took the chance to bring up big business groups, Chaebols which were 'ordered' to reach the plan goals announced by the Government. At the time of seizure by Park Chung Hee of political power there were a small number of companies which enjoyed 'toleration' by the Japanese colonial rule thanks to their cooperation with it, and after the World War II more or less successfully continuing their business owing to their 'crony' behaviors towards the Government, culminating in corruption. This plagued the Rhee Regime causing severe political instability.

President Park (1971) wrote in his book "Potential of the Korean Nation": "one of the most serious impediments for the development is weakness of our companies in all respects and especially in shortage of new entrepreneurship". He must have thought of the situation, in which the government in the Japanese Meiji Period was helpless for embarking on industrialization at the end of 19th century, because it lacked noteworthy businessmen. It took some time until Samurai of Tokugawa Period changed its status into risky entrepreneurs. Which way should Park go in case of Korea in order to bring up market actors?

Park's political legitimacy should lie in eradication of corruption, for which the Cleanup of Illegal Enrichment Law was enacted. About 30 big companies violated this law. Park offered a compromise to these companies that in case of active implementation of the five year plans the Government would alleviate its strict position in anti-corruption policy. Business groups were instrumentalized for Park's economic plans. Around this time the terminology "Chaebol" came to use for the first time. From now on the adage was in full swing. "Plans came from the Park government, Chaebols carried out them"! The privileges Chaebols enjoyed were guarantee by the government of bank loans and foreign loans and grant by it of big specific projects participation, of which experts spoke 'guided capitalism'.

On the top of it, the Government needed a strong association of business groups, as it is the case in advanced countries. Park had probably the powerful Japanese enterprises association Keidanren in mind. He urged business groups to build up an association of enterprises as soon as possible. The currently powerful enterprise association, Federation of Korean Industries (FKI) goes back to this time. As the new Government under Park cleared the framework of the upcoming key industries, SOC, promotion of foreign trade etc., 20 private entrepreneurs such as Lee Byungchul (Samsung), Jung Jeho (Samho), Kim Yunsoo (Samyong), Sul Kyungdong (Dehan), Koo Inhoe (Lucky), Jung Jooyoung (Hyundai) etc. declared their willingness to join in implementation of the first five plan by establishing the Association for Promotion of Economic Reconstruction which was changed into FKI in 1968.

Table 1: Top 10 Chaebols in 50s–80s

Rank	Late 1950s	Mid-1960s	1974	1983
1	Samsung	Samsung	Samsung	Hyundai
2	Samho	Samho	LG	Samsung
3	Gaepung	LG	Hyundai	Daewoo
4	Daehan	Daehan	Hanjin	LG
5	LG	Gaepung	Ssangyong	Ssangyong
6	Tongyang	Samyang	SK	SK
7	Keukdong	Ssangyong	Hanhwa	Hanhwa
8	Hankook Glass	Hwashin	Daenong	Hanjin
9	Donglip	Panbon	Dong-Ah. Const.	Kukje
10	Taechang	Tongyang	HanilSyn. Textile	Daelim

Source: http://www.sjsu.edu/faculty/watkins/park.htm

This Association emphasized its willingness for the new government in more concrete sense: in line with one of the new top policies by the Park government the new Association supported actively the promotion of electrification and dissemination of telephone system which was the first step towards government-business cooperative relations. In the case of Korea's FKI one could speak of the *guided corporatism* instead of the embedded corporatism.

Beside the enthusiastic intention by big business groups to cooperate with the Government in pursuing industrial policies they played an active role in inducing foreign capital. They needed capital, technology, and western management skills. Especially the *foreign capital inducement law* revised just before the second five year plan was enacted with a strong support by FKI. Thanks to the new Foreign Capital Inducement Law the number of direct investment by foreign MNCs rapidly increased. Noteworthy companies were Fairchild, IBM, Signetics, AMC, Motorola, etc. With Japanese firms emerged Japanese-Korea Joint Ventures such as Samsung-Sanyo, Samsung-NEC, Korea Micro Electronic, Komi Industries, Korea-Toshiba, etc. Particular note deserves in this regard the Korean-Japanese Normalization Treaty (1965) which opened for the Japanese business world the path toward their investments in Korea (Park 1969).

Table 2: Inflows of Foreign Capital

(2005: US$ million)				
	First plan (1962–66)	Second plan (1967–71)	Third plan (1972–76)	Fourth plan (1977–80)
Loans	291	2,166	5,432	10,256
Public	116	811	2,389	4,084
Commercial	175	1,355	3,043	6,172
FDI	17	96	557	425
Total	308	2,262	5,989	10,681

Source: cited from Government of the Republic of Korea 1982: 5.

In the time of the First and Second Five Year Plan the loans made up the major part of foreign capital inflow, whilst the foreign direct investment (FDI) stagnated due to market uncertainties caused by the Oil Crisis. As regards the technology import American MNCs were active in direct circuit and transistor related fields, whilst Japanese MNCs in the field of condenser, transformer, speaker, that is to say, electronic/ electric parts. Interesting was also the difference that American MNCs were active in the region of Seoul, Japanese MNCs in the newly opened Economic Special Zone of Masan.

3. Strategy Choice

3.1 Balanced Growth versus Unbalanced Growth

In regards to the allocation of given resources for development there are two alternatives: the one is balanced growth strategy and the other unbalanced growth strategy. The former by Nurkse and Rosenstein-Rodan proceeds on the assumption that ad hoc investment is not sufficient, as demand in underdeveloped country is too low for development to be stimulated. Not even products manufactured at home would be consumed by the labor force which produced them. Here Say's theorem 'supply creates demand' does not work. Thus, what is necessary is 'big push', namely huge coordinated investments to create a demand which would stimulate production. This theory seems not to be tenable in the Third World. The second strategy by Hirschman, Singer and Myrdal stems from real situation of underdeveloped countries, that is to say, shortage of resources, especially financial resources and the lack of experienced entrepreneurs prepared to undertake (risky) investments. Therefore, preference should be given to those leading sectors, for instance, SOC, which entails larger linkage (forward/backward) effects on DPA (direct production activities).

A basic notion of the balanced growth concept is the assumption that all necessary factors must be available in the right place, at the right time and in adequate amounts. For pursuing this concept a centralized authoritarian strong, big state is *conditio sine qua non*. To be short, this strategy requires *a socialist regime*. In contrast, the unbalanced growth concept prefers purposively those sectors, in which available resources are 'concentrated' coupled with expectation that larger linkage effects are created. The attractiveness of this model is to create imbalance in order that those backward sectors should try to catch up with the leading sectors. According to Hirschman the imbalance is to lead to balance which culminates in development.

By taking both strategies into account the Korean Government, particularly the EPB gave more preference to the unbalanced growth strategy, with which the foundation for future economic development plans in Korea was laid. Decisions on construction of the Seoul-Pusan Highway, establishment of the Economic Special Zones such as Gumi, Masan, and further of economic growth centers such as Changwon (Industrial Estate), Pohang (Steel) and Ulsan (Ship-Building), and the Heavy and Chemical Industries Plan in the 70s can be understood in the framework of the unbalanced growth strategy.

Figure 2: Unbalanced growth: investment in SOC or DPA.

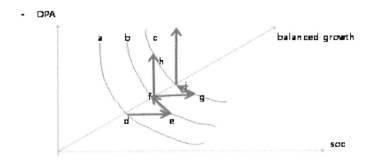

In the framework of the unbalanced growth strategy the Government and the EPB exercised thoroughly the first three five year plans (1962–1976) (*normative planning*). Since the fourth five year plan (1977–81) the plans had character of *indicative planning* which lasted up to the 7th five year plan. The normative planning is state-led plan sticking to the governmental decisions on allocation principles and strategies. Also the late HCI Plan (imperative planning) leaned on the unbalanced growth concept. (see the map)

Figure 3: Economic Development based on Unbalanced Growth Model with extreme Regional Concentration.

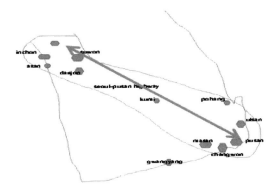

The attitude of the Government towards the plan implementation did not stick to the planned targets. This was also the same with the allocation of resources. To a great degree the *flexibility* in plan implementation played an important role depending on functioning of domestic market forces and especially international market constellations. This means practically the Government tried to rely greatly on the well functioning of market forces for implementation of the plans, for which the incentive system and provision of information by the Government became greatly instrumental.

Table 3: Economic Plans based on unbalanced growth with regional concentration

Taxonomy of planning	priorities
phase of **normative planning:**	
First Five Year Plan (1962–1966):	electrical power, fertilizer production, petroleum refining, cement, synthetic fibers
Second Five Year Plan (67–71):	steel, machines, chemicals
Third Five Year Plan (72–76):	iron & steel, transport equipment, machines, ships, petrochemicals, electronics
phase of **indicative planning:**	
Fourth Five Year Plan (77–81):	iron & steel, machines, ships, petrochemicals, electronics, non-ferrous metals
Fifth Five Year Plan (82–86):	precision, machinery, electronics, technology industries
Sixth Five Year Plan (87–91):	higher technology, R/D, manpower training
Seventh Five Year Plan (92–96):	microelectronics, bioengineering, aerospace, fine chemicals
Phase of **Imperative Planning:**	
(1973–1981)	The Heavy and Chemical Industries Plan

Source: http://www.sjsu.edu/faculty/watkins/park.htm

The private sector also had to deal with uncertainties entailed by the planned targets and plan implementation, and especially the export-led industrialization and international market.

As the following table indicates the realized GNP growth rate exceeded the planned targets which was due to government leadership, efficient resources allocation and, last but not least flexible response by private entrepreneurs. In order to react towards market uncertainties in a better way the Government took the initiative from 1967 on the Annual Overall Resource Budget (ORB) which formed a consistent basis for a short term policy making by taking into account past performance, set short-term targets and allocations, and appropriate implementation policies.

Table 4: Plan Targets and Realized Performance (unit: %)

First Five Year Plan (1962–1966)	
planned 7.1%	realized 8.3%
Second Five Year Plan (1967–1971)	
planned 7.0%	realized 11.4%
Third Five Year Plan (1972–76)	
planned 8.6%	realized 11.2%
Fourth Five Year Plan (1977–81)	
planned 9.2%	realized 5.5%

Source: data collected by the author

Evaluating the five year plans under the Park regime the most important result of them was said to bring the knowledge accumulation process among economic elites and to enhance capability of the private sector as regards how to deal with market forces. Prof. Oh is referring to flexibility of the Government's handling economic plans as follows: " formal planning was only partially successful in mapping a detailed path for the economy to follow. Rather, it turned out to provide a focus for dialogue, training technocrats, articulating the leadership commitment, giving the general guidelines and implicit promises of support that facilitate private planning" (Oh 2011: 8).

3.2 From import substitution to export-led growth strategy

Talking about the alternative strategy between inward-looking and outward-looking strategy for development the author is reminded of the debate evoked by the German dependence theoreticians such as D. Senghaas, and U. Menzel in the 80s. They argued in favor of de-coupling from the dependence on the world economy reflecting on experiences of China, North Korea, Albania, Romania, Cuba, etc. This was called 'dissociative strategy'. The author was and is not sure of success of the dissociative strategy in any country. The question is, as a matter of fact, whether an economy with a small domestic demand should choose import substitution as development trajectory.

An interesting fact was that the Park Government was influenced by the nationalism-disposed self-reliance ideology culminating in import substitution policy. The first five year plan with priorities on petroleum refining and key raw materials producing industries such as fertilizer, cement, iron and steel, and synthetic fibers aimed at import substitution-based industrialization. It was expected to reach self-sufficiency during the first five year plan by increase in productivity by means of multiple cropping which was to be intensively associated with the New Village Movement later. The Government exercised import dampening policy especially for consumer goods and intermediates. The import prohibition and import quota system was introduced in 1965. The outcome of the first five year plan was ambivalent. The growth rate with more than 8% exceeded the planned goal of 7%, the industrial production increased also by 50%. Nevertheless the import substitution contributed to an increase of imported goods by 75%. The trade deficit boosted immensely. Poverty remained unchanged, with 2/5 of all households falling below the absolute poverty line. In sum, the supply of especially consumer goods was not sufficient, the effective demand was very low. Before the end of the first five plan the Government shifted the industrial policy from the import substitution to export-centered strategy (Adelman, op.cit.)

The revision of the import substitution was substantiated by concentration on use of comparative advantage of labor-intensive goods. "The combination of low-per capita income with small population (28.5 million) suggested that a domestic market oriented (import substitution) could not provide the scope for diversification need to achieve greater economic performance" (Adelman, op.cit).

This paradigm change was accompanied by increase in import of foreign capital, foreign technology and capital goods as well as import of raw materials. The first effort is opening of the Kuro Export Industry Zone in 1964 followed by the Gumi Industrial Zone in 1969. The Government hurried up to enact the Foreign Investment Law in 1974, according to which four kinds of industrial zone for export promotion were introduced.

- Government-guided Industrial Zone: Changwon, Ulsan, Gumi, Banwol
- Free Export Processing Zone: Masan and Iri
- Local Industrial Zone: Gwangjoo and Daegu
- Private Industrial Zone[3]

---

3   These efforts were supported by the following measures:
   1. The government set up a strict export target system. Firms having reached these targets they were awarded with special prizes.

To sum up, the Outward Export-led Strategy which had begun mid- 60s the export of labor-intensive goods (e.g. whigs, textiles, etc.) had highest priority. Gradually it shifted from the labor-intensive phase to export of capital-intensive goods which was possible thanks to the HCI Plan standing for import of raw materials, foreign technology and foreign capital, for which the Chaebols played a decisive role. Iron and steel, electronics, petro-chemical products, cars, ships and machines made up the major share of the export. (cf. the following table)

Table 5: Share of Manufacturing Goods in Export 1962–1979

Share of Manufacturing Goods in Export:	
1962	27.0%
1970	83.6%
Share of Heavy and Chemical Industry Goods in Export:	
1970	15.5%
1979	43.1%

Source: Ministry of Finance and Economy

4. Conclusion: Lessons from Korea?

Park Chung-Hee who ruled the country for about 20 years has successfully exercised the first attempt in the Third World to pursue the overcoming of under-development by means of state-led strategies, rationality-based developmental institutions and their knowledge accumulation and bringing up market actors (Chaebols). He laid the foundation for Korea to become an advanced country under the capitalistic system. Significant fact is that the path Korea went was overcoming legacies of the colonialism and two wars having shown that the state-led capitalism making in the Third World in the relatively short period is possible, however, needs at least two prerequisites: first, economic rationality – centered bureaucrats and second, firms, big and small, as market actors.

A significant advantage of Park's politics was his leadership commitment and confidence which he put in developmental institutions and policy making machinery to the effect that they were able to establish constructive and reliant relations with other relevant institutions on the basis of rationality. The fact that Korean

---

2. The Government opened up Korea Trade Promotion Agency (KOTRA) in foreign countries in order to provide firms with information about new market and marketing strategies in foreign countries.

3. The President hosted the monthly export meeting in its Blue House.

institutions proved to be working as rational institutions and making expedient decisions oriented towards pragmatism betrays the Weberian notion that economic rational behavior is solely in monopoly of the Western civilization. Of special advantage was that military personnel and previous bureaucrats did not seize those developmental institutions and policy making machinery.

The development policy by Park Chung Hee was *efficiency-oriented*. Almost all projects related to five year plans he launched had only the efficiency criteria. The quality-accentuating and structure-forming efforts were given the second priority. Park Chung Hee always was in a hurry to bring projects to an end even by ignoring market principle. He, thus, associated this efficiency with his political legitimacy. The effectiveness and sustainability were for him foreign words.

His growth-centered policy later continued in the 80 ties entailed massive external diseconomies, of which the legacies are still noticeable in its full length.

Especially two aspects accompanied this growth-centered policy: *first*, regional concentration, and *second*, concentration of economic and knowledge power in Chaebols.

The growth strategy based on unbalanced growth was regionally *in toto* concentrated on the Eastern region (Youngnam) of South Korea by means of heavy and chemical industries and Economic Special Zones and Export Processing Zones, and highly developed infrastructures. As already stressed this development policy was carried out in tandem with active engagements by Chaebols, of which most of them stem from the Eastern region.

Adding these aspects together one could regard the development of South Korea essentially as *that of the Eastern region* which has been also criticized by people of the Western region (Honam). There has been an extreme income and developmental gap between both regions which has been forming a lasting theme of political and economic debates. One can go so far to argue that the origin of the left wing (current opposition party) versus right wing (ruling party) struggle in Korea may be abortive in Park's unbalanced growth strategy. The thesis by Hirschman attached to the Unbalanced Growth Model that the SOC investment would be accompanied by DPA (Direct Productive Activities) thanks to forward and backward linkage effects proved not to be verified in the period of the Park Chung Hee regime.

Making the balance sheet on the developmental state under President Park one can resume that he was successful in overcoming the absolute poverty Korea was faced with, and pursuing 'economic development' by planning at the same time through bringing up market actors. However, the planning in Korea was to a great degree characterized by resilience in beginning with normative planning in the time of absence of efficiently working enterprises, and gradually by developing actors for implementation of plans; Chaebols, then with indicative planning. Lastly President Park put imperative planning into effect for developing of heavy and chemical industries contrary to market principle – despite worsening international market constellations and shrinking demand caused by the oil crisis at the beginning of 70ties and Korea's shortage of capital, technology and skilled workers. This was really a risky decision which finally led to a great success two decades later.

Last, but not least. Park's economic success had to be compensated for by political and social costs. Without the authoritarian dictatorship his economic success would not have been possible. This experience gives a momentum to reflect on western modernization theories which conceptualize the synchronic development between economic growth and democratization possible. The case of Korea cannot provide an evidence for validity of these theories. It seems that a certain level of economic growth – hand in hand with other variables such as SOC, education, dissemination of information etc. – is necessary.

Lessons from Korea's experiences?

The author would be hesitant to offer any formulaic advices. The experiences Korea made under Park Chung Hee were 'unique' in many respects. Most Korea-concerned experts forget to consider the *state of war* lasting since the Korean War as an *essential development catalyst*. Korea has been living in crisis since more than 6 decades. In this context the author is allowed to give a reference to the book by Dan Senor and Saul Singer "Start-Up Nation. The Story of Israel's Economic Miracle".

References

Adelman, Irma (190?) From Aid Dependence to Aid Independence: South Korea retrieved March 2, 2013.

Amsden, Alice H. (1989) Asia's Next Giant: South Korea and Late Industrialization, Oxford: Oxford University Press.

Andreff, W. (1993) The Double Transition from Underdevelopment and From Socialism in Vietnam, in: Journal of Contemporary Asia 23, No.4, pp. 515–531.

Cho, D. (1990) A study of chaebols, Maeil Economic Daily (korean)

Choi, Byung-Sun (1987) Institutionalizing a Liberal Economic Order in Korea: The Strategic Management of Economic Change, PhD Diss., Harvard University.

Crouch, Colin (2005) Models of Capitalism, in: New Political Economy, Vol. 10, No.4, December 2005, pp. 439–456.

Chung, Chung-Kil (1992) Determinants of the Bureaucratic Contribution to Rapid Economic Development, Seoul National University.

Hall, Peter A. / Soskice, David (2003) Introduction to Varieties of Capitalism, in: Hall / Soskice (eds.), Varieties of Capitalism – The Institutional Foundations of Comparative Advantage, Oxford, pp. 1–68.

Johnson, Chalmers (1982) MITI and Japanese Miracle, Stanford.

Kang, David (2002) Crony Capitalism. University of Southern California.

Kim, Hyung-A (2003) Korea's Development under Park Chung-Hee: Rapid Industrialization 1961–1979, Routledge.

Kim, Moon Hee (2005) Human Resources Development for Knowledge Economy – Republic of Korea, ESCAP, Bangkok.

Kohli, Atul (2004) State-directed development, Cambridge: Cambridge University Press.

Lee, Man Hee (1993) EPB nun gijok ul nahanunga? (Did the EPB create a miracle?), Seoul.

Lin, Timothy C. (2001) Corporations and Korean Capitalism, in: Korean Studies, Vol. 25, No.1, pp. 140–142.

Lombardi, Lucia (2011) How capitalism developed in Taiwan and South Korea – any parallels with China today?, Part 2, in: In Defense of Marxism, 15. Sept. 2011, retrieved May 15, 2011.

Mackow, J. (2005) Totalitarismus und danach, Nomos.

Merkl, W. (1999) Systemtransformation. Eine Einfuehrung in die Theorie und Empirie der Transformationsforschung, Opladen: Ldeske-Budrich.

Nam, Duck Woo (1965) Korea's Experience with the Five Year-Economic Development Plan, online: http://www.dwnam.pe.kr/102plan.html

North, Douglass C. (1990) Institutional Change: A Framework of Analysis, retrieved February 10, 2013.

North, Douglass C. (1993) Economic Performance through Time, Lecture to the memory of Alfred Nobel, December 9, 1993.

Park, Chung-Hee (1971) Potential of the Korean Nation, Seoul (Korean).

Park, Sung-Jo (1969) Die Wirtschaftsbeziehungen zwischen Japan und Korea 1910–1968, Wiesbaden.

Park, Sung-Jo (1977) Allokative Effizienz, Buerokratisierung und Partizipation in der Entwicklungsplanung (unter besonderer Beruecksichtigung der partizipativen Planung in der Volksrepublik China, in: Buerokratie, Th. Leuenberger / K.-H Ruffmann (eds.), Lang, pp. 279–297.

Park, Sung-Jo (1980) Entwicklungsplanung und Politische Entwicklung in der Dritten Welt, Campus.

Park, Sung-Jo (2007) The Soviet Type of Industrialization and its Intellectual Legacies in Development and Transformation Theories focusing on the Change of State Functions, in: Mica Jovanovic et al., (eds.) System Transformation in Comparative Perspective, LIT, pp. 9–44.

Senor, D. / Singer, S. (2009) Start-Up Nation. The Story of Israel's Economic Miracle, Twelve, New York.

Sklair, Leslie / Robbins, Peter T. (2002) Global Capitalism and Major Corporations from the Third World, in: Third World Quarterly, Vol. 23, No. 1, pp. 81–100.

Song, J. / Cho, D. (1998) Diversification Strategies and the formation of Korean big Business Groups (Chaebols): Resources-based and Institutional Perspectives, Discussion Papers APEC Study Center Columbia University, Discussion Paper No. 9.

Janno Reiljan and Ingra Paltser[1]

The Implementation of Research and Development Policy in European and Asian Countries

1. Introduction

In order to promote innovation as one of the most important development factors of a country, a complex and efficient national innovation system must be developed. The integrity and harmonious functioning of the national innovation system must be guaranteed by innovation policy, which intermediates the relationship between organisations dealing with innovation (firms, government agencies and NGOs) and institutions (both formal and informal), but also integrates the parts of different policies directed to innovation to a single innovation policy.

The central role in innovation policy development is executed by research and development (R&D) policy, which represents the major complex of government sector measures to initiate and promote innovation. When planning the policies of other fields (e.g. education, labour market, budget and taxes), the interrelationship with R&D policies and activities must be taken into account. The creation of anything new is always connected with uncertainty, with a risk of no positive results, irrespective of the expenses made. The incoordination of R&D policy with other policies, i.e. deficiency of the innovation system, can limit the results of R&D activities in the economy and economic growth; also, the productivity increase or improvement in competitiveness may not be achieved to the desired extent. That is why government sector R&D policy is not solely responsible for the innovation success of a country, but the importance is large enough to consider it as a separate research object.

In the current article, the levels and dynamics of R&D policy resource supply and costs will be analysed by comparing EU member states, countries closely associated with the EU and three Asian countries. As above, we will present the comparable role of R&D policy in innovation systems of different countries. It should be taken into account that different countries (small and large, highly developed and in the transformation phase, with open and closed economies, in

1 Authors acknowledge the support of the Estonian Ministry of Science and Education foundation project No. SF0180037s08.

different development stages) have different innovation policy objectives and measures to achieve them (Czarnitzki/Bento 2010; Hewitt-Dundas/Roper 2010). Still, R&D policy is developed in more general institutional conditions. For instance, in countries with a majority election system the structure of the state budget is shifted towards a smaller share of public services (including scientific research) and a larger share of social transfers (Persson et al. 1997; Persson/Tabellini 1999; Persson et al. 2000). Kim (2011) shows that R&D policy (financing) decisions are influenced by the specifics of a state political system – the location of a state in the political space, the dimensions of which are presidential versus parliamentary system; majority versus proportional election system; federal versus unitary government system; a parliament consisting of one or two chambers; number of parties in the parliament. All of those qualitative aspects must be taken into account when interpreting the results of quantitative comparative analysis of R&D policies in different countries.

The goal of the article is the comparable assessment of R&D policy implementation in EU member states, countries closely associated with the EU and three Asian countries in respect of R&D policy implementation from a resource supply and cost aspect. In order to achieve the research goal, the following research tasks are tackled:

- on the basis of scientific literature the necessity, nature, measures and expected results of R&D policy in a country are identified;
- through empirical analysis an assessment is given to the international position of Estonia and some other countries (South Korea and Germany) in implementing R&D policy among thecountries in scope.

The results of the research help to understand the differences of R&D policy development in different countries, taking into account theoretical approaches and international experience.

2. Theoretical Questions of Research and Development Policy Interventions

Firstly, it is necessary to give a theoretical overview of the justification of government sector intervention in R&D processes. Generally, the intervention of the government sector is considered to be justified in the case of market and system failures. The government sector should intervene with adequate measures on a scale, which is necessary to overcome the abovementioned failures. At the same time, the government sector should avoid overreaction to failures that will lead to the distortion of market processes and not provide state aid in the shade of R&D policy.

2.1 Elimination of Market Failures

Market failures in R&D activities have been researched for decades (Dasgupta/ David 1994) and they appear in several different forms. In the following, the main market failures in R&D activities will be highlighted. Firstly, the nature of invention and innovation has to be considered. For over fifty years, the question whether R&D outcomes are more public than private good in nature has been attended (Nelson 1959; Arrow 1962). The consumption of R&D outcomes has generally no rivalry, i.e. the invention or innovation can be used parallelly and the utility can be acquired by an endless amount of users without changing their nature (see Romer 1990; Grossman/Helpman 1991; Aghion/Howitt 1992). However, market competition between users of R&D results remains – the profit earning capacity of innovation or invention for the first marketer decreases remarkably after others apply it. Thus, for the owner of new product, services, production technology, etc. it is very important somehow to exclude unentitled persons (competitors) from using its R&D work results, i.e. the protection of intellectual property is needed. As the protection of intellectual property is often difficult and expensive, the economic rationality of its application should be considered. Therefore, the intervention of the government sector and the necessity of R&D policy come from the fact that due to the absence of competitive rivalry in use, innovation is not a pure private good and firms cannot afford excluding others from the use of their R&D work results. However, for several cases government sector intervention cannot be justified purely for excluding market competition because of the absence of rivalry in the use of the R&D results; better reasoning is needed.

For the society as a whole it is useful to emphasise the public good nature of research work results and involve as many organisations (firms and institutions) and members of the society as quickly as possible in the consumption of the R&D results. Thus, the government sector should fund research activities that create public goods. As the result of public institutions' R&D activities, knowledge available to all interested parties is created (Edquist 2006). Public sector R&D activities are financed with an objective to support innovation from research offered as a public good mainly in private firms, but also in public sector institutions. It is expected that fundamental research at universities or scientific research establishments lead to discoveries, the value of which is recognised by firms that apply this new knowledge in implementing innovative projects (Pavitt 2006). The influence of public sector R&D activities on private sector R&D investments and productivity was assessed with macroeconomic models a few decades ago (Levy/Terleckyj 1983).

The practical usefulness of fundamental scientific research is very difficult to assess (Greenberg 1967; Sherwin/Isenson 1967). Normally it takes years or decades until the results of fundamental research are being practically applied (Gellman Associates 1976; Adams 1990; Mansfield 1991/98; Branstetter/Ogura 2005), whereas their application in practice and usefulness develop in the interrelation of many factors (Rogers/Bozeman 2001; Bozeman/Rogers 2002). The profitability of fundamental scientific research is therefore very unsteady. This means that the results of fundamental research can only be offered to society commissioned by public sector organisations and funded from the state budget.

Development work has less characteristics of a public good. The R&D activities conducted by firms are more development work than fundamental research: the objective is to find application possibilities for new knowledge so the profit of the firm would increase (Edquist 2006). That is why funding by the government sector is justified only exceptionally and in a limited amount. Besides supporting development work with resources, the government sector should consider applying intellectual property protection measures in order to constrain the usage of results as public goods. The elimination of market competition and the creation of private monopoly with the help of the government sector are justified only in areas where it is necessary to stimulate firms to provide funds for research activities. In addition, it should be examined whether government sector R&D subsidies increase (supplement) the R&D costs in firms or replace (substitute) them (Leyden/Link 1991; Lach 2002). Government sector R&D costs increase total social R&D costs when the government sector support influences the private sector to allocate R&D funds to projects that without the support would not be profitable (Klette et al. 2000; Wallsten 2000; Jaffe 2002; Tokila et al. 2008). However, the threat that the government sector support will substitute private sector R&D costs emerges inevitably in cases where the private sector has resources but they are more expensive than those offered by the government sector (Jaffe 2002; Blanes/Busom 2004). It is difficult to assess the impact of R&D activities for country as a whole since some firms get them and others do not (Hujer/Radic 2003). A lot of empirical research has been directed to finding out the effect of government sector R&D support on private sector R&D expenditure. These will be reviewed in the second part of the current research.

Generally, research has a positive externality (transfer of knowledge), which is revealed both between research institutions and from research institutions to organisations (firms and institutions) that apply the new knowledge (see Romer

1990; Audretsch et al. 2002). In the case of fundamental research, the international transfer of knowledge must be accounted for (Funk 2002). The private utility of R&D activities to organisations creating new knowledge is much smaller than the social utility because of positive externalities and thus there would be an under demand for R&D (see Griliches 1988). That is why the task of the government sector is to bring the demand for research at the social utility level by applying R&D policy measures.

Development work usually takes place in the organisation implementing the results, which is why it does not have such important direct externalities. In respect of development work, the government sector has a task to promote more externalities (transfer of knowledge and technical solutions). By giving the results of development work the nature of a public good, the government sector has a responsibility to promote development work in firms in order to hedge risks connected with R&D. Of course, it should be checked whether government sector subsidies for firm-level R&D will liquidate market failure or, on the contrary, serve as the distortion of competition (Klette et al. 2000).

Research is characterised by important informational failures (the asymmetry of information) between market participants and by large sunk costs that constrain market exit, which in turn prevents private firm activities in R&D (Carboni 2011). Private firms do not risk making sufficient long-term investments in research due to the uncertainties of R&D results (Dosi 1998). The task of the government sector is to reduce these risks by promoting the creation of inventions and scientific discoveries, but also by promoting the wide consumption of innovations as public goods.

A market failure is also a situation where a firm does not have sufficient resources for innovation (Martin/Scott 2000). In order to promote innovation, the government sector tries to fulfil that resource shortage with its support.

To overcome market failures, the main policy measures related to R&D work have traditionally been subsidies from the government sector budget to create new knowledge and the protection of intellectual property by laws (Edquist et al. 2004). In addition, the form of government sector intervention should proceed from the nature and impact scope of market failures, in order not to excessively reduce government sector's initiative and responsibilities in the design and implementation of development measures.

2.2 Eliminating System Failures

When promoting R&D work the government sector must help to eliminate system failures that prevent research results reaching the phase that is necessary for practical implementation. Overcoming system failures that reduce the impact of R&D means developing the national innovation system in such a way that all parties involved have good cooperation in promoting R&D activities and implementing research results. According to the OECD (1997), system failures are revealed in the following: lack of cooperation between different parties in the innovation process, incompatibility of public sector organisations' fundamental and applied research, inefficient activities of technology transfer organisations and deficiencies in information distribution. In case those failures are not prevented or treated, the resources meant for R&D work will not have the expected effect in guaranteeing economic development. In order to overcome system failures, policy instruments should be directed to creating missing components of the system, developing cooperation relationship and correcting mistakes made in system development. (Metcalfe 2005) That approach is supported by the position (Arnold 2004) that the government sector cannot be limited to financing only (traditional) fundamental research, but must guarantee the functioning of the whole innovation system and also eliminate or reduce occurring failures.

System failures restraining the development of R&D work and the usage of R&D outcomes can be classified as follows (Arnold 2004):

- capability failures – the incapability of research institutions to act derived from bad management, lack of competence, weak study capabilities and other deficiencies;
- failures in institutions – the stiffness of the activities of organisations (universities, research institutes, patent offices, etc.) and thus the incapability to adjust to environmental changes;
- network failures – problems in the relationships of innovation system parties, which are characterised by the shortage of relations or their insufficient quality, the incapability to apply new knowledge and tangling in morally aged technology;
- framework failures – deficiencies in legal institutions, intellectual property protection, health and safety requirements and other background conditions, including social values;
- policy failures (Tsipouri et al. 2008) – deficiencies in the government related to R&D policy development, coordination with other policies and the assessment of policy outcomes, etc.

In order to overcome system failures that reduce R&D work efficiency and hinder innovation, the government sector must develop an evaluation system for research institutions, systematically direct research institutions to fulfil tasks important for economic development, create networks to spread new knowledge and implement counselling programs, but also improve regulatory mechanisms (e.g. laws) that are important for development of R&D activities. Still, it should be taken into account that the government sector intervention should be in accordance with the nature and impact of the system failure. Also, the resources should be used efficiently and regulations should not reduce the private sector's initiative that is needed to develop R&D activities. When considering the intervention by the government sector, different failures in the work of public sector institutions and organisations must be considered (e.g. the instability of the political decision process, the increase of bureaucracy, decision makers' irresponsibility for the results, the possibility of corruption, etc.).

The place of institutions dealing with R&D work among organisations belonging to the national innovation system can be defined as follows (OECD 1999):

- government organisations (at local, regional, state and international level) that develop general R&D policy directions;
- bridging organisations, such as scientific councils and societies that are intermediaries between governments and researchers;
- private firms and research institutions that are funded by firms;
- universities and other connected institutions that create new knowledge and skills;
- other public and private organisations that have special R&D policy roles in the national innovation system (open laboratories, technology transfer institutions, common research and exploratory institutes, patent offices, educational institutions, etc.).

The diversity of R&D activities suggests that when designing public R&D policy, all above-mentioned institutions should be directed to cooperate for achieving common goals, i.e. an institutional environment favouring interactions between organisations should be created. Institutions are defined as the collection of habits, norms, routines, practices, rules or laws that regulates relationships and interactions between individuals, groups and organisations (Edquist/Johnson 2000). The importance of institutions in guaranteeing the development of innovation is emphasised by Klun/Slabe-Erker (2009). Formal and informal institutions, fundamental and supportive institutions, strict and soft institutions, deliberately and spontaneously created institutions must all be taken into account (Edquist/Johnson 2000).

The main components of the institutional environment influencing organisations are the legal system, norms, routines, standards, etc. Different institutions can support and strengthen each other, but they can also be in conflict or restrain one other. (Edquist 2006).

When developing the central element guaranteeing the functioning of the national innovation system, the R&D policy, the size of organisations (firms and institutions) must be taken into account. In the case of the dominance of small firms, an innovation system and R&D policy, which takes into account their specifics, must be developed (Reinkowski et al. 2010).

2.3 Considering the External Sources of Knowledge in R&D Policy

When designing R&D policy, it should be considered that R&D activity is not the only engine for the development of state innovation. Mainly small countries should consider whether and in which areas new knowledge is created and to what extent its procurement from other (outside) sources should be supported. Coe/Helpman (1995) and Keller (2004) emphasise the importance of using international channels in procuring new knowledge especially in the context of small open economies. Firstly, imports are emphasised as the (outside) source of new knowledge promoting national development (Coe/ Helpman 1995), thus the structure of imports should be deliberately shaped to favour innovation. In the last decade exports have also been emphasised as an important source of learning from foreign experience (Delgado et al. 2002; Baldwin/Gu 2003; Alvarez/ Lopez 2006; Greenaway/Keller 2007). Still, the attitude towards foreign direct investments as the source of the procurement of new knowledge has been controversial: in studies conducted by Braconier et al. (2001) and Grünfeld (2002) the transfer of knowledge from foreign direct investments was not discovered, however it was discovered in studies by van Pottelsberghe/Lichtenberg (2001) and Damijan et al. (2004).

The usage of an external source of new knowledge has to be combined in the best way that the state is capable to create new knowledge in the R&D system. Thus, when designing the R&D policy, the need to integrate R&D activities with the national innovation system must be taken into account.

In small open economies the importance of using external sources of knowledge does not reduce the importance of promoting R&D activities in order to guarantee economic development. Cohen/Levinthal (1989) and especially Griffith et al. (2004) mention two objectives for R&D development: on the one hand the creation of new knowledge and on the other hand the development of the absorption possibility of new knowledge from external sources. Diao et al. (1999) also note the importance of absorbing new knowledge from foreign sources to small open economies. The final objective is to improve the innovation performance of firms, but in a small country more attention has to be directed to new knowledge absorption capability development. Verbič (2011) notes in the Slovenian case the share of foreign countries as the source of the development of technology.

The systematic development of R&D policy to eliminate system failures must create favourable conditions to promote innovation in the public sector. At the same time, several application problems have to be solved.

3. Comparative Analysis of Research and Development Policy Implementation

3.1 Data and Variables Used in the Analysis

Diverse and complicated issues of government sector interventions in R&D processes presented in the previous section of the article signify the broad extent of alternatives for policy decisions. Each country forms its own R&D policy corresponding to historical traditions, situation and long-term goals of the development. Increasingly, the EU influence has to be taken into account. As result, the content of R&D policy is qualitatively different in different countries. The same value of resources supply or expenditures to R&D activities can represent qualitatively different policy measures. On the one hand, this is a limitation for quantitative comparable analysis which has been taken into account by interpretation of results. On the other hand, through quantitative comparison we can highlight the differences in the level and structure of the resources supply and expenditures of R&D policy in different countries helping us to understand the qualitative differences of this policy between countries.

In the current study, the government sector position of some European and Asian countries in R&D policy implementation among the investigated sample of countries will be assessed as there is a database created on common principles. Therefore, the results of countries analysed are directly comparable.

In total, 35 countries are used in the analysis (27 EU member states, Croatia, Turkey, Iceland, Norway, Switzerland, South Korea, China and Japan). The statistical data used is from the Eurostat online database and OECD Statistics database.

The results of comparative analysis of R&D policy implementation are more thoroughly analysed in three countries: an "old" EU member country Germany that is internationally recognised for its R&D achievements; Estonia as a successful "new" member country where efforts are made to foster R&D policy; South Korea as an Asian country that has achieved remarkable development success. In appendix, an aggregated assessment of R&D policy implementation for all analysed countries is given.

In the current study, data from six years is applied in order to follow the dynamics of different policy aspects. All variables in analysis have been taken from the years 2000, 2002, 2004, 2006, 2008 and 2010. This way the whole decade is covered by the data.

Many theoretical approaches and empirical research (European Commission 2003; Falk 2004; OECD 2005; Koch et al. 2007; Manjón 2010) have highlighted several variables that describe government sector R&D policy and which can be used to assess the level and structure of R&D policy in different countries. In the current study, the following variables will be used to comparatively assess government sector R&D activities in the investigated sample of countries (see tables 2.1 and 2.2). The tables also note previous research where given variables have been applied before. Analysing different variables separately would give fragmented results. In the current analysis, data describing government sector R&D activities are considered as a whole complex, taking into account the interconnections of variables.

One of the goals of R&D policy is to develop R&D activities carried out by the public sector. This aspect is described by the first set of variables (see table 2.1). The first four variables describe R&D activities carried out in the public sector. For those variables it must be taken into account that not all R&D expenditure in education, and especially in the higher education sector are financed by the government sector – some of the funding is provided by the business and nonprofit sectors, but also from the external sources. Therefore, it is important for each country to highlight those variables that describe R&D expenditure funded by the government sector of that country (variables 5–6). Variable 7 describes the government budget – more specifically its share in R&D financing. The last two variables in table 2.1 describe the share of public sector R&D personnel in total employment, which describes the supply of work force in public sector R&D activities.

Table 2.1: Variables describing public sector R&D activities

No.	Abbreviation	Variable description	Source
1	GOVgdp	Government sector R&D expenditure (% of GDP)	European Commission 2003; Falk 2004; OECD 2005; Koch et al. 2007; Manjón 2010
2	GOVshr	Share of government sector R&D expenditure (% of total R&D expenditure)	European Commission 2003; Sanchez, Bermejo 2007

3	HESgdp	Higher education sector R&D expenditure (% of GDP)	Falk 2004; OECD 2005; Koch et al. 2007; Manjón 2010
4	HESshr	Share of higher education sector R&D expenditure (% of total R&D expenditure)	European Commission 2003; Sanchez, Bermejo 2007
5	GOVtoGOV	Government sector R&D financing from the government sector budget (% of GDP)	OECD 1999; European Commission 2003
6	GOVtoHES	Higher education sector R&D financing from the government sector budget (% of GDP)	Added by the authors
7	GBAORD	Share of government budget appropriations or outlays on R&D in government sector total costs (%)	European Commission 2003; OECD 2005; OECD 2007; Sanchez, Bermejo 2007
8	empGOV	Share of government sector R&D personnel in total employment (% according to data converted to full time equivalents)	Manjón 2010
9	empHES	Share of higher education sector R&D personnel from total employment (% according to data converted to full time equivalents)	Manjón 2010

Source: compiled by the authors

The second important area of R&D policy is supporting business sector R&D activities. Variables describing public sector support to private sector R&D activities are given in table 2.2. In this research, two business sector R&D financing indicators are used that measure the level of government sector financial support to business sector R&D activities. When analysing the government support for business sector R&D in European countries, data from Community Innovation Survey (CIS) study could also be used. However, this data is not available for Asian countries and thus these variables are left out of the analysis.

Table 2.2: Variables describing public sector support to business sector R&D activities

No.	Abbreviation	Variable description	Source
1	GOVto BESgdp	Business sector R&D financing from the government sector budget (% of GDP)	Falk 2004
2	GOVto BESshr	Share of government sector financing in business sector total R&D expenditure (%)	OECD 2005; Koch et al. 2007
*	funPUB	Share of innovative enterprises that received any public funding (% of total innovative enterprises)	CIS; Koch et al. 2007; Nina 2009; Manjón 2010
*	funLOC	Share of innovative enterprises that received funding from local or regional authorities (% of total innovative enterprises)	CIS; Manjón 2010
*	funGMT	Share of innovative enterprises that received funding from central government (% of total innovative enterprises)	CIS; Manjón 2010
*	funEU	Share of innovative enterprises that received funding from EU (% of total innovative enterprises)	CIS; Manjón 2010

* Variable is not used in the current analysis
Source: compiled by the authors

3.2 Results of the Empirical Analysis

Table 2.3 shows the statistical parameters of variables describing public sector R&D activities and the level of government sector support for business sector R&D activities. The indicators are centred for each year to eliminate the common trends – the data characterises for each year the difference of country value from average value in the year observed (i.e. the standard deviation). In the table, the indicators' average values of six years observed are presented.

Table 2.3 indicates that the values of variables for countries vary remarkably, in both absolute (the difference between minimum and maximum levels) and relative terms (the relationship of standard deviation to mean).

Table 2.3: Statistical characteristics of variables describing public sector R&D activities and the level of government sector support for business sector R&D activities[2]

Variable	Mean	Standard deviation	Min value	Max value	Value in			Difference from mean (in standard deviations)		
					Estonia	South Korea	Germany	Estonia	South Korea	Germany
GOVgdp	0.21	0.12	0.03	0.63	0.14	0.37	0.36	-0.60	1.34	1.25
GOVshr	17.79	11.59	0.99	61.12	14.80	12.51	13.95	-0.26	-0.46	-0.33
HESgdp	0.36	0.20	0.05	0.82	0.45	0.31	0.44	0.44	-0.23	0.38
HESshr	26.40	12.25	3.79	55.61	44.56	10.61	16.76	1.48	-1.29	-0.79
GOVtoGOV	0.24	0.38	0.02	2.37	0.11	0.35	0.32	-0.34	0.29	0.21
GOVtoHES	0.28	0.17	0.03	0.62	0.35	0.23	0.36	0.39	-0.32	0.46
GBAORD	1.32	0.56	0.41	2.92	1.33	2.92	1.75	0.01	2.85	0.75
empGOV	0.16	0.10	0.02	0.49	0.14	0.08	0.21	-0.21	-0.74	0.55
empHES	0.32	0.15	0.03	0.70	0.41	0.21	0.28	0.60	-0.70	-0.23
GOVtoBESgdp	0.06	0.04	0.00	0.15	0.04	0.13	0.10	-0.49	1.84	0.93
GOVtoBESshr	7.52	6.37	1.25	34.99	8.15	5.92	5.40	0.10	-0.25	-0.33

The Estonian, South Korean and German position in public sector R&D activities and in the level of government sector support for business sector R&D activities can be seen in three last columns of table 2.3 and in figure 2.1.

In the figure, the difference between minimum and maximum values (in standard deviations) and Estonian, South Korean and German mean value for each indicator is given.

The figure shows that the position of Estonia is the best for the share of higher education sector R&D expenditure in total R&D expenditure (*HESshr*). However, the position of South Korea and Germany is the worst for this variable. The position of Estonia is the worst for government sector R&D expenditure (*GOVgdp*), where the position of Germany is the best. The position of South Korea is the best for the share of government budget appropriations or outlays on R&D in government sector total costs (*GBAORD*).

---

2   Values have been calculated as the mean of six years (2000, 2002, 2004, 2006, 2008 and 2010).

Figure 2.1: Estonian, South Korean and German position among variables describing
public sector R&D activities and the level of government sector support for
business sector R&D activities.

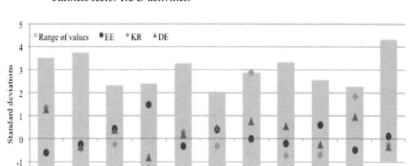

Figure 2.1 indicates that according to variables describing higher education sector R&D financing, the share of higher education sector R&D personnel and the share of government sector financing in business sector total R&D expenditure, Estonia holds a higher position than the countries' average. For the rest of the variables describing public sector R&D activities and the level of government sector support for business sector R&D activities, Estonia has average or lower than average values. This indicates that the main contribution of innovation promotion in Estonia is expected from the higher education sector.

South Korea holds a higher position than the countries' average according to variables describing government budget appropriations or outlays on R&D, government sector R&D financing and the business sector R&D financing from the government sector. This indicates that in South Korea the main contribution of innovation promotion is expected from the government sector. Germany has higher than average position according to seven out of eleven variables and both higher education and government sector are seen as contributors of innovation.

The results of the comparison of R&D policy of countries on the base of eleven variables are controversial and difficult to generalise due to a large number of variables and internal correlations between variables. Approaches to compress the information through constructing a small number of complex indexes of R&D policy with the help of deterministic methods (through weighing and summarising variables' values) cannot be successful because these methods do not take into account the correlations between variables. Therefore, we have to use multiple statistical analysis methods to reduce the number of R&D policy indicators without significant information loss.

Subsequently, to bring out the factual dimensions of R&D policy activities, principal component analysis is conducted with the variables describing public sector R&D activities and the level of government support for business sector R&D activities. For the component analysis, the data of 210 observations (35 countries in six years) is used and the data has been standardised across years. The results of component analysis (table 2.4) show the structure of public sector activities promoting and supporting R&D. Component analysis is based on the internal connections in the set of variables, including the connections between the areas of public sector R&D activities and support measures.

Table 2.4: Component analysis in the set of variables describing public sector R&D policy Rotation method: Varimax

	K1 Level of higher education sector R&D financing	K2 Level of government sector R&D financing	K3 Level of business sector R&D financing by the government sector
HESgdp	**0.96**	-0.03	0.06
GOVtoHES	**0.94**	0.01	0.07
empHES	**0.80**	0.10	-0.18
GOVshr	**-0.70**	0.45	-0.21
GBAORD	**0.67**	0.32	0.38
GOVgdp	0.10	**0.94**	0.22
GOVtoGOV	0.09	**0.93**	0.27
empGOV	-0.03	**0.87**	-0.17
GOVtoBESgdp	0.31	0.07	**0.86**
HESshr	0.12	**-0.45**	**-0.64**
GOVtoBESshr	**-0.49**	-0.19	**0.49**
Component eigenvalue	3.92	3.14	1.51
Cumulative variance explained	35.62	64.19	77.90
Significance of Bartlett test	0.00		
KMO	0.69		

The component analysis covering the indicators describing government sector R&D policy highlighted three independent (non-correlated) synthetic complex indicators (components) describing the internal structure of the variables. As a result of component analysis the number of variables describing public sector R&D policy decreased more than 70% (i.e. from 11 to 3), but less than 25% of the information (variation) included in initial variables set was lost (77.9% of the variance of initial variables is explained through synthetic components).

Explaining the nature of synthetic components and giving adequate names for the new indicators is a complicated task. In the current study, the method applied by Karu/Reiljan (1983) is used to explain the nature of the components.

With the first component (K1) three variables that describe higher education sector R&D funding and the share of higher education sector R&D personnel in total employment are closely correlated. In addition, variables that describe government budget appropriations or outlays on R&D and the share of government sector R&D expenditure in total R&D expenditure are strongly correlated with the given component. In the case of the last variable a reciprocal association exists that explains the crowding out effect of higher education sector R&D funding by government sector R&D funding. The nature of the first component is described as "level of higher education sector R&D financing", whereas the level of funding also affects the possibility of employing R&D personnel.

With the second component (K2) three variables that describe government sector R&D financing and the share of government R&D personnel in total employment are strongly associated. With the given component, the variables *GOVshr* (the share of government sector R&D expenditure in total R&D expenditure) and *HESshr* (the share of higher education sector R&D expenditure in total R&D expenditure) are weakly associated. The association with *HESshr* is negative, which indicates the substitution of government sector R&D financing with higher education sector R&D financing. This component is characterised by the name "level of government sector R&D financing".

With the third component (K3) two variables that describe the level and share of government sector financing in business sector R&D are correlated. The variable *HESshr* (the share of higher education sector R&D expenditure in total R&D expenditure) has a negative correlation with the component. The nature of the given component is best explained by the name "level of business sector R&D financing by the government sector".

Component scores describe each country in the analysis. As each country is represented in the sample with data from six years, there are six component scores for every country. In order to compare countries, they are characterised with the mean of six component scores (see appendix 1). Component scores indicate that the structure of government sector R&D policy varies remarkably through countries – countries emphasise different R&D policy areas. Figure 2.2 illustrates the results of the international position of Estonia, South Korea and Germany.

In figure 2.2 Estonian, South Korean and German average positions among the analysed countries are shown using three complex indicators (components) that explain government sector R&D policy in a way that the difference from the mean value and the distance from the extreme values of the investigated country sample can be seen. While in general Estonia is below the average level of R&D policy implementation, Estonian activities can still be considered balanced – in the case of all components the difference from the average level is smaller than the distance from the extreme values. According to all components, the performance of South Korea and Germany is above the average level.

According to component K1 (the level of higher education sector R&D financing), the Estonian average component score is higher (by 0.44 standard deviations) than the average of analysed countries and Estonia is situated in the first half among all countries analysed (11th position out of 35). Thus, the government sector finances higher education sector R&D to a higher level than the countries' average. The component scores for South Korea (0.26) and Germany (0.39) are almost equal to Estonia and the countries are ranked 16th and 13th position respectively. The highest component values are in Finland (1.8) and Sweden (1.7), the lowest (negative) values in Romania (-2.1) and Bulgaria (-1.9).

In the case of component K2 (the level of government sector R&D financing), Estonia is 0.56 standard errors lower than the average of analysed countries and is in 24th position. This means that the government sector with its research and scientific personnel does not create remarkable support potential for the business sector and neither is a supportive cooperation partner. In order to find out whether setting such objective would be reasonable at all, it is necessary to study the impact of government sector R&D activities on the business sector. The comparison with other countries offers a few standpoints in this respect. The component scores for South Korea (0.74) and Germany (0.95) are higher than the average level and countries are located in 6th and 5th position respectively. The highest values are in Iceland (3.3) and Bulgaria (1.9) and the lowest in Malta (-1.5) and Turkey (-1.3).

Figure 2.2: Estonian, South Korean and German position among analysed countries using the four components describing public sector R&D policy.

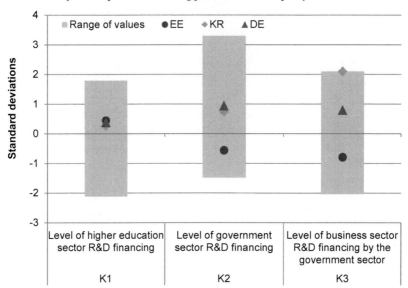

According to the component K3 (the level of business sector R&D financing by the government sector), Estonia is situated below the average level (component score -0.79) and is in 28th position out of 35 countries. The financing of business sector R&D by the government sector demands enough competence to create long-term innovation policy strategies at government level, but also the capability to set and solve very specific development tasks to eliminate market and system failures. Profound research is needed to find out the presence of such competence and capabilities in Estonia. Thus, the modesty of Estonia in this R&D field can be considered natural. South Korea has a very high component score value (2.10) and is ranked first. Thus, in South Korea the government sector supports business sector R&D to a high level. Germany is situated higher than the average level (component score 0.80) and holds the seventh position. The highest component scores besides South Korea are in Romania (1.8) and France (1.4). The lowest levels are in Lithuania (-2.0) and Greece (-1.6).

As the component analysis includes data from six years, it is also possible to view the dynamics of the component scores. In table 2.5 the dynamics of Estonian, South Korean and German component scores for each year have been given.

Table 2.5: Component scores describing Estonian, South Korean and German public sector
R&D policy in 2000, 2002, 2004, 2006, 2008 and 2010

		Estonia	South Korea	Germany
K1: Level of higher education sector R&D financing	2010	0.68	0.48	0.33
	2008	0.68	0.43	0.30
	2006	0.52	0.22	0.25
	2004	0.43	0.17	0.35
	2002	0.23	0.13	0.52
	2000	0.13	0.15	0.56
K2: Level of government sector R&D financing	2010	-0.55	1.38	1.21
	2008	-0.55	1.06	1.14
	2006	-0.69	0.73	0.91
	2004	-0.53	0.59	0.90
	2002	-0.59	0.41	0.78
	2000	-0.43	0.28	0.74
K3: Level of business sector R&D financing by the government sector	2010	0.21	2.55	0.46
	2008	-0.53	2.09	0.55
	2006	-0.63	1.93	0.60
	2004	-1.35	1.84	0.98
	2002	-0.98	2.16	1.03
	2000	-1.46	2.02	1.19

Table 2.5 shows that for two components (K1 and K3) Estonian component scores have grown over time and the position in comparison to the average level of analysed countries has risen. For component K3 (the level of business sector R&D financing by the government sector), the Estonian position in 2010 was higher than the countries' average, compared to the lower than average component score in 2000. According to component K2 (the level of government sector R&D financing), the Estonian position has decreased and moved slightly away from the average of counties.

The South Korean position has improved for all components in 2010 compared to 2000 and the values of component scores have always been over the average level (i.e. positive). Thus, South Korea has a higher than the average position in respect of R&D policy implementation.

In addition, German component scores have been always positive for all three components. However, the position of Germany according to components K1 (the level of higher education sector R&D financing) and K3 (the level of business sector R&D financing by the government sector) has decreased during the analysed period.

Finally, a cluster analysis is performed on the three components describing public sector R&D policy. Single linkage hierarchical clustering method is used to group the countries. The dendrogram (figure 2.3) indicates that the most similar country to Estonia is Portugal. Figure 2.3 also shows that Germany is the most similar to its neighbouring country France. South Korea does not have any specific countries that are highly similar to it; however, Germany is slightly more similar to South Korea than Estonia. Compared to the other countries in the scope, the public sector R&D policy is the most different in Iceland, Bulgaria and Romania.

Figure 2.3: Dendrogram grouping countries using components K1, K2 and K3.

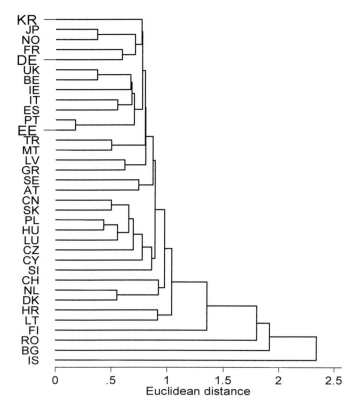

4. Summary

Designing the national R&D policy is a difficult task for the public sector from the aspects of making a choice among the variety of instruments, as well as the nature of the impact that different instruments create. The current study systematised available theoretical approaches for government intervention through R&D policy and gave an assessment to the international position of Estonian, South Korean and German R&D policy implementation based on the empirical analysis of EU member states, countries closely associated with the EU and three Asian countries.

The main reason for public sector R&D policy implementation is to eliminate the market and system failures restraining R&D progress. Market failures are mostly derived from the aspect that in terms of rivalry, innovation and R&D outcomes have a mainly public good nature and it is often impractical to exclude others from the usage of R&D results. Also, the positive externality of R&D must be taken into account, because the private demand is inevitably lower than the social rational level and with R&D policy measures the demand must be brought to the social utility level. In addition, information constraints do not enable firms to risk long-term R&D investments and the public sector must fulfil this investment gap.

Sometimes, due to a system failure cooperation between different parties of a national innovation system does not function smoothly or some institutions and/or organisations do not fulfil their tasks efficiently. The creation of formal institutions and cooperation organisations that promote R&D development in the country is the responsibility of the public sector. Innovation policy determines the tasks of the R&D policy in promoting innovation in a country and reciprocal connections with the supportive components of the innovation policy (i.e. education policy, cooperation development policy and business environment policy).

Still, intervention by the public sector needs careful analytical justification, because incompetent public sector intervention can distort market processes and create ineligible R&D policy.

Empirical analysis showed that according to most of the indicators that describe public sector R&D activities and the level of government sector support for business sector R&D activities, Estonia and South Korea are below the average level and Germany above the average level among the countries analysed. Component analysis brought out three dimensions of public sector R&D policy:

- K1 – the level of higher education sector R&D financing;
- K2 – the level of government sector R&D financing;
- K3 – the level of business sector R&D financing by the government sector.

Only in the case of K1 (the level of higher education sector R&D financing) is the Estonian average level of six years (2000, 2002, 2004, 2006, 2008, 2010) higher than the average of the analysed countries, whereas according to other R&D policy components Estonia is below the average level. This is a somewhat expected result, as in the case of a small open country external sources are considered important for obtaining innovative knowledge.

South Korea and Germany have a higher than average level of performance in all three components. Thus, South Korea and Germany have a higher than average position in the respect of R&D policy implementation.

Although the position of Estonia according to most components describing government sector R&D policy is relatively modest, an important progress has occurred during the ten-year period (2000–2010). For two components (K1 and K3), the Estonian position in 2010 was relatively higher than in 2000. Also, in South Korea an important progress has occurred during the ten-year period; component scores for all three components have increased. However, the position of Germany has decreased during the ten years: the level of higher education sector R&D financing and the level of business sector R&D financing by the government sector has decreased in 2010 compared to 2000.

We have to take into account quantitative measures of level and changes in R&D policy financing though the government sector brings out only the general features of qualitative nature of this policy in different countries (synthetic components characterise general dimensions of government activities R&D financing). Component scores and their changes do not give the possibility to understand the nature of specific policy measures implemented in different countries in this financial framework.

References

Adams, J. D. (1990) Fundamental stocks of knowledge and productivity growth, in: Journal of Political Economy, Vol. 98, No. 4, pp. 673–702.

Aghion, P. / Howitt, P. (1992) A Model of Growth Through Creative Destruction, in: Econometrica, Vol. 60, No. 2, pp. 323–351.

Alvarez, R. / Lopez, R. (2006) Is Exporting a Source of Productivity Spillovers? Working paper 2006/012, Center for Applied Economics and Policy Research, Indiana.

Arnold, E. (2004) Evaluating research and innovation policy: a systems world needs systems evaluations, in: Research Evaluation, Vol. 13, No. 1, pp. 3–17.

Arrow, K. J. (1962) Economic welfare and the allocation of resources for invention, in: The rate and direction of inventive activity. Edited by R. Nelson. Princeton: Princeton University Press, pp. 609–625.

Audretsch, D. B. / Bozeman, B. / Comb, K. L. et al. (2002) The economics of science and technology, in: Journal of Technology Transfer, Vol. 27, No. 2, pp. 155–203.

Baldwin, J. / Gu, W. (2003) Export market participation and productivity performance in Canadian manufacturing, in: Canadian Journal of Economics, Vol. 36, pp. 634–657.

Blanes, J. / Busom, I. (2004) Who participates in R&D subsidy programs? The case of Spanish manufacturing firms, in: Research Policy, Vol. 33, pp. 1459–1476.

Bozeman, B. / Rogers, J. (2002) A churn model of scientific knowledge value: Internet researchers as a knowledge value collective, in: Research Policy, Vol. 31, No. 5, pp. 769–794.

Braconier, H. / Ekholm, K. / Knarvik, K. H. M. (2001) Does FDI work as a channel for R&D spillovers?, in: Weltwirtschaftliches Archiv, Vol. 137, No. 4, pp. 644–665.

Branstetter, L. / Ogura, Y. (2005) Is Academic Science Driving a Surge in Industrial Innovation? Evidence from Patent Citations. NBER Working Paper No. 115. Cambridge, MA: National Bureau of Economic Research.

Carboni, O. A. (2011) R&D subsidies and private R&D expenditures: evidence from Italian manufacturing data, in: International Review of Applied Economics, Vol. 25, No. 4, pp. 419–439.

Coe, D. T. / Helpman, E. (1995) International R&D spillovers, in: European Economic Review, Vol. 39, pp. 859–887.

Cohen, W. M. / Levinthal, D. A. (1989) Innovation and learning: The two faces of R&D. In Economic Journal, Vol. 99, pp. 569–596.

Czarnitzki, D. / Bento, C. L. (2010) Evaluation of Public R&D Policies: A Cross-country Comparison. ZEW Disc. Paper No. 10–073.

Damijan, J. P. / Polanec, S. / Prasnikar, J. (2004) Self-selection, export market heterogeneity and productivity improvements: Firm-level evidence form Slovenia. LICOS Discussion Papers 148/2004, Katholieke Universiteit Leuven, Belgium.

Dasgupta, P. / David, P. A. (1994) Toward a new economics of science, in: Research Policy, Vol. 23, No. 5, pp. 487–521.

Delgado, M. / Farinas, J. / Ruano, S. (2002) Firm productivity and export markets: A non-parametric approach, in: Journal of International Economics, Vol. 57, pp. 392–422.

Diao, X. / Roe, T. / Yeldan, E. (1999) Strategic policies and growth: An applied model of R&D driven endogenous growth, in: Journal of Development Economics, Vol. 60, pp. 343–380.

Dosi, G. (1998) Sources, procedures, and microeconomic effects of innovations, in: Journal of Economic Literature, Vol. 26, pp. 1120–1171.

Edquist, C. (2006) System of Innovation. Perspectives and Challenges, in: The Oxford Handbook of Innovation. Edited by J. Fagerberg, D. C. Mowery, R. R. Nelson. Oxford: Oxford University Press, pp. 181–208.

Edquist, C. / Johnson, B. (2000) Institutions and Organisations in Systems of Innovation, in: Systems of Innovation: Growth, Competitiveness and Employment, Vol. 2. Edited by C. Edquist, M. McKelvey. Cheltenham, Northampton: Edward Elgar Publishing, pp. 165–187.

Edquist, C. / Malerba, F. / Metcalfe, J. S. et al. (2004) Sectoral systems: implication for European innovation policy, in: Sectoral Systems of Innovation: Concepts, Issues and Analyses of Six Major Sectors in Europe. Edited by F. Malerba. Cambridge: Cambridge University Press, pp. 427–461.

European Commission (2003) Third European Report on Science & Technology Indicators. Towards a Knowledge-based Economy. Luxembourg: Office for Official Publications of the European Communities.

Falk, M. (2004) What Drives Business R&D Intensity Across OECD Countries? WIFO Working Papers, No. 236.

Funk, M. (2002) Basic research and international spillovers. In International Review of Applied Economics, Vol. 16, No. 2, pp. 217–226.

Gellman Associates (1976) Indicators of international trends in technological innovation. A Report to the National Science Foundation. Washington, DC: Gellman Associates.

Greenaway D. / Kneller, R. (2007) Firm Heterogeneity, Exporting and Foreign Direct Investment, in: Economic Journal, Vol. 117, pp. F134-F161.

Greenberg, D. S. (1967) The politics of pure science. New York: New American Library.

Griffith, R. / Redding, S. / Van Reenen, J. (2004) Mapping the two faces of R&D: productivity growth in a panel of OECD countries, in: Review of Economics and Statistics, Vol. 86, No. 4, pp. 883–895.

Griliches, Z. (1988) Productivity Puzzles and R&D: Another Non-explanation. In Journal of Economic Perspectives, Vol. 2, No. 4, pp. 9–21.

Grossman, G. M. / Helpman, E. (1991) Innovation and Growth in the Global Economy. Cambridge, MA: The MIT Press.

Grünfeld, L. A. (2002) International R&D spillovers and the effect of absorptive capacity, an empirical study. Paper no 630, Norwegian Institute of Foreign Affairs, Oslo, Norway.

Hewitt-Dundas, N. / Roper, S. (2010) Output Additionality of Public Support for Innovation: Evidence for Irish Manufacturing Plants, in: European Planning Studies, Vol. 18, No. 1, pp. 107–122.

Hujer, R. / Radic, D. (2003) Evaluating the impacts of subsidies on innovation activities in Germany. Working Paper, Goethe-University of Frankfurt.

Jaffe, A. (2002) Building program evaluation into the design of public research-support programs, in: Oxford Review of Economic Policy, Vol. 18, pp. 23–33.

Karu, J. / Reiljan, J. (1983) Tööstusettevõtte majandustegevuse komponentanalüüs. Tallinn: Valgus.

Keller, W. (2004) International Technology Diffusion, in: Journal of Economic Literature, XLII, pp. 752–782.

Kim, J. (2011) Political Institutions and Public R&D Expenditures in Democratic Countries, in: International Journal of Public Administration, Vol. 34, No. 13, pp. 843–857.

Klette, T. J. / Moen, J. / Griliches, Z. (2000) Do subsidies to commercial R&D reduce market failures? Microeconomic evaluation studies, in: Research Policy, Vol. 29, No. 4–5, pp. 471–495.

Klun, M. / Slabe-Erker, R. (2009) Business Views of the Quality of Tax, Environment and Employment Regulation and Institutions: The Slovenian Case, in: International Review of Administrative Sciences, Vol. 75, No. 3, pp. 529–548.

Koch, P. / Pukl, B. / Wolters, A. (2007) OMC Policy Mix Review Report Country Report Estonia, October.

Lach, S. (2002) Do R&D Subsidies stimulate or displace private R&D? Evidence from Israel, in: Journal of Industrial Economics, Vol. 50, No. 4, pp. 369–390.

Levy, D. / Terleckyj, N. (1983) Effects of government R&D on private R&D investment and productivity: A macroeconomic analysis, in Bell Journal of Economics, Vol. 14, No. 4, pp. 551–561.

Leyden, D. P. / Link A. (1991) Why are government and private research and development complement?, in: Applied Economics, Vol. 23, pp. 1673–1681.

Manjón, J. V. G. (2010) A Proposal of Indicators and Policy Framework for Innovation Benchmark in Europe, in: Journal of Technology Management & Innovation, Vol. 5, Issue 2, pp. 13–23.

Mansfield, E. (1991) Academic research and industrial innovation, in: Research Policy, Vol. 20, No. 1, pp. 1–12.

Mansfield, E. (1998) Academic research and industrial innovation: An update of empirical findings, in: Research Policy, Vol. 26, No. 7–8, pp. 773–776.

Martin, S. / Scott, J. T. (2000) The nature of innovation market failure and the design of public support for private innovation, in: Research Policy, Vol. 29, No. 4–5, pp. 437–447.

Metcalfe, J. S. (2005) Systems failure and the case for innovation policy, in: Innovation Policy in a Knowledge Based Economy. Edited by P. Llerena, M. Matt. Berlin: Springer, pp. 47–74.

Nelson, R. R. (1959) The simple economics of basic scientific research, in: Journal of Political Economy, Vol. 49, pp. 297–306.

Nina, B. (2009) Open model of innovation: How Belarus responds to the world trends of development. Paper presented at GLOBELICS 2009, 7th International Conference, Dakar, Senegal, October 6–8.

OECD (1997) National Innovation Systems. Paris: OECD Publications.

OECD (1999) Managing National Systems of Innovation. Paris: OECD Publications.

OECD (2005) Governance of Innovation Systems. Volume 1: Synthesis Report. Paris: OECD Publications.

OECD (2007) Science, Technology and Innovation Indicators in a Changing World. Responding to Policy Need. Paris: OECD Publ.

Pavitt, K. (2006) Innovation Processes, in: The Oxford Handbook of Innovation. Edited by J. Fagerberg, D. C. Mowery, R. R. Nelson. Oxford: Oxford University Press, pp. 86–114.

Persson, T. / Gerard, R. / Tabellini, G. (2000) Comparative politics and public finance, in: Journal of Political Economy, Vol. 108, No. 6, pp. 1121–1161.

Persson, T. / Roland, G. / Tabellini, G. (1997) Separation of powers and political accountability, in: The Quarterly Journal of Economics, Vol. 112, No. 4, pp. 1163–1202.

Persson, T. / Tabellini, G. (1999) The size and scope of government: Comparative politics with rational politicians, in: European Economic Review, Vol. 43, pp. 699–735.

Pottelsberghe, B / van, Lichtenberg, F. (2001) Does Foreign Direct Investment Transfer Technology Across Borders?, in: The Review of Economics and Statistics, Vol. 83, No. 3, pp. 490–497.

Reinkowski, J. / Alecke, B. / Mitze, T. et al. (2010) Effectiveness of public R&D subsidies in East Germany: is it a matter of firm size? Working Paper. Ruhr economic papers, No. 204.

Rogers, J. / Bozeman, B. (2001) Knowledge value alliances: An alternative to the R&D projects focus in evaluation, in: Science, Technology and Human Values, Vol. 26, No. 1, pp. 23–55.

Romer, P. (1990) Endogenous Technological Change, in : The Journal of Political Economy, Vol. 98, No. 5, pp. S71-S102.

Sanchez, A. M. / Bermejo, L. R. (2007) Public Sector performance and efficiency in Europe: The role of public R&D. Institute of Social and Economic Analysis 5 Working paper 01/2007.

Sherwin, C. W. / Isenson, R. S. (1967) Project Hindsight, in: Science, Vol. 156(3782), pp. 1571–1577.

Tokila, A. / Haapanen, M. / Ritsilä, J. (2008) Evaluation of investment subsidies: When is deadweight zero?, in: International Review of Applied Economics, Vol. 22, No. 5, pp. 585–600.

Tsipouri, L. / Reid, A. / Miedzinski, M. (2008) European Innovation Progress Report 2008. Brussels: Directorate-General for Enterprise Policy, European Commission.

Wallsten, S. (2000) The effects of government-industry R&D programme on private R&D: The case of the small business innovation research program, in: RAND Journal of Economics, Vol. 13, No. 1, pp. 82–100.

Verbič, M. / Majcen, B. / Ivanova, O. (2011) R&D and Economic Growth in Slovenia: A Dynamic General Equilibrium Approach with Endogenous Growth, in: Panoeconomicus, Vol. 1, pp. 67–89.

Appendix 1: Component scores describing public sector R&D activities in the analysed countries (the mean for years 2000, 2002, 2004, 2006, 2008, 2010)

	K1	K2	K3
BE	0.40	-0.69	0.32
BG	-1.88	1.91	-0.95
CZ	-0.73	0.38	1.26
DK	1.28	-0.46	-0.29
DE	0.39	0.95	0.80
EE	0.44	-0.56	-0.79
IE	0.01	-0.94	-0.17
GR	-0.23	-0.63	-1.57
ES	-0.03	-0.08	0.55
FR	0.47	0.74	1.35
IT	0.01	-0.22	0.01
CY	-1.30	-0.61	-0.52

	K1	K2	K3
LV	-0.64	-0.70	-1.12
LT	0.14	0.23	-2.03
LU	-1.17	0.51	0.15
HU	-0.77	0.42	-0.23
MT	-0.67	-1.48	-0.93
NL	1.25	-0.02	-0.63
AT	0.95	-1.03	1.11
PL	-1.03	0.08	-0.30
PT	0.32	-0.55	-0.67
RO	-2.12	-0.88	1.82
SI	-0.61	1.11	0.40
SK	-1.24	-0.18	0.42
FI	1.78	1.10	-0.10
SE	1.66	-0.84	1.23
UK	0.66	-0.48	0.50
IS	1.21	3.29	-0.67
NO	0.65	0.32	0.11
CH	1.59	-1.31	-0.11
HR	-0.05	0.47	-1.17
TR	-0.20	-1.32	-0.84
CN	-1.15	0.20	0.72
JP	0.36	0.51	0.24
KR	0.26	0.74	2.10

Herman W. Hoen

Emerging Market Economies and the Financial Crisis: Is there Institutional Convergence between Europe and Asia?

1. Introduction

After the collapse of communism in 1989, the Central and Eastern European countries took the challenge to implement a market economy embedded in a democratic order. Constituent element of the transition was a full-fledged integration with the global economy, for which accession to the European Union (EU) was understood as an important steppingstone. After a period of dramatic economic decline in the 1990s, the emerging market economies in Central and Eastern Europe experienced strong economic growth and a steady catch-up began with average welfare levels in the EU (Kołodko 2002).[1] Recently, however, the countries are severely hit by the financial crisis and many have suggested that it reveals the downside of a market economy (EBRD 2010; see Hoen 2011).

The difficulties that challenge Central and Eastern Europe deviate from developments in emerging markets elsewhere in the world. Many countries in Asia, for example, seem to outperform their European counterparts (Das 2011). Of course, economic performance is not to be confused with economic order, since different institutional settings may yield similar results (Wagener 1992: 24), but the substantial differences in performance between European and Asian emerging markets during the financial crisis may shed new light on the dynamics of institutional change. This article addresses institutional change triggered by the external shock of the financial crisis. The pivotal question is the extent to which globalization leads to converging economic orders or, stated differently, if there is still room for domestic policy manoeuvre that allows to '*make a difference*'.

The development of a market economy, both in Eastern Europe and in Asia, entailed encompassing institutional reform. It is widely considered a complex

---

1   To emphasize the system switch, emerging market economies in Europe as transition countries (Lavigne 1999; Roland 2002). This article focuses on (i) Central European countries (the Czech Republic, Hungary, Poland, Slovakia, Slovenia), (ii) South-Eastern Europe (Bulgaria, Croatia, Romania and Serbia) and (iii) the Baltic States (Estonia, Latvia and Lithuania).

form of institutional change, since it affected the whole economic order and could only be successful in case other elements of the political and social system changed at the same time (Roland 2002: 29–30). Following Douglas North, this article defines institutions as formal and informal *'rules of the game'* (North 1990: 3). Its basic premise is that institutions are neither self-generating nor self-sustaining. Economic, social and political institutions are moulded, employed, and renewed by individuals and organizations. The question, therefore, is: *'why and how do institutions change?'* In addressing and analysing the extent to which there is institutional convergence as a response to the financial crisis, this article follows the approach of *'Varieties of Capitalism'* (Hall/Soskice 2001), which concept in the remainder of this article is abbreviated as VoC.

In the VoC-approach, two *'ideal'* types of capitalism are distinguished: a liberal market economy and a coordinated market economy. Crucial in the distinction is the way in which firms resolve coordination problems (Hall/Soskice 2001: 33–35). In liberal market economies, firms are primarily driven by competition, whereas in coordinated market economies firms coordinate with other actors by strategic interaction. In the VoC-approach, institutions are not only shaped by legal design but also by informal rules and culture. The premise is that countries with a specific set of institutions develop institutional complementarities (ibid 2001: 17–19). Therefore, considering institutional change, liberal market economies and coordinated market economies are expected to respond in a different way to external shocks, such as the global financial crisis. It is the purpose of this article to follow this line of reasoning and to shed some light on evolving varieties in capitalism in emerging market economies across Europe and Asia.

The article is structured as follows. The next section addresses the encompassing institutional reforms of emerging market economies in Central and Eastern Europe that, after the collapse of communism in 1989, took the effort to implement a full-fledged market economy. It explicitly addresses the theoretical debates that underpinned the institutional design of the desired economic order. Following the VoC-approach, it reveals the desired design of liberal market economies.

Section 3, subsequently, focuses on the impact of the global financial crisis on the emerging market economies in Europe and, following a concise analysis of economic performances in this region, pinpoints the possible effects that it triggers as an example of enforced institutional change. The leading threat is the question: *'is there institutional convergence among the emerging market economies in Europe and, if so, which direction is it heading?'*

The succeeding two sections shift focus to emerging market economies in Asia. As is the case for Europe, it is impossible to denote a homogenous group of countries and, a distinction is made between East and Central Asia, whereas China is taken as group on its own.[2]

The analysis resembles the one on emerging markets in Europe. Section 4 addresses the emerging type(s) of capitalism from a perspective of VoC, and shows the prevalence of more state interventionist coordinated market economies, whereas section 5 discusses the institutional responses to the global financial crisis. Essential question, again, is the extent to which there is convergence within the group of emerging market economies in East and Central Asia.

The last section, albeit very tentatively, concludes by comparing the developments of the two huge '*blocs*' of emerging market economies in Europe and Asia and discusses whether or not there is convergence between the two.

2. The Debate Underpinning Emerging Markets in Europe

This section sheds some light on the debates that were held after the collapse of communism to support the transition to a fully-fledged market economy.[3] Notably economists intended to address the system switch by looking at the decline of communism and the climate of rivalry between the co-ordinating mechanisms of the two systems. As a consequence, scholars have focused upon the taxonomy of '*demand-*' and '*supply-constrained*' systems (Kornai 1980). Planned economies are supply constrained, since managers tend to suction the economy in an attempt to maximise output (at any cost). The behaviour of the socialist firm inherently leads to a shortage economy. In a market economy, entrepreneurs do face hard budget constraints and, therefore, maximise profits instead of output. There is no incentive to excess demand.

The transition from a supply-constrained to a demand-constrained system entailed, first and foremost, ending both the queuing caused by rationing and the policy of forced savings (Winiecki 1993). Therefore, the transition was primarily regarded as a matter of stabilization and liberalization. Stabilization implied the enforcement of restrictive fiscal and monetary policies. At the same time, the liberalization of prices, production, and trade was envisaged as a necessary precondition for a market economy, if not the actual institutional design of the

---

2 For arguments explained in Section 4, the following four groups of emerging markets are assessed: (i) the '*Asian Tigers*' (Hong Kong, the Republic of Korea, Singapore and Taiwan), (ii) Central Asia (Kazakhstan, Kyrgyzstan, Tajikistan, Turkmenistan and Uzbekistan), (iii) China, and (iv) some '*New Asian Dragons*' (Malaysia, the Philippines, Thailand, and Vietnam).

3 This section relies heavily on Hoen (2011: 33–35).

market. Since the exchange-rate regimes were understood as an important device for stabilizing the economy, there was specific focus on the price of a currency (Lavigne 1999: 144–146).

The discussion of stabilization and liberalization was a constituent part of the so-called 'shock-versus-gradualism' debate (Hoen 1996). At stake in this debate was the question of how to minimise transition costs and it concentrated on timing and sequencing of reforms. Adherents of the shock approach emphasised the importance of the simultaneous implementation of all the reforms at full speed, rather than a sequential implementation (Åslund 2002). Those in favour of a gradual shift stressed the importance of sequential implementation and were doubtful of the benefits of the rapid implementation of reform (Dewatripont/ Roland 1992: 102; Murrell 1992).

Though the debate was not solely confined to stabilization and liberalization, but also included the speed and sequencing of the microeconomic restructuring of production and the implementation market rules, such as securing property rights, bankruptcy regulations and other economic legislations, the labelling of the strategies applied was usually based on the concepts of stabilization and liberalization rather than on the institutional matters which were also on the agenda of transition (Hoen 1996).[4] The emphasis on stabilization and liberalization, as it manifested in the beginning of the transition, was not solely due to systemic legacies. Of course, an inherited monetary overhang forced policy makers to tackle these problems, but there were other arguments as well to pay particular attention to stabilization and liberalization. It was the result of the dominance of neo-liberal economics underpinning transition (Bönker/Müller/Pickel 2003: 21–23), essentially indicating the endeavour to compete on world markets (Van Brabant 1998).

The first time that the benefits of neo-liberal concepts for transition to a market economy became contested was with the occurrence of the transition crisis, which manifested throughout the region of post-communist countries. In the beginning of the 1990s, stabilization and liberalization of the economies in Central and Eastern Europe were accompanied by an unprecedented decline in economic activity.

---

4   At the beginning of the 1990s, Hungary was conceived of as a transition country that relied upon a gradual shift towards a market economy, building on the reforms of the 1970s and 1980s rather than rejecting them. In contrast, Poland was believed to be a textbook example of shock treatment. However, considering the issues of privatisation and institution building, there were grounds to change these conceptions. Poland was extremely slow in even initiating legislation for privatisation, whereas Hungary was relatively quick in both the transfer of ownership rights and the implementation of bankruptcy law, et cetera (Hoen 1996: 15–18).

Not only the successor states of the Soviet Union faced a deep transition crisis, but also the countries closer to the borders of the EU, which, for reasons of their location, were in a better position to create export-generated growth.

The decline in economic activity, measured in real changes of gross domestic product (GDP), was more severe and protracted than foreseen and its damaging effects even surpassed those of the Great Depression of the 1930s (Poznanski 2002: 61). A decade after the start of transition, only a few transition countries had been able to reach let alone exceed the GDP levels of 1989: Albania, Hungary, Poland and Slovenia. The successor states of the Soviet Union were particularly harshly hit. In some cases, there was a cumulative decline amounting to half of the economy in a time span of just a few years.

Evidently, the use of 1989 as a yardstick to measure the depth of the transition crisis was open to discussion. Besides index number problems – Poland was already suffering from a severe crisis in 1989 – the incompatibility of output registration in planned and market economies turned out pivotal as well. In the context of the shock-versus-gradualism debate, the mismatch of output registration triggered three different views on the transition crisis. Firstly, there were scholars who claimed it has been nominally overestimated. Centrally planned economies were characterized by the registration of output that did not exist.[5] With the transition to a market economy, in which the prevailing tax system may serve as an incentive to underreport production, a nominal overestimation of the crisis was inevitable. Secondly, the view was put forward that although the transition crisis may have been deep, this was unavoidable. This point of view also relied upon systemic differences. It was not so much the registration of non-existent output but rather the production of unwanted if not obsolete output that was considered to be the major cause of the crisis. A centrally planned economy used its resources lavishly and supplied commodities for which, under conditions of a market economy, there was no demand. Therefore, the transition to a market economy coincided with a falling demand for these products.[6] The third view on

---

5   Besides, whereas there was not just the result of lies arising because higher production was rewarded with a bonus, but was also due to greater or lesser degrees of honesty. Hidden changes in the output structure were often reported as growth, whereas they actually entailed a price increase (Winiecki 1993).

6   Besides, available stocks first had to diminish before new production could start. In centrally planned the costs of economies stocks were not taken into account. Due to supply constraints, stockpiling took place on the largest scale possible. Therefore, depleting old stocks took longer than envisaged, which further delayed the process of transition.

the transition crisis expressed severe criticism of the sharp and protracted nature of the decline in economic activity. However, this perspective also ultimately relied upon system differences. In a market environment, radical stabilization and liberalization may effect a relatively quick convalescence in production, but in a situation in which market rules are not yet operational recovery will fail to occur. According to this view, the right policy measures were applied to the wrong system and, therefore, production that could have been viable after restructuring had disappeared (Murell 1995). This analysis was based on a sequencing argument: first markets, then liberalization.[7]

Whatever the gravity of the transition crisis, the advocates of gradual transition remained facing tough resistance and kept fighting an uphill battle. Backed by neo-liberal concepts of economics, the necessity of shock treatment gave the impression to have a firm grounding. To further underline the arguments, the proponents were able to focus on the sustainability of recovery, although it remained a matter of dispute to what extent this sustainability was to be ascribed to policy or legacy (Havrylyshyn/Izvorski/van Rooden 2001). In addition, the concept of gradualism continued to remain under pressure, since it was conceived of as a purely academic justification of the urgings. Even if there were sound arguments to lower transition costs by postponing certain elements of reform, for practical reasons it was still valid to implement them quickly. The political feasibility of painful economic reforms played a crucial role, with the underlying idea being *'Do what you can do!'*

3. Different Modes of Emerging Market Economies in Europe Facing the Financial Crisis

In the second half of the 1990s, there was a wide-ranging improvement of economic activity in Central and Eastern Europe (Kołodko 2002). This improvement foddered the idea that the emerging market economies in Europe should proceed in applying neo-liberally underpinned policies. All the countries in Central and Eastern Europe tried to further integrate into world markets and were quite successful in doing that. At the same time, there emerged a shift in the debate. Whereas in the beginning of the 1990s, it purely focused on an implementation

---

7   In the third view on the crisis, also the argument for the stimulation of aggregate demand prevailed. Most commonly referred to in this respect was the Keynesian-inspired theory of the *'credit crunch'* (Calvo/Coricelli 1993). This suggested that high interest rates discouraged private economic activity, whereas state companies remained in a position to rely on inter-enterprise debts.

of an allegedly known economic order – a market economy – the emergence of diverging market economies was more and more taken into account (Pryor 2005). The view on emerging markets in Europe, as discussed in Section 2, shifted from an instrumental one about the '*means*' to one about the '*ends*' (Bohle/Greskovits 2012: 6). This Section addresses the varieties of market economies emerging in Central and Eastern Europe and discusses these in the context of global financial crisis.

On the way to the turn of the millennium, Estonia, Latvia and Lithuania became the best performing transition countries (EBRD 2001). For a number of subsequent years, they were able to accomplish astonishing GDP-growth and, therefore, came to be known as the '*Baltic Tigers*'. Within the group of quickly emerging Nordic market economies, Estonia was considered the brightest pupil in class. Many have claimed a direct link between the strict market-oriented reforms and outstanding performance (Havrylyshyn/Izvorski/van Rooden 2001). The liberal strands of its reform policies were undisputed, despite the fact that, ironically, it had some difficulties in entering the World Trade Organization (WTO), because the country did not have tariffs. In order to be able to play the WTO-game of tariff reduction, Estonia was requested to implement a suitable tariff-system (Van Brabant 1998: 152–154). In other words, it was too liberal to commit to WTO-rules before it entered the organization in 1999. Within the group of emerging markets in Europe, Estonia, but Latvia and Lithuania as well, came to be known as liberal market economies, as defined in the VoC-approach (Ahrens/Schweikert/Zenker 2011; Ahrens/Toews 2013; Bohle/Greskovits 2012; Buchen 2007; Pryor 2005).

In the VoC-approach two contrasting types of capitalism are distinguished on a scale that reveals a continuum with clusters of countries. The pivotal distinction is the way in which the coordination problem at the supply side, *i.e.* for the firms, is institutionally arranged. Liberal market economies are primarily coordinated by price signals and formal contracting in competitive markets. Coordinated market economies are to a large extent driven by non-market institutions. The VoC-approach focuses on coordination problem in the spheres of (i) industrial relations and the labour market, (ii) education and vocational training, (iii) corporate governance, (iv) inter-firm relations, and (v) relations with companies' own employees (Hall/Soskice 2001: 6–7). The principle VoC-claim regarding the institutional design and development is that liberal market economies and coordinated market economies cultivate institutional complementarities across the five spheres.[8]

The emerging market economies in the heart of Europe, notably Slovenia, Slovakia, Hungary and to a lesser extent the Czech Republic and Poland developed an economic order that relied more on the characteristics of a coordinated market economy, be it that diversity needs to be recognized (Knell/Srholec 2007). Within this group of countries, Poland and the Czech Republic are somewhat more on the liberal side, whereas Slovenia has often been indicated as an economic order most clearly aligning with a coordinated market economy (Buchen 2007; Pryor 2005).

The South-Eastern countries are an even more heterogeneous group. Literature suggests that the emerging markets in the region do reveal some features of coordinated market economies, be it that the state often lacks power to exert policies that belong to such a capitalist mode (Bohle/Greskovits 2012: 191–193). Bulgaria has to be seen as a bit of a liberal outlier though. That is not to say that it has a small albeit strong state but rather that it decided in the mid-1990s to shift policy to a more liberal market economy. In the second half of the 1990s, the role of the government was significantly reduced. Stabilization and liberalization became the main policy objectives (EBRD 2009). Romania had similar intentions, but was far less successful in the implementation of a liberal market economy (Papadimitriou/Phinnemore 2013). In the case the former Yugoslav Republics, Croatia and Serbia revealed a large role for the state and government intervention, which behaviour is common for countries with a legacy of violence and war damage, but at the same time the states often failed to be effectively applying their role as coordinator (Bartlett 2007: 201).

Despite the emerging diversity of types of capitalism in post-communist countries in Europe, the beginning of the new millennium revealed a period of catching-up welfare levels for all the identified groups – Baltic liberal market economies, coordinated market economies in Central Europe as well as the hybrid forms of state coordination in South Eastern Europe (Hoen 2011). GDP-growth in Central and Eastern Europe was significantly higher than in the 'old' member-states of the EU, a process that even accelerated after the accession of eight Central and Eastern European countries to the EU in 2004 and two in 2007 (EBRD 2009/10).

---

8   It is beyond the scope of this article to discuss all the critiques on the VoC-approach. To that end, the reader is *e.g.* referred to Ahrens, Schweikert and Zenker (2011). In the context of this article, suffice it the say that the approach had been applied to developed countries belonging to Organization for Economic Co-operation and Development (OECD) as opposed to developing and emerging markets.

The global financial crisis, which began in 2008, set a temporarily halt to this process of catching up. As can be seen in Table 1, with the notable exception of Poland, all European emerging markets faced negative growth rates in 2009 and two of the Baltic States suffered from negative growth performance already in 2008. It also reveals the GDP-level of 2012 (1989 = 100) and indicates the exchange-rate regimes and creditworthiness. However only very tentatively, the table may reveal a possible link between economic performance and the mode of capitalism. The GDP-level and recent growth performance disclose long-term and short-term performance, whereas creditworthiness as an indicator for financial stability is always seen as an import precondition for economic growth in the post-communist countries (Roland 2002).

Regarding financial stability, the Baltic States made more efforts than other transition countries. Soon after their independence, they had introduced a currency board.[9] With such an exchange-rate regime, the authorities do have only limited degrees of policy freedom, since growth of domestic money supply is made dependent upon the stock of foreign reserves. In South-Eastern Europe, the Bulgarians followed the Baltic example in 1997. Elsewhere the introduction of a currency board was not implemented. Initially, in an attempt to enhance stabilization, fixed exchange rate regimes were implemented in Central Europe, but subsequently these were substituted with managed floats.

Meanwhile, Slovenia (2007), Slovakia (2009) and Estonia (2011) have joined the euro. To be able to so, these countries had to successfully join the exchange-rate mechanism for a period of two years. The trial showed that budget deficits were under control (less than 3% of GDP), there were low inflation rates (less than 1.5%-point above the rates in the three countries with the lowest inflation), and a modest government debt (less than 60% of GDP).[10] Given the currency board that Estonia was so far relying on, the trial was not a serious proving, since *de facto* they did already have the euro.

---

9   A currency board is a monetary authority that has to secure a fixed exchange-rate. The Central Bank is subordinate to this authority. The institutional device is meant to show the outside world commitment to restrictive monetary and fiscal policy. Latvia soon abandoned the currency board and introduced a system of fixed exchange rate. But given the extra restrictions that were implemented, the regime *de facto* remained a currency board.

10 These are the so-called '*convergence criteria*', also known as '*Maastricht criteria*', referred to in Article 121 of the European Communities. See *European Central Bank*, http:www. ecb.int/ecb/orga/escb/html/convergence-criteria.en.html (retrieved April 2013). In the context of this article, the long-term interest rates are not taken into account.

Table 1: *GDP-level of 2012 (1989 =100), annual GDP-growth in Central Europe, South-Eastern Europe and the Baltic States (2008–2012 in percentages), and core data on the financial sector (2012)*

Year	GDP 2012 1989=100	2008	2009	2010	2011	2012*	Exchange-rate regime	Credit-rating[#]
Central Europe								
Czech R.	140	3.1	-4.7	2.7	1.7	0.1	Floating	AA+
Hungary	125	0.6	-6.8	1.3	1.6	-1.5	Floating	BBB-
Poland	200	5.3	1.6	3.9	4.3	2.0	Floating	A+
Slovakia	190	6.4	-4.9	4.2	0.6	-2.1	€uro (2009)	AAA
Slovenia	142	3.8	-7.8	1.2	0.6	-2.1	€uro (2007)	AAA
South-Eastern Europe								
Bulgaria	110	6.0	-5.5	0.4	1.7	1.1	Currency board	A
Croatia	100	2.4	-6.9	-1.4	0.0	-1.9	Floating	BBB+
Romania	120	7.1	-8.0	-1.7	2.5	0.3	Floating	BBB+
Serbia	65	5.4	-3.5	1.0	1.6	-1.9	Floating	BB-
Baltic States								
Estonia	145	-1.0	-14.1	3.3	8.3	3.3	€uro (2011)	AAA
Latvia	105	-4.6	-17.7	-0.9	5.5	5.4	Fixed	A
Lithuania	122	2.8	-14.8	1.4	5.9	5.2	Currency board	A

Source: European Bank for Reconstruction and Development (various years), *Transition Report* (London) and Standard & Poor's (www.standardandpoors.com).

Note: Figures for 2012 are estimates.

[#] The best rating is a Triple A (AAA), which indicates highest confidence in creditworthiness. In order of declining confidence, the range is : AAA, AA+, AA, AA-, A+, A, A-, BBB+, BBB, BBB-, BB+, BB, BB-, B+, B, B-, CCC+, CCC, CCC-, CC, D. With a D-rating, a country is unable to service its debts.

Considering the impact of the financial crisis on the distinguished groups of emerging capitalist's modes in Europe in terms of long-term and short-term performance, it is important to distinguish external shocks from domestic failures, In Central Europe, Hungary is an abysmally performing country. It did not so much suffer from the external financial crisis, but first and foremost faced the consequences of erroneous policies in the past. Due to a political stalemate, budget deficits have risen enormously over an extended period of time. Long before the financial crisis materialized during the course of 2008, the country suffered from lower growth rates and it could by no means qualify for the stabilization-pact of the euro. The Hungarian forint rapidly lost its value since the autumn of 2008 and, therefore, it became harder and harder for the Hungarian to service mortgages which were set in Swiss francs. On top of that, since interest rates on Swiss credits were low, many Hungarians also borrowed francs for private consumption. Therefore, Hungary faces hard times, which manifests in a large negative growth of GDP (-6.5% in 2009) and declining creditworthiness (EBRD 2009: 172–175). Considering a longer time perspective, Hungary is falling back. Its GDP is 125% of the 1989-level. All the other Central European countries did perform better, while Poland even doubled its real GDP since the collapse of communism in 1989.

Slovenia, Slovakia and the Czech Republic are in a slightly better position than Hungary, be it for different reasons. Slovenia and Slovakia benefit from having the euro. It gives the countries better credit ratings. At the same time, this seems to be offset by severe losses in export markets. A relatively expensive euro makes these countries less attractive. Being the largest car producer in the world (over 100 cars per 1000 inhabitants in 2008) and exporting 90% of the produced cars, Slovakia severely suffers from the global decline in car sales (Hoen 2009). The Czech Republic does not suffer from expensive exports, but it lacks the standards of Slovenia's and Slovakia's creditworthiness. That may have consequences for attracting foreign direct investments.

Poland is the genuine exception in the region of Central Europe. For quite some time now, it meets the conditions of the stabilization-pact and, therefore, has low budget deficits and moderate inflation. This also indicates the shift to a more liberal policy over the last decade and the demise of post-communists who shaped the economic order after the collapse of communism (Bohle/Greskovits 2012: 243). But due to the fact that it did not join the euro, it could also benefit from a relatively cheap złoty. Even as a large steel producer, Poland was able to expand it exports. Given the fact that the global demand dramatically declined since the global crisis in 2008/2009, it implies that it has gained market shares (EBRD 2009: 204–207).

In the cluster of South-Eastern Europe, all the countries are disproportionately hit by the recession. Declining economic activity replaces a period of excessive growth in the beginning of the new millennium (EBRD 2005). Since it only faced negative growth in 2008, and regained moderate growth afterwards, Bulgaria seems to be in a slightly better position than the other South-Eastern European countries. Moreover, it is able to sustain relatively favourable credit ratings due to its currency board, which institutional arrangement guarantees low budget deficits and, therefore, small debt burdens. The overall conclusion is nevertheless that the counties perform out of sorts both from a long-term and short-term perspective.

All the Baltic States were certainly hurt by the crisis and performed badly especially in 2009. Estonia was the first member-state of the EU that suffered from a recession and, due to popular unrest, Latvia was urged to ask for IMF-support (IMF 2013). Within these countries, the other side of a currency board manifested. When operating with such an exchange-rate regime, governments cannot opt for monetary financing and, consequently, one is to rely upon private credits. It has been done so at a very large, with all the well-known negative results. The economies have tremendously deteriorated and experienced a collapse which was comparable to that in the beginning of the 1990s right after independence.

All in all, it is safe to conclude that the post-communist emerging markets in Europe have inherently become more vulnerable to market shocks. The moulded market systems, in whatever form it was shaped, allowed the countries to benefit during the booming period at the end of the 1990s and the beginning of the new millennium. Growth figures were higher than elsewhere in Europe and these could to a large extent be ascribed to participation in world markets.

The downside of a market economy was revealed by the financial crisis that spread out over the transition countries rather quickly after 2008. During the economic upswing the performance of the emerging market economies was better than elsewhere. However, the countries faced gloomy perspectives during the sudden downturn. Whereas the 'old' EU-members realized growth figures of on average -4% in 2009 (World Bank 2013), the 'new' member-states did perform much worse. That holds especially for the liberal Baltic states (nearly -16%). At the same time, Estonia, Latvia and Lithuania also experienced a quick and very strong recovery with which they outperformed all the other emerging markets in Central and South-Eastern Europe. Apparently, the liberal nature of the countries' economic order made them more vulnerable to worldwide recessions as well as more conducive to growth. This observation seems to run runs counter to the idea that varieties of capitalism do not so much differ in economic performance but rather in the extent to which incomes are incomes are redistributed (Pryor 2005).

The markets that emerged in Europe after the fall of communism strongly committed to become member of the EU. With the accession of Croatia as from the first of July 2013, Serbia is the only non-member of the countries under scrutiny in this section. Despite EU-membership different modes of capitalism developed. The diversity in modes of capitalism and, as a conceivable result of that, the variances in economic performance underline the importance of domestic intuitions in a globalised economy. It is save to conclude that the best performing emerging market economies in Europe – both short-term and long-term perspectives taken into account – are the ones that are on the liberal continuum of VoC. These are the Baltic States and Poland. Given the economic performance, a likely change in institutional design among the emerging markets in Europe is one moving in that direction. It implies a prospective convergence towards the ideal type. Despite all the theoretical and empirical qualms that the VoC-approach goes along with, the converging institutional development is visualised in Figure 1, in which it is pointed out by the dotted arrow.

Figure 1: European emerging markets in the VOC-framework.

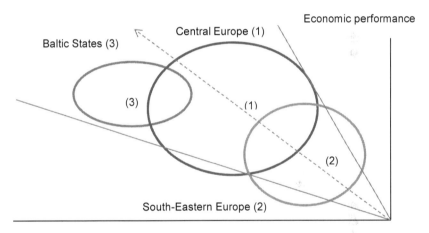

4. Debating the Design of Emerging Markets in Asia

It is hard, if not impossible, to conceive emerging market economies in Asia as a homogenous group of countries. As a matter of fact, as is the case for Europe, there are no pure groups, let alone that there is one group to be clearly identified on the VoC-scale. Institutional structures cannot be defined owing to the different initial conditions that all emerging market economies face in terms of development, economic structure and political culture (Ahrens 2002).

Without claiming to do the impossible, this section nonetheless intends to come to grips with some differences in institutional design *vis-à-vis* the emerging markets in Europe. Given the communist and Soviet legacy of the five Central

Asian countries – Kazakhstan, Kyrgyzstan, Tajikistan, Turkmenistan, and Uzbe-kistan – it makes sense to consider these as a group for which there is a common denominator. That communist legacy need also be taken into account for China, be it that this huge and astonishing fast developing country stands more or less as a case on its own. Whatever criterion is taken, the choice of East Asian emerging market economies is problematic. One could align with the concept of '*Newly Industrializing Economies*' (Amsden 1989) and indicate Hong Kong, Korea, Singapore, and Taiwan as a group, but meanwhile many other countries seem to qualify as '*emerging*' as well.

In this paper, Malaysia, the Philippines, Thailand and Vietnam have been included as a separate group of late industrializers, whereas Indonesia and India have not.[11]

The five Central Asian successor states of the Soviet Union have received much less attention by transition economists than, for example, countries in Central and Eastern Europe or the Russian Federation. In addition, the region distingu-ishes itself by at least four other characteristics. Firstly, Central Asia is extremely well-endowed. The proven stocks of oil and gas, and other natural resources can be perceived as a special legacy that makes the region distinct form other emer-ging market economies. Secondly, these countries' endowments give the region a special geo-political position. Exports of natural resources are becoming an important tool to gain political influence in the world. Thirdly, all the countries are land-locked and far away from major international markets, but they may gain an economic importance as transit countries. Fourthly, and in contrast to the transition countries in Europe, the Central Asian countries are non-democracies, or in the case of Kyrgyzstan contested democracies. Credible commitments to establish liberal democracies do not exist and cannot be expected (Ahrens/Hoen 2012: 6–8).

The Central Asian countries seem to have the characteristics of a dual eco-nomy. There is a state dominated core and a periphery consisting of small-scale enterprises and informal businesses. Contrary to what '*classic*' literature suggests about a dual economy (Lewis 1954), market conditions do prevail in the periphery, whereas in the state-dominated core the coordination mechanisms is completely different. There are extensive non-market incentives, such as tax advantages and

---

11 This is a debatable choice, but one that is based on the following arguments. India, being one of the BRICS (an association of emerging national economies: Brazil, Russia, India, China and South-Africa), is too large to be included in a group, whereas for Indonesia the same holds. Moreover, Indonesia does not have a strong trade integration with the United States of America (USA), whereas the chosen Asian countries do.

price controls, as well as bureaucratic procurements and, very important, there is coercive political power.

This mode of institutional design in Central Asia fits in the debate about the emergence of state capitalism, for which notably China stand as a successful example. Since the collapse of communism at the end of the 1980s and the beginning of the 1990s the term lost its appeal. At that time, a *'third way'* of organizing an economic order with a mixture of socialist planning and liberal market economy was utterly disproved. Some scholars even expressed the idea that what was observed at the end of the 1980s designated *'not just the end of the cold war, or the passing of a particular period of post-war history, but the end of history as such: that is, the end point of mankind's ideological evolution and the universalization of Western liberal democracy as the final form of human government'* (Fukuyama 1992, *xi*). The liberal market economy as the final state of political and ideological evolution made the discussion about alternative economic orders obsolete.

Recently, state capitalism as a new form of political and economic organization became socially acceptable again and returned on the agenda of politicians, journalists and academics (Bremmer 2009; The Economist 2012). The revival is due to the global financial and economic crisis in liberal market economies and it seems to triumph since the incontestable success of the world's largest economy: China. In other words, state capitalism is on the march. It remains unclear, however, what kind of politico-economic order is actually perceived as state capitalism.

The Economist (2012) dissociates itself from *'old'* state capitalism. It indicates that it can no longer be understood as a form of capitalism in which the state owns and controls most of the means of production and, therefore, is in control of the industry and natural resources, as it was functioning in Central and Eastern Europe. Without defining *'new'* state capitalism more specifically, it deliberately coins it as a *'meld of the power of the state with the power of capitalism'* (The Economist 2012: 2–3).

However difficult, a few remarks on defining the rivaling new and oncoming economic order are to be made. Firstly, the way in which states – as pivotal actor in the economic order – interfere in business is quite distinct from the organization and behavior of a centrally-planned economy (Lavigne 1999: 10–15). Planning and control is non-mandatory and the state refrains from decreeing orders regarding what, how much and for whom to produce. The state, however, is visible in the management of enterprises. Managers need to be a member of the ruling political parties. Besides, the state is lending a willing ear to cheap loans, favorable prices or guaranteed demand. In all the varieties of capitalism, ranging from Russia's *'Kremlin capitalism'* or China's *'metropolis capitalism'* to *'energy capitalism'* conducted in Brazil and the Middle East, politicians do have more power than in a liberal market economy. Most of the respective states can be referred to as authoritarian, with the exception of Brazil, and as such the system often serves the interest of the elites (Bremmer 2009: 52).

Secondly, the businesses in which the state seems to be the dominating power are often export-oriented, contrary to what is known from the behavior of centrally-planned economies (Holzman 1987: 91–109). Considering the performance of the enterprises, state capitalism can by no means be characterized as autarkic. On the contrary, many of the best performing and globally competing companies are state-owned. Many of these are oil firms or natural-gas companies, but they also operate in the field of consumer goods, *e.g.* mobile phones. State-owned companies are amongst world-wide well-performing enterprises. In short, state capitalism is outward-looking, be it that the global firms are predominantly in the energy sector.[12]

Thirdly, state capitalism does not imply the exclusion of private enterprises. In the countries that are seen as state capitalist there are significant or large private sectors. What is more, these private sectors seem to coexist very well with the flourishing state sectors. Whereas in centrally-planned economies the small private sector – to the extent that it was allowed – suffered from supply constraints (Kornai 1980), the private businesses in state capitalist countries do not. Crucial, however, is the extent to which these sectors benefit from booming business of state-owned companies. Do they mutually benefit or is there a crowding-out of the two sectors? This question brings back state capitalism as a particular form of a dual economy to the fore.

With respect to the *'classic'* Asian tigers – Hong Kong, Korea, Singapore and Taiwan – institutional design of the economics was distinct and it is problematic to typify these economies as a specific mode of state capitalism.[13] One simply cannot (Chowdhury/Islam 1993: 46–52). The early developers of an export-oriented strategy, which dates back to the 1960s, did not so much rely on a strong state, but first and foremost on a strong and efficient bureaucracy (Amsden 1989; Stark 2012). In neo-liberal thought, bureaucracy is often perceived as a burden to market development. The underlying premise of the Asian tigers has been that bureaucracy not just coincides with market development but rather that it is a precondition for the developments of markets. Furthermore, the strong conglo-

---

12 Russia's *'Gazprom'* is the largest natural-gas company in the world and the biggest oil firms are all state-backed (The Economist 2012: 4–5).

13 In this article, the Republic of Korea, also known as South Korea, is referred to as Korea.

merates of family business, such as the 'chaebol' in Korea, revealed the importance of close ties between businesses and bureaucrats. These ties guaranteed financial credits in times of recession.[14]

Due to the long-term economic success of the Asian tigers, they stood model for a large number of other East and South-East Asia. In a vastly globalizing world economy, these countries have tried to catch up. In their export strategies they have tries to join a process of 'upgrading'. Malaysia and Thailand are examples of countries that appeared as newly emerging economies two decades ago, whereas currently the Philippines as a country which a very large number of inhabitants is seen as one of the 'new dragons'. In some way or another, all these countries do rely on a large role of the state bureaucracy (Tigno 2012). That holds for communist Vietnam, which seeks to implement market reforms in a model of state planning (Anh 2012).

5. Different Modes of Emerging Markets in Asia Facing the Financial Crisis

Just as anywhere else in the world, the emerging markets in Asia suffered from the global financial crisis (Das 2011). The year 2008 revealed hardship, even more so since a number of these countries were still recovering from the blow of the Asia crisis a decade earlier. Having indicated that, the economic performance of the Asia emerging market economies is better than their European counterparts.

Table 2 shows annual GDP-growth for the emerging markets in East and Central Asia under scrutiny. It shows that, with the notable exception of Kyrgyzstan, none of the Central European countries suffered from negative economic growth.[15] Their economic performance seems to be steady over more than a decade. It goes without saying that in the case of Central Asia one has to take reliability of the official statistical data into account, especially for Turkmenistan (Pomfret 2012: 65), but economic performance seems strong. The same holds for China, which country experienced a nearly 10 percent annual growth for more than a decade and it was only in 2012 that it faced somewhat more 'moderate' growth.

---

14 The Asia crisis of 1997 is beyond the scope of this article. It is important to note, though, that in particular these close triggered the financial crisis and declining economic activity in Korea and other emerging markets in East Asia (Mishkin/Eakins 2012: 225–226).

15 Kyrgyzstan's negative growth rates have first and foremost to be ascribed to domestic political upheaval.

Table 2: GDP level of 2012 (1989=100), annual GDP-growth in emerging market economies
in East and Central Asia (2008–2012 in percentages), and core data on the financial
sector (2012)

Year	GDP 2012 1989=100	2008	2009	2010	2011	2012*	Exchange-rate regime	Credit-rating#
The four 'Asian Tigers'								
Hong Kong	361	2.4	-2.9	6.8	5.8	1.3	Currency board	AAA
Korea	490	2.2	0.2	6.1	3.6	2.0		AA
Taiwan	396	0.1	-1.9	10.8	4.0	1.6	Floating	AA+
Singapore	647	1.1	-1.3	14.5	4.9	1.2	Managed float Currency board	AAA
Some new 'Asian Dragons'								
Malaysia	540	4.6	-1.7	7.2	5.1	4.6	Managed float	A+
Philippines	218	3.8	1.1	7.3	3.7	4.2	Floating	BBB-
Thailand	361	2.6	-2.9	7.8	0.1	6.2	Managed float	A
Vietnam	512	8.4	3.1	7.0	5.9	7.5	Multiple rates	BB-
Central Asia								
Kazakhstan	175	4.3	1.2	6.0	7.5	5.5	Floating	BBB+
Kyrgyzstan	110	6.5	2.5	-1.4	5.7	-1.1	Managed float	..
Tajikistan	110	5.0	3.4	6.5	7.4	6.0	Managed float	..
Turkmen.	335	12.0	6.1	9.3	14.7	10.0	Fixed	..
Uzbekistan	220	9.0	8.1	8.5	8.3	7.5	Multiple rates	..
China								
China	1460	9.0	9.1	10.3	9.2	7.8	Managed float	AA-

Source: European Bank for Reconstruction and Development (various years), World Bank (http://www.
worldbank.org/data) and Standard & Poor's (www.standardandpoors.com).
Note: Figures for 2012 are estimates.
The best rating is a Triple A (AAA), which indicates highest confidence in creditworthiness. In order of
declining confidence, the range is : AAA, AA+, AA, AA-, A+, A, A-, BBB+, BBB, BBB-, BB+, BB, BB-, B+,
B, B-, CCC+, CCC, CCC-, CC, D. With a D-rating, a country is un-able to service its debts... No data
available.

The picture for the other emerging markets in Asia is more diffuse. Considering
the more developed newly industrializing market economies, referred to as four
Asian tigers, most of the countries suffered from negative growth rates directly
after the outbreak of financial crisis, Korea being the noticeable exception with
a very modest positive growth. But there was a strong recovery in 2010, which
was moderated in the years after. The new dragons also suffered from economic
decline and their recovery was robust. Regarding the financial stability one can

clearly observe that international markets did have more trust in the more developed markets of the classic for Asian tigers. This can be ascribed to a more mature status of development. On top of that, it can be observed that the countries with a currency board – Hong Kong and Singapore – do have triple A-status. Where the emerging markets in Europe find stability by tightening up with the EU, either by having a currency board of by actually joining the euro, the Asian emerging markets do so by focusing on the USA and the dollar.

Where does it leave us in terms of expected institutional change triggered by the global financial crisis? It can be concluded that (i) the Asian emerging markets seem to be performing better than their European counterparts, among which latter the best performing seem at least more volatile in their economic achievements; (ii) the best performing emerging markets in Asia are those countries for which state interventionism is the biggest. The role of the state, and in particular a state bureaucracy, is much more taken for granted to realize sustained economic growth. Despite all the problems involved with qualifying such a huge and heterogeneous region one can position the Asian emerging market economies as coordinated market economies on the VoC-continuum. What is more, the best-performing state capitalist countries are the most straightforwardly categorized. Given their success, a convergence in institutional change can be expected. This is conceptually exposed in Figure 2.

Figure 2: Asian emerging markets in the VOC-framework.

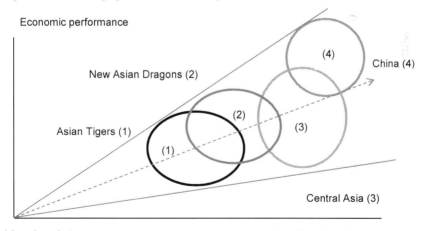

6. Conclusion: Is there Convergence between the Blocs of Emerging Market Economies?

This article focuses on institutional design of economic order and zooms in on emerging market economies in Europe and Asia. These are understood as distinct from fully-developed market economies in terms of (i) volatility in economic performance, (ii) vulnerability to global economic shocks and (iii) the ability to shift the track of reforms as response.

It addresses the question to which extent a convergence of institutional change can be observed as a response to the global financial crisis. It needs to be stated explicitly that the article, therefore, is rather stocktaking or hypothetical in nature than assenting in its conclusions. Taking all these uncertainties into account, the following can be established.

Firstly, in relative terms, the emerging market economies in Europe seem to be designed more as liberal market economies rather than coordinated market economies, whereas in Asia it is rather the other way around. The Asian emerging markets are better tagged as coordinated market economies.

Secondly, the Asian emerging market economies have performed better than their European counterparts in the period immediately following the financial crisis that started in 2008. The decline in economic activity was rather moderate, though significant for the '*classic*' Asian tigers, or absent in the case of China and the Central Asian countries (excluding Kyrgyzstan).

Thirdly, the best-performing emerging market economies in Europe were those most genuinely following the institutional track of a liberal market economy – Estonia, Latvia and Lithuania – and those heading towards that capitalist mode – Poland. As such these countries set an example for other less well-performing emerging market economies in Europe. Therefore, a hesitant convergence in institutional change is likely to materialize of the next years.

Fourthly, the best-performing emerging market economies in Asia are those most genuinely following the institutional track of a coordinated market economy. As such these countries might set an example for other less-well performing countries. The word '*might*' needs to be stressed, since the four Asian tigers seem much more mature in their institutional design and, therefore, less willing or able to redesign. It is also important to note that the four tigers

Fifthly, whereas one can hesitantly conclude that there is a convergence in institutional change within the two blocs of emerging market economies, it seems justified to conclude that there is no institutional convergence between the blocs. On the contrary, a most likely pattern is one that discloses divergence, in which the European emerging markets tentatively converge to a more liberal market economy, without however closing the gap, whereas the Asian emerging markets move timidly and little by little toward the opposite design of a coordinated market economy. This development is pictured in Figure 3.

Figure 3: Divergence of Emerging markets?

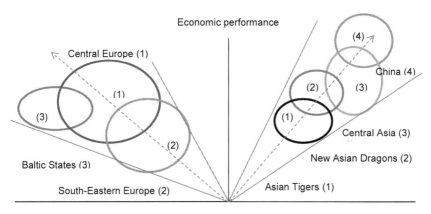

It is important to keep in mind that this article's conclusions can only be tentative and should be considered conjectural rather than confirmative. The expressed need for further research is, however, not to be taken as just another disclaimer. The article plainly reveals that, despite an ongoing process of globalization, there are firm grounds to expect room for national institutional deviations that stem from legacies that are poles apart.

References

Ahrens, Joachim (2002) Governance and Economic Development: A Comparative Institutional Approach. Cheltenham: Edward Elgar.

Ahrens, Joachim / Schweikert, Rainer / Zenker, Juliane (2011) Varieties of Capitalism, Governance and Government Spending – A Cross-section Analysis. PFH Research Papers 1, Göttingen.

Ahrens, Joachim / Hoen, Herman W. (2012) Economic Transition and Institutional Change in Central Asia, in: Institutional Reform in Central Asia: Politico-economic Challenges, edited by Joachim Ahrens and Herman W. Hoen, pp. 3–17. London: Routledge.

Ahrens, Joachim / Toews, Gerhard (2013) Varieties of Capitalism in Developed and Transition Countries: an Emperical Investigation of Economic Convergence of OECD and Post-Soviet Countries. Unpublished paper, Göttingen: PFH.

Amsden, Allice H. (1989) Asia's next Giant: South Korea and the late Industrialization. Oxford: Oxford University Press.

Åslund, Anders (2002) Building Capitalism. The Transformation of the former Soviet Bloc. Cambridge: Cambridge University Press.

Anh, Dang N. (2012) The Urban Poor During the Global Financial Crisis and Economic Downturn in Vietnam, in: Poverty and Global Recession in Southeast Asia, edited by Aris Ananta and Richard R. Barichello, pp. 383–396. Singapore: ISEAS.

Bartlett, Will (2007) The Western Balkan, in: Varieties of Capitalism in Post-Communist Countries, edited by David Lane and Martin Myant, pp. 201–218. Houndmills: Palgrave.

Bohle, Dorothee / Greskovits, Béla (2012) Capitalist Diversity on Europe's Periphery. Ithaca: Cornell University Press.

Bremmer, Ian (2009) State Capitalism Comes of Age. The End of the Free Market?, in: Foreign Affairs 88, pp. 40–55.

Buchen, Clemens (2007) Estonia and Slovenia as Antipodes, in: Varieties of Capitalism in Post-Communist Countries, edited by David Lane and Martin Myant, pp. 65–89. Houndmills: Palgrave.

Calvo, Guillermo A. / Coricelli Fabrizio (1993) Output Collapse in Eastern Europe: The Role of Credit. IMF Staff Papers 40, pp. 35–52.

Chowdhury, Anis / Islam Iyanatul (1993) The Newly Industrializing Economies of East Asia. London: Routledge.

Das, Dilip K. (2011) The Asian Economy. Spearheading the Recovery from the Global Financial Crisis. London: Routledge.

Dewatripont, Mathias / Roland, Gerard (1992) The Virtues of Gradualism and Legitimacy in the Transition to a Market Economy, in: The Economic Journal 102, pp. 291–300.

The Economist (2012) Special Report – State Capitalism. The visible Hand, January 21st.

European Bank for Reconstruction and Development (various years) Transition Report. London: EBRD.

European Central Bank (2013) Convergence Criteria, online: http://www.ecb.int/ecb/orga/escb/html/convergence, retrieved May 1.

Fukuyama, Francis (1992) The End of History and the Last Man. London: Hamilton.

Hall, Peter A. / Soskice, David W. (2001) Varieties of Capitalism: The Institutional Foundations of Comparative Advantage. Oxford: Oxford University Press.

Havrylyshyn, Oleh / Izvorski, Izvaldo / van Rooden, Ron (2001) Recovery and Growth in Transition Economies, 1990–97, in: Good Governance in Central and Eastern Europe. The Puzzle of Capitalism by Design, edited by Herman W. Hoen, pp. 26–53. Cheltenham: Edward Elgar.

Hoen, Herman W. (1996) 'Shock versus Gradualism' in Central Europe Reconsidered. Comparative Economic Studies 38, pp. 1–20.

Hoen, Herman W. (2009) Slowaakse Auto-industrie onder Druk. Ablak 14, pp. 10–13.

Hoen, Herman W. (2011) Crisis in Eastern Europe: The Downside of a Market Economy Revealed? European Review 19, pp. 31–41.

Holzman, Franklyn D. 1987 The Economics of Soviet Bloc Trade and Finance. Boulder: Westview Press.

Index Mundi (2013) Country Facts, online: http://www.indexmundi.com/, retrieved April 15.

International Monetary Fund (2013) IMF Reaches Staff-Level Agreement with the Latvian Authorities on First Review under Stand-by Arrangement, online: http://www.imf.org/external/np/sec/pr/2009/pr09269.htm, retrieved May 1.

Kornai, János (1980) The Economics of Shortage. Amsterdam: North-Holland.

Knell, Mark / Srholec, Martin (2007) Diverging Pathways in Central and Eastern Europe, in: Varieties of Capitalism in Post-Communist Countries, edited by David Lane and Martin Myant, pp. 40–62. Houndmills: Palgrave.

Lavigne, Marie (1999) The Economics of Transition. From Socialist Economy to Market Economy. Basingstoke: Macmillan.

Lewis, William A. (1954) Economic Development with Unlimited Supply of Labour. Manchester School of Economics and Social Studies 22, pp. 139–191.

Mishkin, Frederic S. / Eakins, Stanley G. (2012) Financial Markets and Institutions. Boston: Pearson.

Murrell, Peter (1992) Evolution in Economics and in the Economic Reform of the Centrally Planned Economies, in: The Emergence of Market Economies in Eastern Europe, edited by Christopher Clague and Gordon C. Rausser, pp. 35–53. Cambridge: Cambridge University Press.

Murrell, Peter (1995) Transition according to Cambridge Mass. Journal of Economic Literature 33, pp. 164–78.

North, Douglas C. (1990) Institutions, Institutional Change and Economic Performance. Cambridge: Cambridge University Press.

Papadimitriou, Dimitris / Phinnemore, David (2013) Romania: uneven Europeanization, in: The Member States of the European Union, edited by Simon Bulmer and Christian Lequesne, pp. 263–276. Oxford: Oxford University Press.

Pomfret, Richard (2012) Turkmenistan after Turkenbashi, in: Institutional Reform in Central Asia: Politico-economic Challenges, edited by Joachim Ahrens and Herman W. Hoen, pp. 63–88. London: Routledge.

Poznanski, Kazimierz Z. (2002) The Crisis of Transition as a State Crisis, in: Post-communist Transformation and the Social Sciences. Cross-Disciplinary Approaches, edited by Frank. Bönker, Klaus Muller and Andreas Pickel, pp. 55–76. Oxford: Rowman & Littlefield.

Pryor, Frederic (2005) Market Economic Systems. Journal of Comparative Economics 33, pp. 25–46.

Roland, Gerard (2002) The Political Economy of Transition. Journal of Economic Perspectives 16, pp. 29–50.

Standard & Poor's (2013) Sovereigns Rating List, online: http://www.standardandpoors.com/ratings/sovereigns/ratingslist/en/us/?sectorName=Governmen&subSectorCode=39&subSectorName=Sovereigns, retrieved May 1.

Stark, Manuel (2012) The Emergence of Developmental States from a New Institutionalist Perspective. A Comparative Analysis of East Asia and Central Asia. Frankfurt am Main: Peter Lang.

Tigno, Jorge V. (2012) The Price of Rice and Politics of Poverty in the Philippines, in: Poverty and Global Recession in Southeast Asia, edited by Aris Ananta and Richard R. Barichello, pp. 229–278. Singapore: ISEAS.

Van Brabant, Jozef M. (1998) Eastern Europe and the World Trade Organization. The Present Position and Prospects of Accession, in: Eastern Europe and the World Economy. Challenges of Transition and Globalization, edited by Iliana Zloch-Christy, pp. 141–176. Cheltenham: Edward Elgar.

Wagener, Hans-Jürgen (1992) System, Order, Change – On Evolution and Transformation of Economic Systems, in: Changing Economic Order, edited by Julien van den Broeck and Daniel van den Bulcke, pp. 23–65. Groningen: Wolters–Noordhoff.

Winiecki, Jan (1993) 'Heterodox' Stabilisation in Eastern Europe. European Bank for Reconstruction and Development, Working Paper. London: EBRD.

World Bank (2013) Data by Country, online: http://www.worldbank.org/data, retrieved April 15.

Karmo Kroos

Developmental Welfare Capitalism in East Asia with a Special Emphasis on South Korea

> "[W]hile capitalism cannot coexist *with*, neither can it exist *without*, the welfare state."
>
> (Offe 1984: 153, italics in original).

1. Introduction: Rationale for the Topic and Analytical Framework

This paper investigates the developmental welfare capitalism regimes of Newly Industrialising Countries (NIC) – placing special emphasis on South Korea (henceforth Korea). It takes Kosuke and Johnson's conceptual frame as a basis and structures the analysis of the Korean developmental state within four contested themes: industrial policy versus the market, democracy and the developmental state, the time frame and government-business relationship. Furthermore, it uses the varieties of capitalism (VoC) and welfare state literature to understand the Korean emerging market economy. Although these approaches are first used sequentially, an attempt is made at the final section of the paper to merge these theoretical frames into a holistic approach – link the production and the welfare regimes to the political system, similar to Soskice's (2007) extended VoC framework, in order to show that the Korean political economy arrangement has not been static but has evolved in stages to face the challenges of the era: from the developmental state in the 1960s and 1970s, to the modernisation state in the 1980s and finally to the contradictions of the welfare state in the 1990s and 2000s. To explain the major building blocks of Korean developmental welfare capitalism – the developmental state, the welfare regime and the political system – the conceptual framework followed in this paper will be introduced first.

Although the world is globalising, it is important to recognise that there are still plenty of differences within and among capitalist economic models, including the East Asian NIC. Therefore, political economists and economic sociologists argue that in reality there is no unified (textbook) model of a market economy that all actually existing systems follow. Hence they have proposed the framework of comparative capitalisms instead. This analytical tradition, known as the VoC approach allows one to take into account the differences in special institutional

arrangements between labour, capital and the state. In addition to this, stratifi-
cation and public policy scholars of welfare states and regimes have developed
typologies to understand the components of social policy under different capitalist
formations. However, what is largely missing in the contemporary literature on
VoC and welfare states is an attempt to combine the analyses of the economic
systems with the social and political arrangements.

The VoC approach to the analysis of national economies dates back at least to
the 1960s when the path-breaking books by Gerschenkron (1962) as well as the
research on traditions of diversity of modern capitalism by Shonfield (1965) were
published. Indeed, in the 1960s the triumph of the distinctive national economies
of Austria, France, Italy, Japan, Netherlands, Sweden, Western Germany, the UK
and the USA (just to mention the "usual suspects") triggered a discussion about
the diversity of capitalist systems. Rather than following one unified free-market
model, these national systems encouraged policy makers and electorates around
the world to find unique solutions to their national challenges. As Crouch/Streeck
(1997: 1) sum up the epoch that lasted for two decades before neoliberalism started to spread (symbolised by the triumph of the conservative policies of Reagan
and Thatcher on either side of the Atlantic):

> "Interest in the diversity of modern capitalist economies became widespread as far back
> as the late 1960s, when … technologies and markets were far from fully determinative
> of social life under capitalism, and … societies had non-trivial alternatives with respect
> to how they wanted to run their respective capitalisms and, by implication, what kind
> of society they wanted to be. It was true that sometimes these choices had been made
> long ago and were now deeply entrenched in an established 'culture' that was, at least in
> the short term, beyond the reach of contemporary actors. Nevertheless, the very idea of
> alternatives and choice implied that, to some extent at least, purposeful collective action –
> in one world: politics – could make a difference even and precisely for the nature of
> advanced capitalism. Observed and relentlessly documented capitalist diversity stood
> for the promise that, provided one could create the 'right' political conditions, people in
> twentieth-century societies did have a capacity to reorganise their capitalist economic sys-
> tems in line with collective preferences within a broad band of meaningful alternatives."

The success of national economies survived the oil crisis of the 1970s, and the
academic discussion of the national systems based on a unique competitive advantage reached its peak in the 1980s. Indeed, scholars published innumerable
studies on the models of national political economies, and based on textbooks
on comparative economic systems, courses and entire programmes were taught
at universities around the world. To point out just some of the citation classics on
East Asian economic models, Johnson published the seminal monograph, *MITI*

and Japanese Miracle, in 1982, and the World Bank followed with *The East Asian Miracle* in 1993.

But the 1990s brought deep recession to Japan and Germany, and the neoclassical policy transfer that meant deregulation, privatisation and freedom of trade. Contrary to the expectations of eliminating overregulation, improving efficiency, and increasing the size of a slice of the enlarged pie for all promised by international trade and division of labour based on competitive advantage, Asia instead experienced the financial crisis of 1997–8. As policy advice to rescue the countries, reformers in East Asia received suggestions along the lines of the Washington Consensus to "get the prices right" (also known as the market fundamentalist thesis of getting the state out) during the Washington Consensus mark 1, and when this did not work, to "get the institutions right" during the Washington Consensus mark 2. To the great disappointment of the developers of the parsimonious development and transition models, the output loss in East Asia suggested that the single variable or single set of key determinants (such as getting the prices and institutions right) hardly guaranteed a positive turn-around (W. T. Woo 2004).

Based on this and other recent economic reform experiences in Latin America, Eastern Europe or Central Asia, it seems reasonable to take Hirschman (1986, Ch. 6) as a point of departure and try to complicate the political economy of development. More particularly, what is implied in this paper is that the search for a single variable able to explain the economic development has led to the false arguments on how my variable "trumps" everything else or debates as to whether "my variable can swallow your variable".[1] Yet, one has to be equally careful to avoid falling into the opposite of the single variable approach. That is, one should avoid slipping into another extreme where almost anything counts in the attempt to get a holistic picture of development. For instance, one should be careful of the all-inclusive argument, such as the one put forward by Roy et al. (2012: 26–27), to explain East Asian economic success. On the basis of the success stories of the emerging economies they do not only list different institutional factors from the history of religion, the culture, politics as well as corporate governance, independent technocracy and bureaucracy, but they also add some structural factors, such as geography, a sound financial system, human capital and land reform to the list

---

1   The reader may recognise that there is a link to the orthodox training of economists that tends to ignore social, historical, political, cultural or geographic phenomena (all of which the institutional school and economic geography emphasise) as well as a link to the arguments that there is a need for more interdisciplinary training of social scientists (see Kornai 2007; Kroos 2012; Wallerstein 1996/2000) to understand the development challenges and figure out the solutions.

as success factors that have played an important role in the fast economic growth of East Asian countries. Intuitive as they may sound, there is a danger of falling into the opposite extreme of a parsimonious understanding of development where almost everything is related to the success of the economic policy.

As a middle way between the all-inclusive "everything counts" approach of the sociology of development and parsimonious models of one key (set of) variable of neoclassical economics, this paper follows the attempts to incorporate the economic, political and social spheres into the analysis. While Kang (2006: 6) assesses that the VoC approach offers an ambitious "synthesis" of the major sociology of development approaches that had been developed over half a century, scholars working within this tradition have not stopped there. As shown in Figure 1, Hancké et al. (2007) suggest moving beyond VoC and propose an extension of Hall/Soskice's (2001) original two country ideal types – a comparison and contrast of Liberal Market Economies and Coordinated Market Economies. Nevertheless, even this can be seen as unsatisfactory because it is hardly able to incorporate countries such as Korea into the typology – suggesting that it could be classified together with Italy and Spain under the *Compensating state* type. Since the organised expression of labour interests has not always been allowed in Korea, it is difficult to classify it under *Étatisme's* type either, even though the close relationship between state and economy make it similar to France in some respects. In this context, Kang's (2006) criticism of the VoC tradition that it has been more successful in integrating the state-centred approach (originating, as mentioned above, from the national economic systems of the 1960s) than it has been in incorporating the insights of the society-centred approach (related to the welfare regime literature) is a point well taken.

To overcome these challenges, alternative VoC approaches have been put forward by Amable (2003) with his five types of capitalism and Baumol et al. (2007) with their four types of capitalism. Although Amable (2003) embeds a system design into the social context and places stronger emphasis on the political dimension (within which context the institutions represent the choice of the dominant social coalition), his five types of VoC (the Anglo-Saxon's market based model, Scandinavian welfare state model, Continental European Rhinish economy model, Southern European Mediterranean model and Asian Meso-Corporatist model) seem to be locked into the cultural background conditions. Although the Baumol et al. (2007, Ch. 4) typology of four types of VoC (state-guided capitalism, oligarchic capitalism, big-firm capitalism and entrepreneurial capitalism) is said to be more flexible and sensitive to the level of development (ibid, 61), it fails to identify any possible role for the political and social dimension as drivers or contributors of institutional change over time.

Figure 1: State-economy relations, interest organization, and modes of coordination.

State-Economy Relations

		Close	**Arm's-length**
		Étatisme	*LMEs*
		France pre-1990s	UK, Baltics
		Compensating state	*CMEs*
		Italy, Spain some EMEs	Germany Slovenia

(Left axis: Interest organization — Organized / Fragmented)

Source: Hancké et al. (2007: 25)

Therefore, to find a balance between a single variable and multidimensional / multidisciplinary approaches as well as to avoid the limitations of the above mentioned approaches, an attempt is made here to enrich the analytical tradition of VoC by complementing the examination of the Korean political economy to welfare and political regimes. To that end, Soskice's (2007) analytical approach, which incorporates the production regime, the welfare state and political system into the analysis of VoC, is used in this paper for clarifying the Korean developmental welfare capitalism. Hence, the paper is organised into three parts in order to interpret the Korean developmental welfare capitalism holistically. Starting with an analysis of the Korean political economy we shall first analyse its developmental state. To complement this with the developments in the social and political spheres, we shall then discuss changes in the Korean welfare regime over decades and finally, before drawing conclusions, briefly touch on the changes that have occurred in the political system.

2. South Korean Political Economy

While the tremendous success of East Asian countries' post World War II development has not gone unnoticed among scholars, policy advisors and makers, the region is often treated as unified and its development model, as homogeneous. The prime example of the latter is the World Bank's miracle report titled *The East Asian Miracle* from 1993 (for concise overviews see also World Bank 1993b and

Page 1994a). As a critique of overgeneralization and lack of sensitivity towards country specific nuances of the report, Perkins (1994) argues that *There are at Least Three Models of East Asian Development*. According to him, these three are: "the manufactured export-led state interventionist models of Japan, Korea and Taiwan; the free port service, commerce-dominated model of Singapore and Hong-Kong; and models of those economies rich in natural resources (at least in the beginning) but not in human resources (Indonesia, Malaysia, and Thailand)". In order to understand better the historical background of the sub-type to which Korea belongs, the colonial heritage of the "the manufactured export-led state interventionist model" (also known as the developmental state) will be discussed briefly prior to a more detailed analysis of it central issues.

Unlike many less developed countries that followed Nehru's Indian Consensus model for post-colonial development, Waelbroeck (1998b: 325) argues that the Four Dragons (Hong Kong, the Republic of Korea, Singapore, and Taiwan [China]) followed the Japanese example. This proved to be a good choice and should not be too surprising given the fact that there are three countries in Northeast Asia that formed the core of the Japanese empire in the pre-war period: Japan, Korea and Taiwan. Indeed, as Woo-Cumings (1999a, xi–xii) assesses, "[n]othing succeeds like success, and thus Korea and Taiwan learned lessons and absorbed advanced technologies and capital from Japan, and then embarked on a similar trajectory of light-industrial exporting under multi-year plans, guided by strong state ministries (if less so in Taiwan than Korea). This gave all three economies a highly neomercantilist, nationalist tendency; in Japan and Korea especially, it meant strong state involvement with and promotion of big economic conglomerates."

Nevertheless, the Japanese colonial past of the success stories of the NIC tends to be forgotten in the mountains of academic publications published about the East Asian miracle in general and about Korea in particular. More precisely, one of the first analyses of Korean economic success by Frank et al. (1975) actually devotes a separate chapter to the economic history of the country since the World War II but fails to make the connection to its colonial past as anything positive. As with many other scholars discussing Korean development, Frank et al. (ibid, 226–227) note the possible impact of Japanese colonialism only in passing – in the form of the type of industrial relations between paternalistic employers and loyal employees, the industrial structure and development model to be followed and imitated (despite the extremely unpopular colonisation). Instead, the Japanese colonial past is presented as economic dependency and domination – a development trap to be overcome rather than something to be benefited from. It is also understandable, as the aim of Frank et al. is to analyse the influence of the Korean foreign trade regime and therefore the emphasis on the role of export that has dominated the study of Korean economic success since then.

Also, in other publications, the Korean colonial past has been mentioned in passing (see e.g. Cumings 1984; Goodman/Peng 1996: 195–200; Johnson 1987; J. Woo 1991: 66; Holliday 2005; Pirie 2008: 64 and Ramesh 2004: 3) and its impact on the Korean growth model is systematically analysed in very few cases. And in the few cases in which the challenge is accepted a diametrically opposite position is reached. In other words, there is "disagreement … as to whether Japanese colonisation basically distorted or laid down groundwork for development" (Cheng 1990: 140). On the one hand, Eckert (1992) and Kohli (1994/97/99) argue that despite the brutality of the Japanese colonialism, it was namely this past dependent historical experience that left the imprint of the political economy and allowed Korea to catch up with the developed world in such a short period of time after the World War II. On the other hand, Chang shows that the colonial past (2006, Ch. 4), or more broadly, the culture (2007, Ch. 9) cannot explain the success of NIC. Given the impossibility of collecting contrafactual evidence to learn what would have happened if the countries had not had a Japanese colonial past, the controversy is difficult to settle. Nevertheless, what can be studied more closely is the political economy arrangement known as the "developmental state", which a subgroup of NIC, such as Korea, adopted from Japan and has been implementing quite successfully since the 1960s.

Korea borrowed the developmental state approach to economic development from Japan and implemented it relatively successfully until it was hit by the Asian Financial crisis and serious doubts were raised about her political economy arrangement (sometimes described as "crony capitalism"). Although the authors of the World Bank (1993a) miracle report (see also Page 1994a/b) have attempted to downplay the role of the state in the extraordinary economic progress of East Asia and have tried to emphasise as well as interpret the success story of the East Asian NIC as a confirmation of its neoliberal policy (labelling the actual practices of the region as "market friendly"), the so called "revisionist school" has vehemently criticised the report (see Amsden 1994; Lall 1994; Perkins 1994; Rodrik 1994 and Yanagihara 1994). More specifically, the critics of the miracle report have seriously questioned the selective use and interpretation of data, the lack of attention to initial conditions (education and equality) as well as the total ignorance of any of the countervailing arguments that the area specialists have produced during the decades of research – a practice whose aim seems to be an attempt to downplay the active role of the state in the East Asian (including Korean) political economy of development. While there have been many rounds of debate over the role of the state in the miracle on which literature overviews can be found elsewhere (e.g. Chu 1997), it is clear that the East Asian financial crisis called for the need to rethink the underlying assumptions of the miracle and to formulate a new development paradigm (including the state and the market relationship) for the region (see e.g. Park et al. 2004; W. T. Woo 2004 and Stiglitz/Yusuf 2001).

Irrespective of these academic quarrels over the role of the state in East Asian development (which at times tends to become rather ideological), the theoretical dispute over the applicability of the market and state failures as arguments for and against interventionism in the economy and its development continue (see e.g. Amsden 1992; Wade 1988; Kruger 1974/90; Lall 1994; Rodrik 1995a, 1995b, 1996a, 1996b and Stiglitz 1988: 153–156, 1989). The strongest argument of the revisionist school in this context seems to be the empirical evidence from (not so) distant economic history. According to Chu (1997: 19) and Chang (2002b, 2003, 2009: 8), there is hardly a successful case of economic development where state intervention did not have the upper hand. Starting from the industrialisation of England – a crucial case in this respect that was raised by Polanyi (1944 [1957], Ch. 6) – and ending with the NICs' (including Hong Kong and Singapore as the textbook cases of laissez-faire, which have been studied closely by Lam 2000) successful catch-up with industrialised countries, the state actually has played an important role in industrial development. In other words, even in the cases that are widely believed to be examples of laissez-faire economic policy, the visible hand has been complemented by the invisible one. The paradoxical lesson (even if not yet the widespread consensus) from this is that the market needs a strong government (see e.g. Evans et al. 1985; Deyo 1987; Bardhan 1990 and Stiglitz 2001) and an open economy demands a bigger state than a closed one (Rodrik 1998). Pempel (1999: 139) sums up much of the scholarship as well as popular understanding on the role of state in East Asian economic success stories:

> "The East Asian states, it is argued, have been successful because governments there have acquired control over a variety of things presumed critical to economic success: they can extract capital; generate and implement national economic plans; manipulate private access to scarce resources; coordinate the efforts of individual businesses; target speci-fic industrial projects; resist political pressures from popular forces, such as consumers and organised labour; insulate their domestic economies from extensive foreign capital penetration; and, most especially, carry through a sustained project of ever-improving productivity, technological sophistication, and increased world market shares."

In this context, it is now hardly questioned that the government strongly inter-vened in the East Asian post-World War II development. The close relationship between the government and the market that has been developed in the state interventionist models of Japan, Korea and Taiwan is known as "developmental state". It is a concept that originates from Chalmers Johnson's book *MITI and the Japanese Miracle: The Growth of Industrial Policy, 1925–1975*[2] and can be seen as a label that attempts to capture the essence of one of the three ideal types of states[3]. Unlike the "plan ideological" sub-type of the Soviet developmental state (see White 1984), the East Asian is "plan rational". That is, East Asian NIC, which follow this development strategy, believe that their destinies can be changed – miracles can be created or the initial conditions can at least be combined so innovatively that they allow for the design of a tailor-made solution for the situation that is most suitable for the national development needs. This stands in contrast to accepting the destiny and trying to build on the competitive advantage as suggested by Ricardian inspired neoclassical political economy of development (see Srinivasan 1985). But that is not all; it also presupposes a capable government which is why Leftwich (1995: 401) defines developmental states as "states whose politics have concentrated sufficient power, autonomy and capacity at the centre to shape, pursue and encourage the achievement of explicit developmental objectives, whether by establishing and promoting the conditions and direction of economic growth, or by organising it directly, or a varying combination of both."

Speaking of the origin of the developmental state within the history of economic ideas, Fallows (1994: 179) and Leftwich (1995: 401–402) trace the idea back to List (1885 [1996]: 175–178) who put forward the idea that to catch-up with advanced nations state intervention in less developed countries is necessary – a very similar idea to what Gerschenkron (1962, Ch. 1) later made famous. However, contrary to the Russian state intervention for military aims, List makes a futuristic argument if one observes the success story of the export oriented countries of mass production in East Asia that materialised approximately a century later. He (1885 [1996]: 178) states: "… a perfectly developed manufacturing industry, an important mercantile marine, and foreign trade on a really large scale can only be attained by means of the interposition of the power of the State."

Leftwich (1995, see also 1996) identifies six major components that define the (the model of) developmental state: (i) a determined developmental elite – leadership by determined and relatively incorrupt developmental elites; (ii) the relative autonomy of the state from domestic special interests; (iii) a powerful, competent and insulated economic bureaucracy; (iv) the weak and subordinated

---

2   For the "odyssey of a concept" see also Johnson (1999) and for the genealogy of the term see Cumings (1999) and of the idea see Leftwich (1995).

3   For alternative typologies see White (1984) who identifies state capitalist, intermediate and state socialist; and Evans (1989) who distinguishes between predatory, developmental and other apparatuses of third world states.

civil society; (v) the effective management of non-state economic interest; and (vi) repression, legitimacy and performance. In short, he puts emphasis on politics and state capacity and perhaps not enough on the complicated relationship with big business – a criticism that Leftwich (2001: 152) accepts. Furthermore, as the analysis of the developmental state around these defining features can be found elsewhere (see Clapham 1996) and the different theoretical perspectives on the politics of East Asian development (liberal institutionalism with universalistic policy suggestions; culturalism with emphasis on contingent issues such as culture; and globalism with a focus on geographical and timing factors) are analysed by Zhang (2003), the discussion to follow will take Johnson's understanding of the defining features of the developmental state as the basis. Actually, he has put forward at least two conceptualisations of the developmental state. In the 1987 paper entitled *Political institutions and economic performance* he lists and discusses seven key issues of the capitalist developmental state: financial control; labour relations; autonomy of the economic bureaucracy; autonomy of the state from business interests; balancing incentives with commands in administrative guidance; large business conglomerates; and foreign capital. More than a decade later, however, he (1999: 46–60) narrows them down to four in the reflections on the basis of Oyama Kosuke's review of his seminal book on MITI and Japanese political economy. Since he regards the latter as the best conceptualisation of the defining issues of the developmental state, it is also taken as the starting point of the analysis of the Korean case in the sections to follow. These four fundamental issues related to the developmental state are: (i) industrial policy versus the market, (ii) democracy and the developmental state, (iii) the time frame, and (iv) the government-business relationship. All together these themes characterise the Korean developmental state and economy. Therefore, we shall discuss them one by one.

2.1 Industrial Policy *versus* the Market

Existing literature reviews on state intervention (Block 1994; Chang 2002a), regulation (Chang 1997) and industrial policy (Chang 1994/ 2009; Kosacoff/Ramos 1999; Pack/Saggi 2006; Rodrik 1995b; Shapiro/Taylor 1990 and Shapiro 2007) as well as the seminal original contributions that have been made about these issues within the East Asian development controversy (see e.g. Amsden 1989/92; Amsden/Chu 2003; Barrett/ Chin 1987; Campos/ Root 1996; Chang 1993/2006; Chu 1997; Fishlow et al. 1994; Johnson 1982/84/87/99; E. M. Kim 1997; Krugman 1994a; Lall 1994; Nolan/Pack 2003; Park et al. 2004; Page 1994a/b; Shapiro 2007; Wade 1990 and World Bank 1993a, esp. Ch. 6) indicate that the heated debate about the role of the state and the market in the East Asian economic success story in general and the industrial policy in the Korean one in particular has been active for a while. Despite the length and many rounds of debate (with their reflections on the changes in the international economic environment), the complicated relationship between government and businesses within the East Asian economic development in general and the Korean developmental state approach to catching up in particular continues to be a source of conflicting conclusions. For instance, the issues related to the possibility of moral hazard, the economic impact of state interventions in picking winners instead of protecting losers; getting interventions, structure and prices right (or wrong); engaging in import substitution and/ or export promotion are hardly less controversial after all these years of debate.[4]

To start with, it has to be made clear what is meant by "industrial policy" in this context. In the above mentioned literature on the NIC development experience, it does "not mean any policy that affects industry but a very particular type of policy that affects industries. It is what is commonly known as "selective industrial policy" or "targeting" – namely, a policy that deliberately favours particular industries over others, against market signals, usually (but not necessarily) to enhance efficiency and promote productivity growth" (Chang 2009: 2). As for the "market", it is understood in this context in an oversimplified way[5] as the opposite to state intervention or bureaucratic coordination (for details see Kornai 1984).

---

4   This is clearly an arbitrary selection of a much larger number of issues that have been debated on within the East Asian industrial policy debate. For instance, Chang (2009: 3–4) lists the following topics: (i) coordination of complementary investments (the so-called Big Push); (ii) coordination of competing investments through entry regulation, "investment cartels", and (in declining industries) negotiated capacity cuts; (iii) policies to ensure scale economies (e.g., licensing conditional upon production scale, emphasis on the infant industries starting to export from early on, state-mediated mergers and acquisitions); (iv) regulation of technology imports (e.g., screening for overly obsolete technologies, cap on technology licensing royalties); (v) regulation of foreign direct investment (e.g., entry and ownership restrictions, local contents requirement, technology transfer requirements, export requirements); (vi) mandatory worker training for firms above a certain size, in order to resolve the collective action problem in the supply of skilled workers due to the possibility of "poaching"; (vii) the state acting as a venture capitalist and incubating high-tech firms; (viii) export promotion (e.g., export subsidies, export loan guarantees, marketing help from the state trading agency); (ix) government allocation of foreign exchanges, with top priority going to capital goods imports (especially for export industries) and bottom priority, to luxury consumption good imports.

5   Chang (2002a: 544) for instance states that "defining a free market is at the deepest level a pointless exercise because no market is in the end 'free' as all markets have some state regulations on who can participate in which markets and on what terms."

On the one hand, the supporters of state intervention and believers of the positive impact of the industrial policy in East Asian NIC, such as Korea, argue that the active role played by the state in the late industrialisation is central to their economic success stories. Among these are two slightly different schools of thought that have been advancing this argument: the Weberian (institutionalist) and the neo-Marxist (structuralist/dependent development) perspective. Without going into details here, the Weberian school basically follows Johnson's lead (see e.g. Johnson 1982/87 as well as Page 1994a: 620) and emphasises the role of efficient bureaucracy (such as MITI in the Japanese case). However, the world system theorists of dependent development hold that the "artificial" development of the semi-periphery locks these countries into a dependent position and makes them vulnerable in the world economy, which is controlled by core countries' capital, technology, markets and transnational companies (see e.g. Arrighi et al. 2003).

There are problems with both perspectives. On the one hand, the problem with the good governance argument is that it depicts the state as a homogeneous body of policymaking and implementation which lacks any internal conflict and assumes that the developmental state polices lead to economic growth without actually showing the causality, according to Lie (1990).[6] On the other hand, the problem with the world system theorists is that they fail to see that some developing countries "have been able to beat the system" and have climbed the ladder because they have been able to take advantage of their structural factors, such as size, or institutional advantages, such as human capital, according to Amsden (2003: 37). Furthermore, Deyo (1987: 17–18) summarises the contrafactual evidence from East Asian NIC in the following:

> "East Asian industrialisation departs from the expectations of those writers in the dependency tradition who argue that external economic dependency is associated with long-run economic stagnation and economic inequality, loss of economic autonomy in economic restructuring and the formation of development strategy, and a weakness of domestic states. Rather, the East Asian NICs present a pattern not only of continued high growth rates but also of relatively equitable development, a continuing ability to alter domestic economic structures and world market position to adjust to changing economic circumstances and an enhanced rather than a diminished state power to mobilise and deploy domestic economic resources."

Nevertheless, the supporters of the idea that industrial policy has hardly made any positive impact on East Asian development argue that its success stories should

---

6   The (lack of evidence for) causality between industrial policy and economic development has given birth to a heated debate – see World Bank (1993 Ch. 6) and Lall (1994: 650–652) as well as Chang (2009) and Pack/Saggi (2006).

be associated with market friendly policies instead. This has also been the official line of the World Bank (see World Bank 1993a and Page 1994a/b), and it relates to the neoclassical school's traditional interpretation of industrial policy as a source of market distortion (see Bhagwati 1982; Kruger 1974/90, Nolan/Pack 2003 and Pack/Saggi 2006). Again, drawing on the East Asian economic success story in general and the Korean one in particular, E. M. Kim (1997: 11) problematises the position of the neoclassical school by pointing out that

> "(1) it neglected the role of the state as having an independent and leading role in the economy; (2) it assumed the private sector in Korea to be not very different from the "rational," "free" enterprises found in the West, which tend to work in relatively free markets; and (3) it ignored structural obstacles that may hinder economic development, such as [an] unreceptive international market and MNCs, and [the] destruction of [the] economy caused by war, and so on."

There is also a milder version of the market-cantered school that would accept state intervention if there were negative externalities (Stiglitz 1988: 153–156 and 1989), if the harm arising from government failures were smaller than from market failures (Fishlow 1990) or if it were needed for the promotion of market institutions (Datta-Chaudhuri 1990 and Stiglitz 2001). This middle-ground position does not question the idea of state intervention on technical grounds (as the proper neoclassical school does) or dispute it on ideological positions (as some representatives of the Austrian School of Economics do). Instead, it takes issue with the quality of state intervention. Indeed, Bardhan (1990: 4–5) assesses in the editorial of the *Symposium on the State and Economic Development*:

> "In much of the neoclassical literature the emphasis is on the *extent* of state intervention; mostly, of course, on the harmful effects of that intervention. As a matter of fact, almost all states in developing countries, successful or otherwise, are interventionist, and the important question is not really about the extent but the quality of that intervention. We need to understand why the *quality* of intervention is so different in the different states, even when those states command similar instruments of intervention and sometimes display similar extents of intervention..."

Within this context it has been puzzling for the development scholars such as Rodrik (1996a: 19–21) to understand "How Did East Asian Countries Manage to Intervene without Inviting Rent Seeking?" in general and "Why did trade protection, industrial policy, and subsidised credit work in these countries [Korea and Taiwan] when it failed most everywhere else?" in particular. His honest answer to these questions in the review article of the *Journal of Economic Literature* is that "we do not really know" (ibid, 19). His best guess is that there must have been something special about these countries policy makers' ability to discipline their private and public actors – an acknowledgement that begs rather than answers the questions. That means Rodrik is forced to admit as an answer to his own follow-up question "where this ability came from and whether it can be replicated in other settings remain a mystery" (ibid).

Nonetheless, this does not prevent him from suggesting that development states such as Korea were special in their ability to identify and solve successfully the "coordination failures". According to Rodrik (1996b), these include a form of market failures that middle-income countries, which are locked into low-wage and/or low-tech equilibrium, typically face. More specifically, without government subsidy to solve the private sector's lack of interest in undertaking activities that need specialised inputs, the NIC would not have produced miracles. Rather than getting the prices or institutions right or wrong, they got the "interventions right" by "coordinating and encouraging private (and public) investments with a high degree of linkages within the modern sector" (1995: 97). In other words, what we have here is a kind of merging of the Krugmanian "extraordinary mobilisation of resources" (see Krugman 1994a: 78) and Hirschmanian ideas of forward and backward linkages (see Hirschman 1986, Ch. 3) with a growing understanding of the critical role of technology in economic development (see Freeman 1994 for the literature overview).

Nonetheless, this does not explain how developmental states like Korea managed to intervene successfully when others failed – a puzzle that Rodrik himself highlights.[7] Probably, the most compelling argument offered (at least before the East Asian financial crisis) originates from Westphal (1990: 44), who explains that Korean industrial policy consists of two interrelated parts that relate to the two objectives that Korean economic policy has set for itself since the 1960s: encourage exports and promote infant industries. These components should be acknowledged but not confused with one-another. As described in detail by Westphal, the export promotion, which has used free trade as its primary "incentive scheme", is essentially a policy neutral tool because all it did was to abandon the idea of imposing tariffs and import quotas on the importation of capital and

---

7   Actually Rodrik (1996a: 20) also adds to the above mentioned possible reasons "the special initial conditions". What he means by this is not the colonial past that enabled Korean leaders to intervene successfully, rather the much better educated labour force (given its income level) as well as the equal distribution of wealth and income (around 1960) which may explain the overall economic success story but not the successful state intervention. For more details about his position on the role of Korean education and equality in economic development see Rodrik (1994; 1996a: 20–21) as well as Alesina/Rodrik (1994).

intermediate inputs for sectors and goods where a competitive advantage was detected. However, the infant industry promotion, with the aim of (re)creating comparative advantages, has used protection as its dominant incentive and logically has not been policy neutral. Furthermore, according to Westphal (ibid, 47) it is also important to add that the protection of infant industries in Korea has almost always applied only to non-export sales.

Based on all this, he (ibid, 56–57) offers five lessons from Korean industrial policy: (i) the aim of state intervention has to be the attainment of international competitiveness or self-sufficiency (in the given geo-political context); (ii) policy makers should seek advice and collect relevant information to judge the potential for exploiting or developing the competitive advantage; (iii) the industry specific strategies should not be firmly fixed and followed regardless of the experience and knowledge acquired during the implementation; (iv) the number of industries targeted at any one time should be greatly limited in order not to spread technical and entrepreneurial talent; and (v) the state should not concentrate its intervention efforts on the areas where the country has a competitive advantage because of the possibility of being excessively crowded out in international competition.

In short, Korean industrial policy found a way to enable the visible and invisible hand to cooperate closely, making it incorrect to emphasise one over the other. Rather one should try to understand the way it produced economic progress to catch up. As many nuances in the industrial policy implementation overlap with the relations with big business, we shall suspend the discussion here and postpone it for the upcoming sections. Hopefully, together with this analysis, one gets a better idea of how exactly Korea managed to implement the industrial policy and the extent to which its effect(s) have been positive or distortionary – issues that remain most contested.

2.2 Democracy and the Developmental State

A further characteristic of the developmental state relates to politics and the relationship of the political regime to democracy. While some commentators have associated Johnson's ideas of the developmental state with (soft) authoritarianism (see Benczes 2000 and Gills 1996, 667 respectively) and some others like Rodrik (1996a: 23) have expressed uneasy feelings about speculating that authoritarianism may have been involved in the East Asian ability to intervene successfully (noting that "there are too many mismanaged dictatorships around the world to take the hypothesis seriously"), the complicated relationship between the developmental state and democracy cannot be denied. Although Johnson warns against the dangers of a non-democratic government (1987: 143) and refuses to accept that there is "any necessary connection between authoritarianism and the developmental state," he also acknowledges "that authoritarianism can sometimes inadvertently solve the main political problem of economic development using market forces – namely how to mobilise the overwhelming majority of the population to work and sacrifice for developmental projects" (1999: 52). His Weberian argument is that in a truly developmental state power is held not through cohesive means but by legitimation, typically enjoyed by revolutionaries.[8]

On the one hand, it is true that the East Asian fast growing NIC were not democratic when they concentrated on economic catch-up. On the other hand, it is also correct to say that some of them have become democratic during the process. Indeed, the Korean economy was set on the trajectory of recovery, development and success by the military coup led by General Park Chung Hee on May 16, 1961. It was this authoritarian military regime that directed the nation to "The Road toward Economic Self-Sufficiency and Prosperity" and produced the fastest growing economy (with an average of 8.7% present annual growth) in the world between 1980 and 1991 (E. M. Kim 1997: 2). However, the paradox here is that the very economic success of the Korean developmental state also gave birth to democratisation. Indeed, since the mid-1980s Korea has seriously been on the road to democratisation, ending the authoritarian regime and bringing a democratic transition to the country in 1987. E. M. Kim's analysis of the relationship between big business and the state between 1960 and 1990 demonstrates in detail how the labour movement (both legal and underground) grew and "became a formidable voice for democratisation" (ibid, 4) in the Korean public-private-partnership where big business conglomerates and government repressed labour and excluded them from enjoying the fruits of economic growth for decades. It shows that despite the success of big business in delaying the development of political freedoms in Korea and Taiwan, eventually it happened. In short, "late democratisation followed late industrialisation" (Thompson 1996: 643).

This description matches the expectations of the modernisation theory advanced most prominently by Lipset (1959). To put it simply, the theory argues that countries' political and economic systems go hand in hand – for instance, a liberal democracy needs free markets. Once a country's socio-economic development reaches a certain level, it requires more skilled labour, which leads to expansion of education and development of critical thinking. Before long, demands for

---

8   Reflecting on the Japanese case, it would probably be more appropriate to speak of legitimisation by charismatic leadership – as enjoyed, for instance, by Lenin or Castro. Speaking of the bureaucrats it would be more appropriate to speak of goal-rational legitimisation, which is also known as teleological rule (see Konrad/Szelenyi 1979).

political liberalisation and democratisation are voiced. While many had written the modernisation theory off due to a lack of any serious empirical validity, the events in Eastern Europe, Former Soviet Union as well as in some NIC caused it to resurface. Indeed, Korean socio-economic development since the 1960s and consequent democratic changes in the political sphere since the 1980s match the theory: economic growth has led to social mobilisation associated with modernisation – growth of urbanisation, mass communication, expansion of education and the creation of new social classes demanding political participation. But what has been missing in the classical modernisation theory according to Thompson (1996: 627) is precisely the role played by the developmental state in the less developed countries that start industrialisation under non-democratic political leadership. Therefore, it makes sense to add this component to the modernisation theory, while at the same time realising that the developmental state's relationship to democracy is not static but dynamic. As E. M. Kim (1997) stresses – there is a need to understand the dynamic and changing nature of the state, business, and one may add, labour relations of the Korean political economy as a source of democratisation. That is, one needs to recognise that there has been the evolution from the comprehensive to the limited developmental state in Korea. It may be politically difficult to accept, and it can be easily misinterpreted, but the non-democratic developmental state may be necessary to serve as a catalyst for modernisation and democratisation.[9]

2.3 The Time Frame

Oyama takes issue with Johnson that the description and analysis of Japan as a developmental state in the chosen time frame between 1925 and 1975 is arbitrary – suggesting that if another period were used, a different conclusion could be reached. Indeed, Johnson (1999: 54) accepts that the chosen time frame is somewhat arbitrary, but also defends himself on the grounds that "[t]he mid-1970s saw the end of the era of Japan's catching up and the beginning of its uneasy tenure as an economic superpower, which is why my book ends there." There are two

---

9   India as a counterfactual to Korea in this respect is quite telling. While some scholars like E. M. Kim (1997: 217) argue that "it is not clear whether more political freedom and democracy in the initial phase of economic development would have occurred at a slower pace" in Korea, it can be problematised on the basis of India that chose a democratic development political system but has not been developing anywhere as quickly as the Four Dragons in Northeast Asia (see Herring 1999 and Currie 1996 for details of the Indian case with respect to developmental state and democracy).

important issues that emerge from this exchange of ideas. As mentioned above, the developmental state is not a static formation but a dynamic one. It changes or evolves along the changing geopolitical circumstances and international economic relations as explained on the basis of the Korean example by E. M. Kim (1997). In addition to the exceptional post-World War II era that brought more state intervention to many countries, there is the question of transferability of the policy outside East Asia, which reflects the controversial role of initial conditions in socio-economic development.

Korean development has been described in sequence by a number of scholars, but Gereffi has created a research programme out of it. He (1989/94; see also Gereffi/Wyman 1990) has analysed Korea in comparison to Latin American countries and diagrammed its developmental path as shown in Figure 2. According to this, the era of the Korean colonial past is described as a primary commodity export, and the 1950's introduced the era of primary import substitution industrialisation (ISI) for consumer goods and attempts to take advantage of land surplus (in addition to the struggle to survive with the help of international aid). The 1960's initiated the era of primary export orientation industrialisation (EOI) that tried to take advantage of unskilled labour surplus was introduced in Korea; the 1970's era added increased utilisation of capital as well as the selective use of (secondary) ISI; and the 1980's brought EOI diversification and emphasis on technology-based production as well as liberalisation and democratisation. The 1990's brought the East Asian financial crisis and IMF intervention together with the structural adjustment programme to liberalise further (see Gills 1996). Last but not least, the on-going 2000s have brought globalisation as well as the global financial and economic crises which have hit the export sectors badly and wiped out 1.63 million jobs (Son /San 2009: 23). According to E. M. Kim (1997), all these policy amendments resulted in a fundamental change from a "comprehensive developmental state" to a "limited developmental state" by the end of 1980 when democratisation brought an end to an authoritarian government. Although there are some who have declared the developmental state dead (Fine 1999; Deen 2011), the majority of the scholars who have contemplated its future in the wake of the financial crisis (e.g. Holliday 2005) or in the context of globalisation (e.g. Shin 2005) have found for different reasons that the spread of capitalism demands even stronger government involvement.

Figure 2: *Paths of Industrialisation in Latin America and East Asia: Commonalities, Divergence, and Convergence.*

Mexico and Brazil: 1880–1930	Mexico and Brazil: 1930–55	Mexico: 1955–70 Brazil: 1955–68	Mexico: 1970 – present Brazil: 1968 – present

Secondary ISI

Diversified
Export
Promotion and
Continued
Secondary ISI

Commodity →
Primary ISI

Secondary
ISI and
Secondary EOI

Primary EOI

Taiwan: 1895–1945 Korea: 1910–45	Taiwan 1950–59 S. Korea: 1953–60	Taiwan: 1960–72 S. Korea: 1961–72	Taiwan and S. Korea: 1973 to present

Source: Gereffi (1989: 517)

Instead of making an argument for getting the prices, institutions or interventions right, Gereffi as well as Amsden and Chu make the argument for "getting the structure 'right'". In other words, they explain how latecomers in modernisation and economic development upscale into more technologically complex industries and commercially demanding services. While Gereffi (1994: 222–224) explains on the basis of historical evidence that export oriented countries in East Asia have gone through progressive sophistication of their economies – a process that resembles climbing the ladder starting from primary commodity export, export-processing zones, competent supply subcontracting, original equipment manufacturing, and as the final stage, original brand-name manufacturing; Amsden/Chu (2003) make a late structuralist argument. Contrary to neoclassical economics' understanding of the structural change in developing countries (see Syrquin 1988), the late structuralist argument emphasises the change in the economy as a whole during the country's journey different stages of development (see Dutt/Ros 2003 and Gibson 2003), which provides an explanation for the developmental states' conscious wish, and in some cases such as Korea, the ability to alter the structure of the economy.

The above mentioned structuralist argument resembles in spirit Rostow's (1960) *The Stages of Economic Growth*. Although Rostow's contribution to the economics of development is not perhaps taken as seriously now as it was prior to the triumph of neoclassical economics, one has to admit that retrospectively the post-World War II developments in NIC are not too far from the sequence laid down in his theory along the following milestones: the traditional society, the preconditions for take-off, the take-off, the drive to maturity and the age of high mass-consumption. And despite the infrequent mention of his name in the contemporary literature on NIC catch-up process, the logical description of Korean development in stages, presidential regimes or decades is still rather common. This is not a coincidence as Rostow actually appears to be behind the Korean development model. More precisely, Natsios (2012) refers to an important upcoming book under the title "The Secret Successes of USAID" by Michael Pillsbury on the basis of recently declassified CIA cables. According to these sources, Rostow, as a senior Advisor to Kennedy and later to Johnson, had just finished the above mentioned book, and his ideas formed the theoretical foundation for the tied aid for General Park Chung-hee who had assumed the presidency in 1961 and who, according to Natsios, is said to have complained shortly afterwards to the CIA that USAID economists had taken over the running of the country.

The politics of tied aid relates to the geo-political environment of Korea at the time of the economic catch-up process. In addition to the realisation that the relationship between state, business and society is not constant or static but in a permanent state of change and that there may be lack or scarcity of political commitment, one needs to understand that the circumstances within which the East Asian developmental states managed to catch up with the developed economies were exceptional and may not be replicable elsewhere. Indeed, one has to take into account the outcomes of the Korean War and the Cold War more generally – the military threat from North Korea and possible Soviet expansion as well as the US military presence, political support, economic assistance and access to its markets – to understand the conditions under which the Korean developmental state managed to catch up with developed countries economically. Furthermore, the unique historical conditions in the international political economy during Korea's catch-up stage allow one to cast doubt on the transferability of its developmental state policy elsewhere. As Pirie (2008: 75) argues in his monograph on the Korean developmental state:

> "If there is a central theme to the analysis of the Korean developmental state offered within this thesis[,] it is that the project of state-led industrialisation was a product of, and its success was dependent on the existence of, a complex confluence of circumstances. It is impossible to understand why Korea exhibited such economic dynamism without understanding Korean history, the nature of post-war global political/economic structures, and the particular position Korea occupied within these structures. Such an understanding

highlights two things. First, it exposes the shortcomings of those theorists who argue that it is possible for other states to replicate the Korean experience by simply pursuing the 'correct' policies. Second, and more importantly ... it serves to highlight the essentially time-bound nature of the Korean state-led development project. Global industrial/economic and political structures are by their very nature dynamic, not ossified and static."

2.4 Government-Business Relationship

There is hardly a component in the developmental state structure that is more controversial than the relationship between government and big business. Although Johnson (1999: 56) regards government-business relationships the most important aspect of the developmental state, he adds that "[t]he exact nature and terms of the internal organisation of "Japan, Inc." remain obscure" (ibid, 59). This observation can easily be extended to Korea as her development strategies were largely patterned if not copied from Japan, which functioned as an exemplar for economic progress and catch-up with the West, as mentioned above. Although the corporatist political-economy arrangements can be found also in Western market economies (see e.g. Katzenstein 1984/85), it seems that what Korea has copied from Japan with respect to the business relations is difficult for Westerners to comprehend within the dichotomous conceptual models of public-private, state-civilian, partisan-nonpartisan, formal-informal, official-nonofficial, governmental-market, legal-illegal, regulated-customary and/or procedural-substantial that we have been socialised to view appropriate government-business relationships without the risk of corruption or rent-seeking and hence, welfare loss.

This contrast between Western and East Asian government-business relationships' traditions is crucial. E. M. Kim (1997, Ch. 8) and Ahn (2001: 425–428) describe the *Chaebols*[10] as the central success factor in Korea's EOI. The government used these big business conglomerates for state-led industrialisation in an increasing manner until the boundaries of the two became rather blurred. First, in the 1960's government intervention was automatic and sector neutral as long as they engaged in export activities (see also the discussion on industrial policy above). In the 1970's, the government introduced and implemented seven specific industry promotion acts which led to the development of the heavy and chemical industries in order to upgrade the economic structure, prepare for the exploitation of economies of scale, take advantage of private R&D capacities and build up national security. To achieve these goals, Korean policy makers seem to have used primarily capacity

---

10 The Korean conglomerate known as *Chaebol* is defined as "a business group which consists of varied corporate enterprises engaged in diversified business areas, and typically owned and managed by one or a few interrelated families" (Ahn 2001: 441).

building[11] – taking advantage of the commercial banks, in which the government was a major shareholder or special purpose banks for the distribution of subsidised and unlimited credit. Furthermore, these (almost unrestricted) credit lines were substituted with "preferential interest rates, foreign loans, tax credits, accelerated depreciation allowances and tax holidays" (ibid, 426). According to E. M. Kim (1997), the next step in industrialisation, for which *Chaebols* were used, was to take up the technologically complex industrial projects through imitation and/or innovation. This brought ambitious export targets to be met within the planned time frame. As a result of all this, the Korean economy concentrated considerably: while the top 10 *Chaebols'* share in its economy made up 5.1% in 1973, it increased to 22.7% by 1989 and in the case of the top 30, from 9.8% to 29.6% (Ahn 2001, 426).

It is important to realise that the concentration of a substantial proportion of the Korean economy in *Chaebols* happened within the above described industrial policy context over decades – starting from the absorption of "excess labour" to the development of the absorptive capacity of foreign technology. In other words, following the Japanese model, the Korean government was deeply engaged in the process of promoting industrial development. To achieve its aims, it "blurred the line between industrial and trade policy", according to Ahn (ibid). This, together with the combination of inward and outward oriented polices of import substitution and export promotion, has puzzled some of the most distinguished scholars of development economics like Kruger and Krugman.

Kruger has been forced to change her view on Korea more than once over time. First in 1980, she argues that economic success of countries like Korea was a result of export promotion rather than import substitution polices. Moreover, she states in this connection that "it seems clear that export performance is a function in a large part of governmental policies" (Kruger 1980: 289). In 1993 she adds that: "To be sure, the Korean economy has not been characterised and is not characterised by laissez-faire. But in contrast to the over-controlled, overregulated, highly distorted economies …, the Korean economy has been characterised by diminishing intervention in most spheres of economic activity, and the degree of distortion is considerably smaller" (Kruger 1993: 30). In 1995 she admits that the Korean government was heavily involved in steel, heavy chemicals and car industries, but contrary to her previous positions, she simply claims that these investments were not successful. Rather than seeing the government intervention as the cause of

---

11 McDonnell and Elmore (1987) identify five possible mechanisms of intervention – mandates (rules), inducements (money/procurement), capacity-building (money/ investments) and system-changing (authority).

the extraordinary results, she now interprets Korean success as being due to hard work combined with a sense of national danger or destiny (Kruger 1995: 40). And then in 1998 she returns to the orthodox position and states that "by the early 1960s a few then-developing countries – most notably Korea, Taiwan, Hong Kong and Singapore – had abandoned import substitution and adopted outer-oriented trade strategies. The results were spectacularly rapid growth." (Kruger 1998: 1514)

Krugman (1994a) has interpreted the East Asian economic development as a result of input-driven growth which owes much of its success to the mobilisation of vast amounts of labour and capital which makes the miracle a "myth". Although he (1994b: 153) has advocated that also the US should identify a handful of strategic sectors such as "high technology" for state support, he is better known for his post-factum position on the reasons for the East Asian financial crisis, which claims that it was only a matter of time before the practice of administratively picking the winners produced painful results. According to this line of reasoning, the negative side effects of state intervention had always been part of the developmental state package in the form of bad debts (see Lim 1999), but by the end of the millennium they spiralled into systematic crisis. As Krugman (1998: 74) states:

"By now the outline of how Asia fell apart is pretty familiar. At least in part, the region's downfall was a punishment for its sins. We all know what we should have known even during the boom years: that there was a dark underside to "Asian Values," that the success of too many Asian Businessmen depended less on what they know than on whom they know. Crony capitalism meant, in particular, that dubious investments – unneeded office blocks outside Bangkok, ego-driven diversification by Korean *Chaebols* – were cheerfully funded by local banks, as long as the borrower had the right government connections."

Despite the decades of sustained economic growth that the Korean developmental state had produced, the country was heavily hit by the East Asian financial crisis. As a result, Korea had to negotiate with the IMF and its international partners one of the largest bailouts ever (Pallack 1997; Ahn 2001: 420; Foreign Policy 2008). This meant that Korea had to accept the structural adjustment programme including the liberalisation and deregulation polices – to negotiate the neoliberal paradigm as documented in detail by Pirie (2008, Ch. 7–9) and criticised by Crotty & Lee (2001a/b, 2006). Nevertheless, one should be careful about interpreting that the crisis and the neoliberal policy transfers have changed the close relations between state and big business in Korea. As Woo-Cumings (1999a, x) warns, we should be critical of the mood changes towards the East Asian Miracle in the context where nothing fundamental has actually changed – "[t]he problems of corruption and lack of transparency in Southeast Asia and financial instability in the massively leveraged Korean corporate sector have long been understood and well documented". Lee (2002) goes even further to argue that the old (informal) rules of the game will not end with the introduction of new (formal) regulations (lack of which was assumed to be the underlying reason for the East Asian financial crisis for those who did not accept the speculation argument). For him there is only one solution: one has to change the social relations underlying the political intervention together with getting the state out. For others, the vulnerability of the Korean development model has become apparent only recently in the context of the global financial and economic crises. And now that a growing number of scholars (see e.g. Bugra/Agartan 2007; Joerges et al. 2005; Webster et al. 2009 and Deyo 2012) realise that Polanyi (1944 [1957]) was correct about the contradiction of capitalism – commodification in the form of the deepening of markets to the spheres of life traditionally not controlled by it equals the breeding of insecurity – it makes sense to examine more closely the Korean social model.

3. South Korean Welfare Model

Welfare state and regime literature discusses the macro-sociological and social policy dimensions of contemporary political economies from a comparative perspective. While the comparative analysis of welfare states and regimes goes back to the fifties (see Briggs 1961; Holmwood 2000 and Titmuss 1972 [1987]), it really exploded with the publication of Esping-Andersen's (1990) book entitled *Three Worlds of Welfare Capitalism*.[12] Based on the comparative typology of welfare states in Western societies, Esping-Andersen identified along the lines of the most important political ideologies in the West the social democratic, liberal and conservative/corporatist models. Although the typology was initially limited to Western countries, the idea of classifying welfare systems into typologies has quickly spread beyond Western countries as the overviews of welfare state regime literature (Arts/Gelissen 2002; Pierson 2006) as well as its recent developments and new directions clearly indicate (Castles et al. 2010 and Ferragina/Seeleib-Kaiser 2011).

Within this literature and research tradition, a growing number of scholars of East Asian welfare regimes have realised and criticised the Euro-centric conceptualisation of welfare regimes and their typologies (see e.g. Y. M. Kim 2005). More specifically, researchers attempting to understand the East Asian welfare systems have commonly argued that the region's social sector does not fit into any of the Esping-Andersen's ideal types. While Esping-Andersen (1997: 179) has responded

---

12   For an overview of how the "welfare modelling business" has become an entrance branch of academic industry since the publication of the *Three Worlds of Welfare Capitalism* see Abrahamson (1999). For an alternative approach to that of Esping-Andersen's see Headey et al. (1999).

by warning that "any attempt at labelling the Japanese welfare state is premature since it has not yet sunk its roots, institutionally speaking" and hence has tried to solve the puzzle for the time being by proposing a hybrid model: placing Japan between Europe and America, many others have argued for the extension of the typology by adding the East Asian ideal type. But even this has not satisfied some as there is an on-going debate over the issue as to whether the East Asian welfare regimes can be grouped into one welfare regime subtype or not. Understandably, in order for the typology to make sense, there cannot be too many classes. Yet to put all East Asian welfare systems into one category does injustice to the country specific differences and nuances. One solution that has been suggested is to differentiate between Northeast and Southeast Asian welfare regimes (Tang 2000; Ramesh 2004; Holliday 2005 and Wilding 2008). As a reaction to this, however, there is also a recurrent interest in emphasising the commonalities over differences and identifying the common attributes of the East Asian welfare model (H-J. Kwon 1999: 83–84; White/Goodman 1998: 17–18; Abrahamson 2011).

Richness of terminology to describe the East Asian welfare model in general and the Korean one in particular suggest that there is little consensus about the distinctive features of its nature and/or the fact that the object of analysis has been undergoing fast changes. For instance, the nature of the East Asian welfare model has been described under a large variety of labels – from Oikonomic (C. Jones 1990), Confucian (C. Jones 1993), conservative (Gottfried/O'Reilly 2002), developmental welfare system (White/Goodman 1998: 15), 'hybrid' (Esping-Andersen 1997), informal security (Wood/Gough 2006), informal care regime (Abrahamson 2011:16) Japan-focused (Goodman/Peng 1996: 216), Japanese-style (Peng 2008: 178), oriental (White/Goodman 1998), Pacific (Castells 1992) to tiger social policy and welfare capitalism (Holliday/Wilding 2003), and most recently as welfare developmentalism (Kwon 2010). Within this "politics of development policy labelling" (Wood 1985), the Korean welfare system, as a unique social model, has been labelled as developmental welfare state (Lee/Ku 2007 and Lee et al. 2011), minimalist welfare state (Lee et al. 2011), productive welfare model (Ramesh et al. 2004), productivist welfare capitalism (PWC) (Holliday 2000/05), productivist social policy (Kwon/Holliday 2007), (emerging) productivist (Wood/Gough 2006: 1706), productivist regime (Gough 2004), development-universalist (Ku/Finer 2007: 123) or most recently as weak-productive-protective and as productive + employment protection type (Hudson/Kühner 2011: 50–54), productive welfare under Kim Dae-jung government, participatory welfare under Roh Moo-hyun government (Chan 2006) or as a result of democratic government policies as the active welfare (Lee et al. 2011).

All this indicates that Korean socio-economic model has been understood as a unique type that has prioritised economic developmental goals over social. Therefore, observers often argue that Korea as well as Taiwan and Hong Kong have been able to grow so fast and catch up with the developing countries so quickly because they saved on social costs. Most explicitly, Deyo (1992) and Holliday (2000/05) argue that East Asian NIC have subordinated their social sector to the economy and this very characteristic differentiates them from all other welfare regimes outside or inside East Asia, making them similar to few welfare states like Taiwan. As Holliday (2005) states:

> "Beginning with policy, PWC is characterised by a broad thrust that prioritises economic growth, and makes this the fundamental orientation of policy makers not only across economic sectors but also across social and cultural sectors. Policy spheres that tend to be thought of as straddling the economic/social divide are therefore read in economic rather than social terms. One instance is relations between capital and labour, which are skewed as much as possible towards the needs of capital, with the result that the power of organised labour is severely limited. ... In PWC, funding for social policy is generally low so as not to crowd out entrepreneurial and productive activity. However, because social policy is read in economic terms, and some elements are held to make a positive contribution to growth, funding is not pared back completely. Indeed, some social policy spheres may be characterised by quite significant investment, designed to provide the society as a whole with a competitive edge over its main economic rivals. The clearest instance is education, to which a productivist society may devote quite significant resources. ... Overall, social policy funding is likely to be less extensive than in other worlds of welfare capitalism, because such [a] policy has a strictly subordinate status. Sources of funding may derive from both the public and private sectors. As PWC seeks to promote entrepreneurial activity, it has a natural tendency to favour private funding over public. However, if the private sector fails to meet social policy needs held to be crucial to economic advance, the state can certainly be expected to step in to meet the shortfall."

This view that the subordinated role of the social sector to the economy is so distinctively unique that it can be regarded as a fourth type of welfare capitalism, contradicts the position of some of the most well-known scholars. For instance, Esping-Andersen argues on the basis of the Japanese case that the socio-economic relations of East Asian countries have simply not matured enough to be properly classified among the welfare states. Other scholars such as Habermas (1976), Offe (1984: 147) and Bruce et al. (1999: 22–23) state in different contexts that the promotion of economic efficiency along with social equality, social integration and avoidance of social exclusion and class conflict, the promotion of social stability and autonomy as well as a reduction in poverty are the broadly accepted legitimisation methods for politicians and policy makers in all kinds of welfare regimes. Bruce et al. go on to make a normative argument that high economic growth is more important than anything else in the above mentioned list – it is the supreme goal of any welfare regime. (In fact, they go even so far as to argue that economic growth is not a practical but a moral aim of any welfare regime – not a means towards some more higher-minded end but a goal in its own right). If these assessments and positions were correct, there would be little point in speaking of a special (called productivist or any other of the above mentioned) type of welfare model in East Asia in general or Korea in particular.

It is argued in this paper that the 'Growth First, Distribution Later' (Lee et al. 2011) policy paradigm in East Asia in general and in Korea in particular is special and allows one to speak of a unique socio-economic welfare arrangement. Although it resembles the empirically based theory of Kuznets, known as the Kuznets curve, which shows that inequality rises before it falls in the process of economic development, the productivist/developmentalist welfare regime stands out because its defining feature is the subordination of social policy to economic policy (for details see Holland 2000/05 and Kwo/Holliday 2006). It is special compared to others because social responsibilities, traditionally understood to be the responsibility of the state in Western societies, have been taken over by companies (esp. *chaebols*) in Korea (Woo-Cumings 2001: 370). This has two contradictory implications. On the one hand, the costs of the Korean welfare model could be expected to be greatly underreported in international comparisons (with or without the aim of typology buildings). This "dependent variable problem" (Clasen/Siegel 2007)[13] has typically led to the second best choices in the form of expenditure analysis. Instead of real data on the theoretical concept, the constructs are operationalised via intervening variables or proxies measured with aggregate spending data on the social sector. But if the roles carried out traditionally in advanced welfare capitalisms by the state are taken over by private, non-governmental or international entities in the less developed world, the official data simply does not show the actual level of social protection provided and benefits received. Therefore, in this context where the role of the state is taken over by some other actors, it is important to realise the conceptual difference and implications between "welfare regime(s)" and "welfare state(s)" as the scholars from the University of Bath have been stressing (see Gough 2001, Gouth/Wood with co-authors 2004 as well as Wood/Gough 2006).

The Korean productivist/developmentalist welfare regime is unique because it has produced "growth with equity" according to World Bank (1993a) and Rodrik (1996a: 20–21) while being at the same time "a paradise for big business" according to Woo-Cumings (1999b: 30). This strange formula worked as long as the Korean

---

13 The "dependent variable problem" refers to the methodological challenges that research on welfare states and regimes has been suffering due to conceptual and data access limitations.

conglomerates were able to compete in the global marketplace. Paradoxically, what has been described as a paradigm shift in the welfare capitalism literature from 'Keynesian welfare national state (KWNS)' to 'Schumpeterian workfare post-national regime (SWPR)' (Jessop 1993/94/99, 2002) seems to have worked the other way around in Korea. Developmental policies place emphasis on growth enhancing factors such as human capital and infrastructure and only later extend the social benefits to people as social rights. Indeed, the policy tools promoted under SWPR such as "permanent innovation and flexibility in relatively open economies by intervening on the supply-side and strengthening as far as possible their structural and/or systemic competitiveness" (ibid 1999: 355) is very similar to the socio-economic policies that have been implemented in Korea for decades. In that sense, the emergence of KWNS in Korea was a combined result of democratisation and the need to offset the negative side-effects of the global financial and economic crises. In other words, instead of promoting efficiency, flexibility and innovativeness, Korea faces in the short and medium term the challenge of deepening welfare provisions, increasing spending on and improving access to social benefits. Unlike most other developed countries, Korea needs to direct its welfare policies from SWPR to KWNS.

Indeed, only recently has Korea been under real pressure to provide more welfare benefits based on social rights in addition to its decade long concentration on SWPR with the aim of securing structural or systematic competitiveness in the economic catch-up process. While Offe (1984: 148) explains that "[i]n the light of the Keynesian doctrine of economic policy, the welfare state came to be seen not so much as a burden imposed upon the economy, but a built-in economic and political stabilizer which could help to regenerate the forces of economic growth and prevent the economy from spiralling downward into deep recessions", it has not quite been the case in Korea. Only minimum welfare was provided to selected beneficiaries as long as the state was repressive and authoritarian and the economy was growing fast. Nevertheless, the Keynesian logic as an argument for state provision of safety-nets has been developing together with the democratic forces even in countries like Korea and has intensified with the economic, demographic and social changes – just as the modernisation theory would suggest. Indeed, several scholars of the Korean welfare regime (see e.g. Croissant 2004: 520) report increased popular (democratic) pressure to widen the accessibility to social benefits and deepen the welfare provisions due to the low fertility rate and an ageing population, intensified female labour market participation, growing divorce rates, spreading of one-generation or single-person households, urbanisation and rising post-materialistic and individualistic values.

However, the controversy over the Korean welfare regime does not stop here. On the one hand, Hort and Kuhnle (2000: 168) question the position held above about the Korean productivist welfare model (i.e. prioritisation of that has allowed the developmental state to save on social costs in order to promote economic growth. According to them,

"... chronological latecomers in social security legislation were not latecomers in terms of 'developmental' time. Rather than arresting or retarding welfare state development, our Asian countries even preceded European nations in the sense that they adopted state welfare programmes at lower levels of modernisation. This casts doubt on the idea that the Asian economic development was based on growth without welfare. Instead, here as in Europe, modernisation was accompanied by the adoption of social security programmes."

On the other hand, Kwon/Holliday (2007: 242) argue that the image that Korea has now become more welfare oriented after the East Asian financial crisis is a myth. They state that:

"When the Asian financial crisis took a heavy toll on Korea in the late 1990s, policy makers responded by extending [the] welfare policy. For many analysts, this was a paradoxical move, marking a fundamental reconfiguration of the social policy system. This article contests that interpretation. It examines the changes made to Korean social policy in recent years, and considers their impact on the Korean welfare state. It notes both that welfare extensions have been comparatively limited, and that they have often formed part of wider attempts to boost labour market flexibility. It thus concludes that [the] limited expansion of the Korean welfare state is chiefly an attempt to bolster industrial competitiveness and economic growth. For now, Korea retains the productivist social policy orientation that has long characterised it. It also concedes, however, that in the future underlying social change, notably a rapidly ageing population, may prompt policy makers to make significant changes to the Korean welfare state."

One could propose a resolution to this controversy by arguing that education must be seen as part of social sector and its costs. Although the connection between the educational policy and welfare states/regime analysis has traditionally been weak and has been connected to the social policy in social policy literature in general (see Room 2002; Midgley/Tang 2001: 251) or to the national welfare models in particular (see e.g. Heidenheimer 1981 for the US), it has been the accepted view within the new political economy of development. For instance, the Washington Consensus (Williamson 1990) (the cookbook used to reform the economies of East and Central Europe on the development lessons gained in Latin America) suggested transferring the social sector expenditures to the sectors which can be considered as investments, such as education. Also, the World Bank (1993a) emphasised in its miracle report on East Asia that the success of this region has been biased (in addition to export orientation and what they interpreted as market friendly economic policies) with a strong emphasis on education. Indeed, within the welfare state literature, the connection between education and the social sector has been brought more directly into the discussion only within the East Asian welfare state regime literature. Indeed, most comparative research on East Asian welfare regimes has claimed that the miracle of fast growth with equity has been possible only due to the absence of the big and expensive welfare state in these NIC. As mentioned above, the argument has been that instead of depending on taxpayers' money, these East Asian welfare systems have depended heavily on the family and allowed the government to pursue different developmental goals. But this is so only if one assesses and conceptualises the productivist welfare regimes and their typologies by the Euro-centric standards and concepts. If one gives up the "cunning of imperialist reason" (Bourdieu/Wacquant 1999) and if education is seen as part of the social sector and its costs, the essence of developmental welfare capitalism becomes clearer.

In this context, the Korean welfare policy, previously oriented towards economic competitiveness and currently being redirected slightly more towards social security, contrasts with many Western welfare models. The former has depended more on informal security mechanisms while the latter has traditionally provided benefits funded from taxes instead of helping to overcome obstacles needed to find more sustainable solutions. However, both have recently started to reorient the emphasis towards an active labour market and innovation polices. The global economic and financial crisis and the accumulation of local social problems in the East and West will probably make the welfare regimes more similar in the upcoming years and decades. This convergence is reflected in the analytical models such as the one suggested by Choi (2007) that merges Gough's and his collaborators' informal security regimes approach with Esping-Andersen's inspired welfare capitalism analysis.

This realisation that there is a strong connection between education and social sector polices is likely to gain wider acceptance, the more alarming the future of welfare state in the demographically critical nation states become and the more these economies have to compete globally. This has already led some scholars (see Cerny/Evans 2000/04; Evans/Cerny 2003) to suggest that the welfare state is being replaced with a "competition state" that channels the social sector costs towards education and training. (One only needs to consider the numerous active labour market or life-long-learning polices that have been implemented and are being funded by taxpayers' money in high income countries or by donor money in not so high income countries). Others have gone even further to argue that the welfare states have (had) to respond to the emergence of the globalised, post-industrial knowledge society with emphasis on human capital investment. (One only needs to consider here the number of polices directed towards building innovation and knowledge capacities).

4. South Korean Developmental Welfare Capitalism and its Major Challenges

This section augments the previous sections in order to link the production and the welfare regimes to each other as well as to the political system. Last but not least, an attempt is made to point out the major challenges that the system faces. Using Soskice's (2007) extended VoC framework, it will be shown that the Korean political economy arrangement has not been static but has evolved in stages to face the challenges of the era: from the developmental state in the 1960s and 1970s, to the modernisation state in the 1980s and finally to the contradictions of the welfare state in the 1990s and 2000s. Hancké et al. (2007: 7–8) review the criticism that has been raised against the original VoC's analytical frame of Hall/ Soskice (2001) and show that it can be questioned for being static, functionalistic, ignorant of the endogenous sources of national transformation and within-system diversity, mechanistic in its conception of institutional complementarities and, and hence, institutionally deterministic. In other words, VoC neglects the role of state and class relations, interpreting a firm as a passive 'institution-taker' rather than understanding it as an active and creative entrepreneur who can take a variety of forms within a national system. It has limited the number of possible varieties of capitalisms to just two (classifying them either as coordinated or liberal market economies), which reflect its bias towards manufacturing and insensitivity towards service economies. Furthermore, it misrepresents economies as isolated entities without linkages between them or the forces of globalisation, and is unrealistic about the compromise and conflict (by emphasising the former and understating the latter). Finally it neglects the gender (inequality) issues and as Kang (2006) adds, has a strong rational-choice view of institutions.

Such criticism seems to be relevant within the discussion of Korean production and welfare regime literature because the two research traditions hardly build on each other's strengths in order to overcome the limitations. Despite the discussion about the importance and value of interdisciplinary research, there is hardly any systematic attempt to relate VoC in political economy literature and "welfare capitalisms" in comparative social policy and sociology literature with each other. On the one hand, political economists do not appear to read or show interest in the comparative social policy and sociology literature on welfare states and regimes. On the other hand, the comparative social policy scholars and sociologists appear to care equally little for the political economy of development literature. Indeed, a reader who is new to the social models literature would be surprised to learn that there is little to be found in the welfare capitalism literature about political economy, VoC or what former comparative economic systems scholars now call "new comparative economics" (see Shleifer 2002; Djankov et al. 2003). Although Esping-Andersen's (1994: 720–726) chapter in the *Handbook of Economic Sociology* makes some cautious moves to relate the welfare states to economic performance, and Block's (1994) entry in the same handbook manages almost the impossible – to provide an overview of "The Roles of the State in the Economy" (including an attempt to relate the different ideal types of state interference to the functioning of the economy), these are rather abstract and hesitant moves.

In this context, efforts made by E. M. Kim (1993), Holliday (2005) and H.-J. Kwon (2007) to merge production and welfare regime literature as well as an attempt made by W. Kim (2010) to link changes in politics to economics and labour struggles in order to understand the Korean case are less universalistic but actually offer more practical guidance. To build on these analyses, the following paragraphs will relate the previously discussed Korean developmental state and social model to the changes in its political arrangement. It uses the above mentioned Soskice's (2007) extended VoC framework in order to show how the Korean political economy arrangement has evolved. Similar to Peng & Wong (2008) and Lee et al. (2011) the evolution is arranged in three stages: from the developmental state in the 1960s and 1970s, to the modernisation state in the 1980s and finally to the contested welfare state the 1990s and 2000s. Indeed, to comprehend the Korean developmental welfare regime and the reasons for its past success, one has to understand not only its economic progress but also dynamic changes that have been introduced and institutionalised into its social and political arrangements. In addition to the changes in the economic and social systems described in the previous sections, the developmental welfare capitalism that has been evolving over decades in Korea has a clear connection to its political situation as has been shown among others by Asami (2011), Chan (2006), Lee et al. (2011) and Peng/ Wong (2008). Indeed, as shown in the following tables, Korean political arrangements at any given point in time reflect the level of economic development and starting conditions, on the one hand, and the balance of power between labour, capital and political establishment, on the other hand.

Table 1: The Politics of Institutional Evolution, Source: Peng & Wong (2008: 70)

	Developmental state, 1960s and 1970s	Democratisation, 1980s and 1990s	Post-industrialism, 1990s and 2000s
Problems	Economic under-development; political legitimacy gap	Social and economic inequality; societal mobilization	Economic restructuring; reinvigorate economic growth
Window of opportunity	Post-war and post-colonial reconstruction	Democratic opening; electoral competition	1997 financial crisis; demographic change; globalization
Dominant political coalition	Productivist coalition	Progressive coalition (civil society, the state)	'New' productivist coalition (social policy advocates, economic reformers, international partners)
Purpose of social policy	Rewarding productivist sectors of society; facilitating economic / industrial development	Social justice, socio-economic redistribution, household protection	Activation of productive labour market; human capital investment

Table 2: The Development of Welfare Policies, Source: Lee et al. (2011, 8)

Periods	Regime	Economic policies	Welfare policies
Authoritarian dictatorship	Park Jung-hee (1961–1979) Chun Doo-hwan (1980–1987)	Exported oriented Industrialisation (Government dominant growth strategy)	Growth First, Distribution Later (Developmental Welfare State or Minimalist Welfare State)
Democratisation	Roh Tae-woo (1988–1992) Kim Young-sam (1993–1997)		Transition period
Democratic government	Kim Dae-jung (1998–2002) Noh Mu-hyun (2003–2007) Lee Myung-bak (2008-present)	Globalization and postindustrialisation (balance between growth and distribution)	Productive Welfare Participatory Welfare Active Welfare

Figure 3: South Korean Developmental State in 1960s and 1970s.

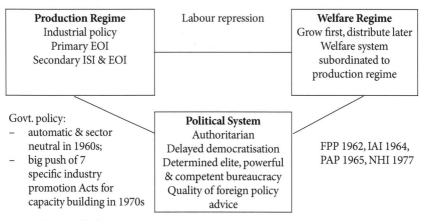

Source: Composed by the author

As shown in Figure 3, Korea in the 1960s and 1970s can be described as a de-velopmental state in which the industrial policy was used to promote economic growth and the social sector was subordinated to the economic sector. While government economic policy was automatic and sector neutral in the 1960s, it introduced seven specific industry promotion acts for capacity building in the 1970s. In Gereffi's terminology, the emphasis was on primary EOI and secondary ISI & EOI at this stage of economic development. Although labour was severely repressed during these two decades and the social policy could be symbolised by the slogan "Grow first, distribute later" the government did actually introduce the first welfare programmes already in this period: the Family Planning Programme (FPP) in 1962 (to bring down the fertility rate that was as high as 6.0 in 1960), the Industrial Accident Insurance (IAI) in 1964 (to provide some assurance for work related injuries), the Public Assistance Programme (PAP) in 1965 (for the poorest of the poor), and the National Health Insurance (NHI) in 1977 (for the emplo-yed in the public sector). All this was implemented by the powerful bureaucracy that benefited from competent foreign policy advisers/partners such as USAID under the apparently authoritarian political regime that purposefully delayed democratisation. In short, the limited coverage welfare regime was devoted to the promotion of economic growth.

Figure 4: South Korean Modernisation State in 1980s.

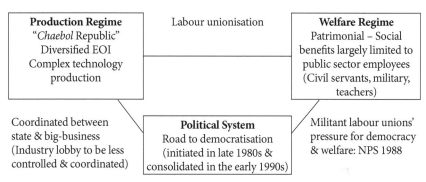

MODERNISATION STATE
1980s

Production Regime "*Chaebol* Republic" Diversified EOI Complex technology production	Labour unionisation	**Welfare Regime** Patrimonial – Social benefits largely limited to public sector employees (Civil servants, military, teachers)
Coordinated between state & big-business (Industry lobby to be less controlled & coordinated)	**Political System** Road to democratisation (initiated in late 1980s & consolidated in the early 1990s)	Militant labour unions' pressure for democracy & welfare: NPS 1988

Source: Composed by the author

As can be seen from Figure 4, Korea in the 1980s can be described as a modernisation state. This was the era of big business in the Korean economy, which is why some journalists labelled it "*Chaebol* Republic". Indeed, as mentioned in the first half of the paper, while the share of the top 10% of *Chaebols* in 1973 was 5.1%, it increased to 22.7% by 1989. Behind this concentration was the diversified EOI and complex technology production. Big business-government relations were characterised as well coordinated and dominated by the industry lobby. Welfare regime during this decade can be described as patrimonial or conservative – referring to the fact that social benefits were still largely limited to civil servants, the military and teachers. Apart from the introduction of the National Pension Scheme (NPS) in 1988, not much was done during this decade to deepen the welfare provisions even though there was pressure for social justice, redistribution and family protection. This led instead to unionisation and militarisation of labour, opening up the road to democratisation, which was initiated in the late 1980s and consolidated in the early 1990s.

As shown in Figure 5, Korea in the 1990s and 2000s can be described as contested welfare state. While big business had grown stronger and the state had grown weaker due to the internationalisation and global competitiveness of the economy in the 1980s, the state had to democratise and start responding to the popular pressure for more welfare benefits in the 1990s. In addition to this, Korea in the 1990s and 2000s has been facing major challenges: the economy went through the East Asian financial crisis in 1997–8, and it has been heavily hit as an export oriented economy by the global financial and economic crisis. It now also needs to compete globally, which means constant pressure not only for efficiency and

productivity but also from business to eliminate the social responsibilities developed during the previous stages of development. As Chang (1999: 34–35) reports:

> "In 1996, the Korea Federation of Industries, the association of the *chaebols* prepared
> a report arguing for the abolition of all government ministries except the ministries
> of defence and foreign affairs and for the consequent reduction of government staff by
> 90%. The report had to be officially withdrawn because it was unfortunately leaked in
> advance by a careless reporter and created a popular uproar. While the chance of such
> proposal being taken seriously was non-existent even in Korea that was then (and still is
> to a large extent) in the grip of an anti-statist reaction, but the incident is illustrative of
> the aggressiveness that the *chaebols* were showing in pushing for greater business freedom
> in the recent period."

The political system has been democratising, which also means that politicians
are looking for votes and thus hesitate to implement reforms with high short term
costs and incremental benefits over the long term. Last but not least, the welfare
state has to find solutions to challenges, a task that has been postponed for decades.
For instance, R. S. Jones (2008) lists the following challenges related to the social
sector: an ageing population (that is the fastest in OECD countries), low fertility
rate (that has dropped to 1.2 – suggesting a low tax base for years to come), a postponed pension system reform (reflecting the fact that the reform with an aim to
find a sustainable solution has been blocked at parliament level several times since
2003), unemployment and NEET phenomena (that have affected 20% of the 15–29
age group and 25% of the holders of tertiary education), health care accessibility
due to heavy dependency on the ability to pay out of the pocket[14] and raising
public expenditure.[15] There is also tremendous pressure on students to perform
well at all levels of the education system (reflected in twice as high private tutoring
than OECD average, which appears to kill creativity instead of contributing to the
innovation society – a factor that should provide the opportunity to pay for the
increasing social costs in an ageing society (OECD 2012: 23–25).

Although the government has started to seek solutions, the postponement of
the timely dealing with social sector problems and the subordination of the sector to economic priorities have resulted in a backlog over the decades, which is
anything but easy to solve. For instance, the government introduced Infant-Child
Care Programme (ICCP) in 1991 and expanded it later; launched Mother-Child
Welfare (MCW) programme in 1999 and reformed it into Mother-Father-Child
Welfare Programme (MFCWP) in 2002; set up a committee on Low Fertility and

---

14 According to OECD (2012: 21) Korea's private share is the fourth largest in OECD.
15 According to Jones (2008: 27–28) Korean public expenditure on health care is the
    fastest growing in OECD.

Population Ageing Policy (LFPAP) in 2005 in order to find solutions to the challenges related to demography. As shown by S. Kwon (2008) and Kwon et al. (2009), it also strengthened and enlarged the Livelihood Protection Programme into the National Basic Livelihood Security System (NBLSS) through which most assistance is being provided, and it introduced the Long-Term Care Insurance (LTCI) and Earned Income Tax Credit (EITC) to boost work incentives in 2008. Last but not least, the government has attempted on numerous occasions to reform the National Pension Scheme (NPS) which has, however, been blocked several times at parliament level.

Figure 5: South Korean Contested Welfare State in 1990s and 2000s.

CONTESTED WELFARE STATE
1990s & 2000s

Production Regime Political (crony) capitalism *Chaebols* too big to fail	Education & training	**Welfare Regime** Explosive due to accumulated demographic, economic & social inequity problems

IMF bailout & market liberalisation; increased pressure from big business for radically smaller state	**Political System** Democratic (but not yet fully consolidated democracy)	Challenges: ageing society; low fertility rate; rising divorce rate, income inequality, unemployment & NEET problems; access to pensions, health care & other social benefits; pressure on the education and training system. Search for solutions: ICCP, MCW/MFCWP, LFPAP, LTCI, EITC, (attempts to) reform NBLSS & NPS.

Source: Composed by the author

The situation remains alarming despite the introduction of these and other programmes (see Chan 2006 and Peng 2008: 174). Indeed, based on a number of policy analyses and progress reports provided by Cho (2006), Elekdag (2012), Goishi (2011), R. S. Jones (2008), OECD (2012) and Peng & Wong (2008) about the Korean ability to cope with the social problems, the situation remains extremely challenging. One can even say that the Korean low fertility rate and the rapidly ageing society, the rising divorce rate, low labour force participation (i.e. NEET problem and raising unemployment), inadequate income and long-term care for the elderly, limited access to public pensions, health care and other social benefits, rising inequality and relative poverty, pressure on the education and training system (reflected in the heavy reliance on private tutoring) make the socio-economic and political situation under the circumstances of the worldwide economic recession and intensified globalisation almost explosive.

5. Conclusion

There is growing interest among political economists, comparative public policy scholars and sociologists towards understanding the national differences between different forms of welfare capitalisms. In this context, the decades of sustained economic growth in East Asia have earned the admiration of policy makers, making it an exemplar for economic development that others were recommended to follow. But it has also amplified an academic discussion on how governments in countries like Korea seemed (at least initially) to be able to intervene without inviting rent seeking or distorting the market. As the East Asian miracle has not been replicated in the rest of the developing world, it suggests that the reasons behind the unique development path are more complex and context specific than any single variable analysis could indicate. This paper took a closer look at three unique and interrelated sets of arrangements with respect to the Korean developmental welfare capitalism in order to understand better the kind of capitalist society that is emerging in Korea as well as to study what others could learn from its experience.

As shown in the first part of the paper, the Korean developmental state has its origin in the Japanese model. It had to find a balance between direct intervention through the industrial policy and the market in order to promote economic growth. As a result of these peculiar methods of state intervention (including industrial policy and special arrangements between the government and big business) Korea, went through stages where the ordination from primary ISI was followed by primary EOI and then by secondary ISI and EOI. But one has to agree with scholars who are "extremely sceptical" about the transferability of the Korean development state and its experience to other countries because it would demand drastic changes in national economic policy making and implementation – "an overriding commitment to meaningful economic development, commitment that few political leaders of less developed countries appear capable of making" (Waelbroeck 1998a: 42/58). Furthermore, one has to be even more sceptical about the desirability to transfer these political economy arrangements, given the vulnerability that the sequences of financial and economic crises have exposed and the obvious emergence of cumulative social problems.

It has been claimed that the East Asian miracle in countries like Korea has been possible only due to the absence of the big and expensive welfare state. The argument has been that instead of taxpayers' money, the welfare system has depended heavily on the family and allowed the government to pursue the national developmental goals. Although the economic development model had to respond to social and political pressures and much has been done to make the welfare regime more inclusive and increase the coverage, some scholars like Hwang (2011: 9) argue that the fundamental aim of the system to limit the social sector to a subordinate role has not changed, and the amendments have been made so that the social policies would not undermine the growth potential of the Korean economy. Directing the social costs to areas which could be considered as investments is in accordance with the Washington Consensus (Williamson 1990) and the World Bank's (1993a) interpretation of the reasons behind the East Asian economic miracle. It also corresponds with the criticism that has been inspired from the Euro-centric conceptualisation of welfare regimes by Midgley & Tang (2001: 251) and Room (2002) who suggest that education must be seen as part of social sector and its costs. Furthermore, as shown in the last sections of the paper, the suppressed role of the social sector has led to the accumulation of a long list of challenges and problems in Korean society that are difficult to solve with or without education – so much so that the Korean welfare situation can be considered as explosive.

The Korean case indicates that the developmental welfare capitalism can produce economic growth under an undemocratic political system if the latter has elite committed to development, a powerful and competent bureaucracy as well as strong foreign partners and advisors to rely upon. But along the lines of Polanyi, Korean developmental welfare capitalism shows that (spread of) markets indeed breed insecurity – especially for the export oriented economy with a relatively limited domestic market that relies heavily on global financial capital and consumer demand. It also suggests that as long as the political system was undemocratic, the social sector could only care about the production related issues and provide security and safety-net for the state employed. Nevertheless, once the economy became sophisticated and started to require a better educated labour force, the demands for political democratisation and wider access to social benefits emerged. Paradoxically, it has become apparent that some of the social sector reforms, such as the aim of making pension system more sustainable, are actually more difficult to carry out under the democratic government than it would have been before.

Dynamic changes in the Korean political economy and social model during the past five decades suggest that the role and relationships between socio-economic arrangements and political institutions are not fixed but subject to change over time. While the original conceptualisations of VoC or welfare capitalism could lead one to suggest that fundamental socio-economic and political institutions in society are change resistant, recent updates to VoC literature (see Hall 2003/07 and Hall/Thelen 2009) envision also the possibility of evolution over time. As the analysis presented in this paper shows, there is actually no contradiction as the Korean socio-economic and political arrangements reflect the balance of power between labour, capital and the political establishment of the particular era, on the one hand, and the level of economic development and starting conditions, on the other hand. Now that the political system has been democratised and the social sector problems, which were repressed for decades have surfaced, no longer to be ignored, Korean developmental welfare capitalism faces a major challenge to keep the economy competitive while the political system is under democratic pressure to find solutions to the enormous social sector problems.

References

Alesina, Alberto / Rodrik, Dani (1994) Distributive Politics and Economic Growth, in: Quarterly Journal of Economics, Vol. 109, No. 2, pp. 465–490.

Abrahamson, Peter (1999) The Welfare Modelling Business, in: Social Policy & Administration, Vol. 33, No. 4, pp. 394–415.

Abrahamson, Peter (2011) The welfare modelling business revisited: the case of East Asian welfare regimes, in: Hwang, Gyu-Jin (Ed.) New Welfare States in East Asia, Cheltenham UK & Northampton US: Edward Elgar, pp. 15–34.

Ahn, Ghoong Yong (2001) A search for robust East Asian development models after the financial crisis: mutual learning from East Asian experiences, in: Journal of Asian Economics, Vol. 12, No. 3, pp. 419–443.

Amable, Bruno (2003) The Diversity of Modern Capitalism. Oxford: Oxford University Press.

Amsden, Alice (1989) Asia's Next Giant: Korea and Late Industrialisation. Oxford: Oxford University Press.

Amsden, Alice (1992) A theory of government intervention in late industrialization, in: L. Putterman and D. Rueschemeyer (eds.) State and Market: Rivalry or Synergy? Boulder, Co.: Lynne Rienner, pp. 53–84.

Amsden, Alice (2003) Comment: Good-bye Dependency Theory, Hello Dependency Theory, in: Studies in Comparative International Development, Vol. 38, No. 1, pp. 32–38.

Amsden, Alice H. / Chu, Wan-Wen (2003) Getting the structure "right": upscaling in a prime latecomer, in: Amitava Krishna Dutt and Jaime Ross (Eds.) Development

Economics and Structuralist Macroeconomics. Essays in Honor of Lance Taylor, Cheltenham & Northampton: Edward Elgar Publ., pp. 263–281.

Arrighi, Giovanni / Beverly J. Silver / Brewer, Benjamin D. (2003) Industrial Convergence, Globalization, and the Persistence of the North-South Divide, in: Studies in Comparative International Development, Vol. 38, No. 1, pp. 3–31.

Arts, Wil / Gelissen, John (2002) Three Worlds of Welfare Capitalism or more? A State-of-the-art report, in: Journal of European Social Policy, Vol. 12, No.2, pp. 137–158.

Asami, Yasuhito (2011) Overview of the Evolution of Social Security in Asian Countries, in: Expert Meeting on Building Social Safety Nets for Employment – Strategies in Asia. Ministry of Health, Labour and Welfare, Japan, February 21–22, pp. 15–38.

Bardhan, Pranab (1990) Symposium on the State and Economic Development, Journal of Economic Perspectives, Vol. 4, No. 3, pp. 3–7.

Barrett, Richard E. / Chin, Soomi (1987) Export-oriented industrializing states in the capitalist world system: similarities and differences, in: Deyo, Frederic C. (ed.) The Political Economy of the New Asian Industrialism, Ithaca: NY: Cornell University Press, pp. 23–43.

Baumol, William J. / E. Litan, Robert / Schramm, Carl J. (2007) Good Capitalism, Bad Capitalism, and the Economics of Growth and Prosperity. New Haven: Yale University Press.

Benczes, István (2000) Gerschencronian anachronism. Progress report on East Asia's miracle, crisis and transformation, in: Bara, Z. /Csaba, L. (Eds.) Small Economies' Adjustment to Global Challenges, Budapest: Aula, pp. 129–149.

Bhagwati, Jagdish N. (1992) Directly Unproductive, Profit-seeking (DUP) Activities, in: Journal of Political Economy, Vol. 90, No. 5, pp. 988–1002.

Block, Fred (1994) The Roles of the State in the Economy, in: Neil J. Smelser and Richard Swedberg (eds.) The Handbook of Economic Sociology, Princeton: Princeton University Press and NY: Russell Sage Foundation, pp. 691–710.

Briggs, Asa (1961) The Welfare State in Historical Perspective, in: Archives Europeennes de Sociologie, Vol. 2, pp. 221–258.

Bugra, Ayse / Agartan, Kaan (2007) *Reading Karl Polanyi for the Twenty-First Century.* NY: Palgrave Macmillan.

Campos, Jose Edgardo / Root, Hilton L. (1996) The Key to the Asian Miracle: Making Shared Growth Credible. Washington DC: Brookings Institution, 1996.

Castles, Francis G. / Leibfried, Stephan / Lewis, Jane et al. (2010) (eds.) The Oxford Handbook of the Welfare State. Oxford: Oxford University Press.

Castells, Manuel (1992) Four Asian tigers with a dragon head: a comparative analysis of the state, economy, and society in the Asian Pacific Rim, in: Richard Appelbaum and Jeff Henderson (eds.), State and Society in the Pacific Rim. London: Sage, pp. 33–70.

Cerny, Philip G. / Evans Mark (2000) New Labour, Globalization and the Competition State. Harvard Papers 70, 2000, Center for European Studies, Harvard University, Cambridge, MA.

Cerny, Philip G. / Evans Mark (2004) Globalisation and Public Policy under New Labour, in: Policy Studies, Vol. 25, No 1, pp. 51–65.

Chan, K. H., Raymond (2006) Participatory welfare in Korea: meaning and issues, in: CAPS Working Paper Series Paper 9, online: http://commons.ln.edu.hk/capswp/9.

Chang, Ha-Joon (1993) The political economy of industrial policy in Korea, in: Cambridge Journal of Economics, Vol. 17, No.2, pp. 131–157.

Chang, Ha-Joon (1994) *The Political Economy of Industrial Policy*. London and Basingstoke: Macmillan, 1994.

Chang, Ha-Joon (1997) The economics and politics of regulation, in: Cambridge Journal of Economics, Vol. 21, No. 6, pp. 703–728.

Chang, Ha-Joon (1999) Industrial Policy and East Asia – The Miracle, the Crisis, and the Future, a revised version of the paper presented at the World Bank workshop on "Re-thinking East Asian Miracle". San Francisco: 16–17 February.

Chang, Ha-Joon (2002a) Breaking the Mould – An Institutionalist Political Economy Alternative to the Neo-Liberal Theory of the Market and the State, in: *Cambridge Journal of Economics* Vol. 26, No. 5, pp. 539–559.

Chang, Ha-Joon (2002b) Kicking Away the Ladder – Development Strategy in Historical Perspective. London: Anthem Press.

Chang, Ha-Joon (2003) Kicking Away the Ladder: The "Real" History of Free Trade, in: Foreign Policy In Focus, Silver City, NM: Interhemispheric Resource Center.

Chang, Ha-Joon (2006) The East Asian Development Experience: The Miracle, the Crisis and the Future. London: Zed Books & Penang: Third World Network.

Chang, Ha-Joon (2009) Industrial Policy: Can We Go Beyond an Unproductive Confrontation? A Plenary Paper for ABCDE (Annual World Bank Conference on Development Economics) Seoul, Korea, 22–24 June, online: http://hajoon chang.net/wp-content/uploads/ 2012/01/ABCDE2009-Changpaper.pdf.

Cheng, Tun-jen (1990) Political Regimes and Development Strategies: Korea and Taiwan, in: Gary Gereffi and Donald Wyman (eds.) Manufactured Miracles: Patterns of Development in Latin America and East Asia. Princeton: Princeton University Press, pp. 139–178.

Cho, Nam-Hoon (2006) New Challenges for Low Fertility and Policy Responses in Korea. Paper prepared for Policy Forum on Low Fertility and Ageing Society, Seoul, September 13–14, online: http://www.neaef.org/public/neaef/files/doc uments/publications_pdf/ young_leaders/4th/Population%20-%20Cho%20 Nam%20Hoon%20YLP%20paper.pdf.

Choi, Young Jun (2007) Coming to a standstill? A New Theoretical Idea of East Asian Welfare Regimes. Barnett Papers in Social Research 2007/3, Oxford: University of Oxford, online: http://www.spi.ox.ac.uk/fileadmin/documents/pdf/ BarnettPaper20073YJC.pdf.

Chu, Wan-wen (1997) The "East Asian Miracle" and the Theoretical Analysis of Industrial Policy: A Review. Mimeograph, Academia Sinica, Taipei, online: http:// idv.sinica.edu.tw/wwchu/SURVEY.pdf.

Clapham, Christopher (1996) Introduction: Liberalisation, regionalism and statehood in the new development agenda, in: Third World Quarterly Vol. 17, No. 4, pp. 593–602.

Clasen, Jochen / Siegel, Nico A. (2007) (eds.) Investigating Welfare State Change. The 'Dependent Variable Problem' in Comparative Analysis. Cheltenham UK & Northampton US: Edward Elgar.

Croissant, Aurel (2004) Changing Welfare Regimes in East and Southeast Asia: Crisis, Change and Challenge, in: Social Policy & Administration, Vol. 38, No. 5, pp. 504–524.

Crotty, Jim / Lee, Kang-Kook (2001**a**) Korea's Neoliberal Restructuring: Miracle or Disaster? Dollars & Sense No.236, p. 28.

Crotty, Jim / Lee, Kang-Kook (2001**b**) Economic Performance in Post-Crisis Korea: A Critical Perspective on Neoliberal Restructuring. University of Massachusetts, Amherst, October 3, online: http://www.networkideas.org/featart/ dec2001/james_lee.pdf.

Crotty, Jim / Lee, Kang-Kook (2006) The Effects of Neoliberal 'Reforms' on the Post-Crisis Korean Economy, in: Review of Radical Political Economics Vol. 38, No. 4, pp. 669–675.

Crouch, Colin / Streeck, Wolfgang (1997) The Future of Capitalist Diversity, in: Crouch, Colin and Streeck, Wolfgang (eds.) Political Economy of Modern Capitalism Mapping Convergence and Diversity. Sage Publications, pp. 1–19.

Cumings, Bruce (1984) The origins and development of the Northeast Asian political economy: industrial sectors, product cycles, and political consequences, in: International Organization Vol. 38, pp. 1–40.

Cumings, Bruce (1994) The Origins and Development of the Northeast Asian Political Economy: Industrial Sectors, Product Cycles, and Political Consequences, in: International Organization Vol. 38, No. 1, pp. 1–40.

Cumings, Bruce (1999) Webs with No Spiders, Spiders with No Webs: The Genealogy of the Developmental State, in: Meredith Woo-Cumings (ed.) The Developmental State, Ithaca and London: Cornell University Press, pp. 61–92.

Currie, Bob (1996) Governance, democracy and economic adjustment in India: conceptual and empirical problems, in: Third World Quarterly Vol. 17, No. 4, pp. 787–807.

Datta-Chaudhuri, Mrinal (1990) Market Failure and Government Failure, in: Journal of Economic Perspectives Vol. 4, No. 3, pp. 25–39.

Deen, Ebrahim Shabbir (2011) The developmental state: An illusion in contemporary times, African Journal of Political Science and International Relations Vol. 5, No. 9, pp. 424–436.

Deyo, Frederic C. (1987) Introduction, in: Deyo, Frederic C. (ed.) The Political Economy of the New Asian Industrialism, Ithaca: NY: Cornell University Press, pp. 11–22.

Deyo, Frederic C. (1992) The Political Economy of Social Policy Formation: East Asia's Newly Industrialized Countries, in: Richard P Appelbaum and Jeffrey Henderson (eds.) States and Development in the Asian Pacific Rim, Newbury Park, CA: Sage, pp. 289–306.

Deyo, Frederic C. (2012) Reforming Asian Labor Systems: Economic Tensions and Worker Dissent, Ithaca: Cornell University Press.

Djankov, Simeon / Glaeser, Edward / La Porta, Rafael et al. (2003) The new comparative economics, in: Journal of Comparative Economics Vol. 31, pp. 595–619.

Dutt, Amitava Krishna / Ros, Jaime (2003) Development economics and political economy, in: Amitava Krishna Dutt and Jaime Ros (eds.) Development Economics and Structuralist Macroeconomics. Essays in Honor of Lance Taylor, Cheltenham & Northampton: Edward Elgar, pp.3–28.

Elekdag, Selim (2012) Social Spending in Korea: Can it Foster Sustainable and Inclusive Growth? IMF Working Paper WP/12/250, online: http://www.imf.org/external/pubs/ft/wp/2012/wp12250.pdf.

Eckert, Carter J. (1992) Offspring of Empire: The Koch'ang Kims and the Colonial Origins of Korean Capitalism, 1876–1945. Seattle: University of Washington Press.

Esping-Andersen / Gøsta (1990) The three worlds of welfare capitalism. Cambridge, UK: Polity Press.

Esping-Andersen / Gøsta (1994) Welfare States and the Economy, in: Neil J. Smelser and Richard Swedberg (eds.) The Handbook of Economic Sociology, Princeton: Princeton University Press and NY: Russell Sage Foundation, pp. 711–732.

Esping-Andersen / Gøsta (1997) Hybrid or Unique? The Japanese Welfare State Between Europe and America, in: Journal of European Social Policy Vol. 7, No. 3, pp. 179–189.

Evans, Mark / Cerny, Philip G. (2003) Globalisation and Social Policy, in: Nick Ellison and Chris Pierson (eds.) Developments in British Social Policy 2, London: Palgrave, pp. 19–40.

Evans, Peter B. (1989) Predatory, Developmental, and Other Apparatuses: A Comparative Political Economy Perspective on the Third World State, in: Sociological Forum Vol. 4, No. 4, pp. 561–587.

Evans, Peter B. / Rueschemeyer, Dietrich / Skocpol, Theda (1985) (eds.) Bringing the State Back In. Cambridge: Cambridge University Press.

Fallows, James (1994) Looking at the Sun: The Rise of the New East Asian Economic and Political System, NY: Pantheon.

Ferragina, Emanuele / Seeleib-Kaiser, Martin (2011) Welfare Regime Debate: Past, Present, Futures?, in: Policy & Politics Vol. 39, No. 4, pp. 583–611.

Freeman, Chris (1994) The Economics of Technical Change, in: Cambridge Journal of Economics Vol. 18, No. 5, pp. 463–514.

Fine, Ben (1999) The Developmental State Is Dead – Long Live Social Capital?, in: Development and Change Vol. 30, No. 1, pp. 1–19.

Fishlow, Albert (1990) The Latin American State, in: Journal of Economic Perspectives Vol. 4, Nr. 3, pp. 61–74.

Fishlow, Albert et al. (1994) (eds.) Miracle or design? Lessons from East Asia. Washington DC: Overseas Development Council.

Foreign Policy (2008) The List: The World's Biggest Bailouts. Foreign Policy, September 15, 2008.

Frank, Charles R. Jr. / Kim, Kwang Suk / Westphal, Larry E. (1975) Foreign Trade Regimes and Economic Development: Korea, Cambridge MA: NBER.

Gereffi, Gary (1989) Rethinking Development Theory: Insights from East Asia and Latin America, in: Sociological Forum Vol. 4, No. 4, pp. 505–533.

Gereffi, Gary (1994) The International Economy and Economic Development, in: Neil J. Smelser and Richard Swedberg (eds.) The Handbook of Economic Sociology. Princeton: Princeton University Press and NY: Russell Sage Foundation, pp. 206–233.

Gereffi, Gary / Wyman, Donald (1990) *Paths of Industrialization: An Overview*, in: Gary Gereffi and Donald Wyman (eds.) Manufacturing Miracles: Paths of Industrialization in Latin America and East Asia, Princeton N.J.: Princeton University Press, pp. 3–31.

Gerschenkron, Alexander (1962) Economic backwardness in historical perspective, a book of essays. Cambridge, Massachusetts: Belknap Press of Harvard University Press.

Gibson, Bill (2003) An essay on late structuralism, in: Amitava Krishna Dutt and Jaime Ros (eds.) Development Economics and Structuralist Macroeconomics. Essays in Honor of Lance Taylor, Cheltenham & Northampton: Edward Elgar, pp. 52–76.

Gills, Barry K. (1996) Economic liberalisation and reform in Korea in the 1990s: A 'coming of age' or a case of graduation blues?, in: Third World Quarterly Vol. 17, No. 4, pp. 667–688.

Goodman, Roger / Peng, Ito (1996) The East Asian Welfare States: Peripatetic Learning, Adaptive Change, and Nation-Building, in: Gøsta Esping-Andersen (ed.) Welfare States in Transition, National Adaptations in Global Economies. London: SAGE Publishing, pp. 192–224.

Goishi, Norimichi (2011) Social Safety Net for the Working Poor in Japan, Korea and Taiwan, in: Hwang, Gyu-Jin (ed.) New Welfare States in East Asia, Cheltenham UK & Northampton US: Edward Elgar, pp. 108–124.

Gottfried, Heidi / O'Reilly, Jacqueline (2002) Reregulating bread-winner models in socially conservative welfare systems: comparing Germany and Japan, in: Social Politics Vol. 9, No. 1, pp. 29–59.

Gough, Ian (2001) Globalization and regional welfare regimes, in: Global Social Policy Vol. 1, No. 2, pp. 163–189.

Gough, Ian (2004) East Asia: the limits of productivist regimes, in: Gough, Ian and Wood, Geof with Armando Barrientos, Philippa Bevan, Peter Davis and Graham Room (eds.) Insecurity and Welfare Regimes in Asia, Africa and Latin America: Social Policy in Development Contexts. Cambridge: Cambridge University Press, pp. 169–201.

Gough, Ian / Wood, Geof / Barrientos, Armando et al. (2004) (eds.) Insecurity and Welfare Regimes in Asia, Africa and Latin America: Social Policy in Development Contexts. Cambridge: Cambridge University Press.

Habermas, Jürgen (1976) Legitimation Crisis (Trans. by Thomas McCarthy). London: Heinemann.

Hall, Peter A. (2003) Varieties of Capitalism and Institutional Change: A Response to Three Critics, in: Comparative European Politics Vol. 1, No. 2, pp. 241–250.

Hall, Peter A. (2007) The Evolution of Varieties of Capitalism in Europe, in: Robert Hancké, Martin Rhodes and Mark Thatcher (eds.) Beyond Varieties of Capitalism. Conflict, Contradictions, and Complementarities in the European Economy. Oxford: Oxford University Press, pp. 39–85.

Hall, Peter A. / Soskice, David (2001) An Introduction to Varieties of Capitalism, in: Hall, Peter A. and Soskice, David (eds.) Varieties of Capitalism: The Institutional Foundations of Comparative Advantage, Oxford: Oxford University Press, pp. 1–68.

Hall, Peter A. / Thelen, Kathleen (2009) Institutional change in varieties of capitalism, in: Socio-Economic Review Vol. 7, No. 1, pp. 7–34.

Hancké, Robert / Rhodes, Martin / Thatcher, Mark (2007) Introduction: Beyond Verities of Capitalism, in: Robert Hancké, Martin Rhodes and Mark Thatcher (eds.) Beyond Varieties of Capitalism. Conflict, Contradictions, and Complementarities in the European Economy. Oxford: Oxford University Press, pp. 3–38.

Headey, Bruce / Robert, E. (1999) Goodin and Ruud Muffels. Real Worlds of Welfare Capitalism. Cambridge: Cambridge University Press.

Heidenheimer A. J. (1981) Education and social security. Entitlements in Europe and America, in: Flora P. & Heidenheimer A. J. (eds.) The development of welfare states in Europe and America. New Brunswick, NJ: Transaction Publishers, pp. 269–304.

Herring, Roland J. (1999) Embedded Particularism: India's Failed Developmental State, in: Meredith Woo-Cumings (ed.) The Developmental State. Ithaca and London: Cornell University Press, pp. 306–334.

Hirschman, Albert O. (1986) Rival Views of Market Society and Other Recent Essays, Cambridge MA: Harvard University Press.

Holmwood, John (2000) Three pillars of welfare state theory: T.H. Marshall, Karl Polanyi and Alva Myrdal in defence of national welfare states, in: European Journal of Social Theory Vol. 3, No. 1, pp. 23–50.

Holliday, Ian (2000) Productivist Welfare Capitalism: Social Policy in East Asia, in: Political Studies Vol. 48, No. 4, pp. 706–723.

Holliday, Ian (2005) East Asian Social Policy in the Wake of the Financial Crisis: Farewell to Productivism?, in: Policy and Politics Vol. 33, No. 1, pp. 145–162.

Holliday, Ian / Wilding, Paul (2003) (eds.) Welfare Capitalism in East Asia. Social Policy in the Tiger Economies. Basingstoke & NY: Palgrave Macmillan.

Hwang, Gyu-Jin (2011) New global challenges and welfare state restructuring in East Asia: continuity and change, in: Hwang, Gyu-Jin (ed.) New Welfare States in East Asia, Cheltenham UK & Northampton US: Edward Elgar, pp. 1–14.

Joerges, Christian / Stråth, Bo / Wagner, Peter (2005) (eds.) The Economy As a Polity: The Political Constitution of Contemporary Capitalism, London: UCL.

Johnson, Chalmers (1982) MITI and the Japanese Miracle: The Growth of Industrial Policy 1925–1975. Stanford: Stanford University Press.

Johnson, Chalmers (1984) (ed.) The Industrial Policy Debate, San Francisco: Institute for Contemporary Studies.

Johnson, Chalmers (1987) Political Institutions and Economic Performance: The Government-Business Relationship in Japan, Korea, and Taiwan, in: Frederic C. Deyo (ed.) The Political Economy of the New Asian Industrialism, Ithaca, NY: Cornell University Press, pp. 136–64.

Johnson, Chalmers (1999) The Developmental State: Odyssey of a Concept, in: Meredith Woo-Cumings (ed.) The Developmental State, Ithaca and London: Cornell University Press, pp. 32–60.

Jones, Catherine (1990) Hong Kong, Singapore, South Korea and Taiwan: Oikonomic Welfare States, in: Government and Opposition Vol. 25, No. 4, pp. 446–462.

Johnson, Chalmers (1993) The Pacific challenge – Confucian welfare state, in: Catherine Jones (ed.) New Perspectives on the Welfare State in Europe, London: Routledge, pp. 199–217.

Jones, Randall S. (2008) Public Social Spending in Korea in the Context of Rapid Population Ageing, in: Economics Department Working Papers No. 615, OECD Publishing.

Jessop, Bob (1993) Towards a Schumpeterian workfare state? Preliminary remarks on post-Fordist political economy, in: Studies in Political Economy Vol. 40, pp. 7–39.

Jessop, Bob (1994) The transition to post-Fordism and the Schumpeterian workfare state, in: R. Burrows and B. Loader (eds.) Towards a post-Fordist Welfare State? London: Routledge, pp. 13–37.

Jessop, Bob (1999) The changing governance of welfare: recent trends in its primary functions, scale, and modes of coordination, in: Social Policy and Administration Vol. 33, No. 4, pp. 348–359.

Jessop, Bob (2002) The Future of the Capitalist State. Cambridge: Polity.

Kang, Nahee (2006) A Critique of the "Varieties of Capitalism" Approach, No. 45–2006 ICCSR Research Paper Series, Nottingham University Business School, Nottingham University.

Katzenstein, Peter J. (1984) Corporatism and Change: Austria, Switzerland and the Politics of Industry. Ithaca and London: Cornell University Press.

Katzenstein, Peter J. (1985) Small Sates in World Markets – Industrial Policy in Europe. Ithaca and London: Cornell University Press.

Kim, Eun Mee (1993) Contradictions and Limits of a Developmental State: With Illustrations from the Korean Case, in: Social Problems, Vol. 40, No. 2, pp. 228–249.

Kim, Eun Mee (1997) Big Business, Strong State: Collusion and Conflict in Korean Developments, 1960–1990. Albany: SUNY Press.

Kim, Wonik (2010) Simultaneous Transitions: Democratization, Neoliberalization, and Possibilities for Class Compromise in Korea, in: Review of Radical Political Economics Vol. 42, No. 4, pp. 505–527.

Kim, Yeon Myung (2005) The Re-examination of East Asian Welfare Regime: Methodological Problems in Comparing Welfare States and Possibility of Classifying East Asian Welfare Regimes. Paper presented at Bath University Workshop on East Asian Social Policy. 13ʰ–15ʰ, 2005, online: https://www.google.ee/ur l?sa=t&rct=j&q=&esrc=s&source=web&cd=1&cad=rja&ved=0CCwQFjAA &url=http%3A%2F%2Fwww.welfareasia.org%2F1stworkshop%2Fdata%2Fc ontribution_YM%2520Kim2.doc&ei=5npqUYzJEYqw0AWJ5ICACw&usg= AFQjCNEGeK9HH0kUi8E4lHOsq6SDLORyQw&bvm=bv.45175338,d.d2k.

Kohli, Atul (1994) Where Do High-Growth Political Economies Come From? The Japanese Lineage of Korea's "Developmental State", in: World Development Vol. 22, No. 9, pp. 1269–1293.

Kohli, Atul (1997) Japanese Colonialism and Korean Development: A Reply, in: World Development Vol. 25, No. 6, pp. 883–888.

Kohli, Atul (1999) Where Do High-Growth Political Economies Come From? The Japanese Lineage of Korea's Developmental State, in: Meredith Woo-Cumings (ed.) The Developmental State. Ithaca and London: Cornell University Press, pp. 93–136.

Konrád, George / Szelényi, Ivan (1979) The Intellectuals on the Road to Class Power: A Sociological Study of the Role of the Intelligentsia in Socialism. NY and London: Harcourt Brace Jovanovich.

Kornai, János (1984) Bureaucratic and Market Coordination, in: *Osteuropa Wirtschaft Vol. 29, No. 4, pp. 316–319.*

Kornai, János (2007) Disciplines of Social Sciences: Separation or Cooperation?, in: Francois Bourguignon, Yehuda Elkana and Boris Pleskovic (eds). Capacity Building in Economics Education and Research, Washington DC: The World Bank, pp. 13–25.

Kosacoff, Bernardo / Ramos, Adrián (1999) The industrial policy debate, in: CEPAL Review Vol. 68, pp. 35–60.

Kroos, Karmo (2012) Eclecticism as the Foundation of Meta-theoretical, Mixed Methods and Interdisciplinary Research in Social Sciences; in: Integrative Psychological and Behavioral Science Vol. 46, No. 1, pp. 20–31.

Krugman, Paul R. (1994a) The myth of Asia's Miracle, in: Foreign Affairs Vol. 73, pp. 62–78.

Krugman, Paul R. (1994b) The Age of Diminished Expectations. Cambridge MA: MIT Press.

Krugman, Paul R. (1998) Saving Asia: It's Time To Get Radical. The IMF plan not only has failed to revive Asia's troubled economies but has worsened the situation. It's now time for some painful medicine, in: Fortune Vol. 76, pp. 74–81.

Kruger, Anne O. (1974) The Political Economy of the Rent-Seeking Society, in: American Economic Review Vol. 64, No. 3, pp. 291–303.

Kruger, Anne O. (1980) Trade Policy as an Input to Development, in: American Economic Review Vol. 70, No. 2, pp. 228–292.

Kruger, Anne O. (1990) Government Failures in Development, in: Journal of Economic Perspectives, Summer Vol. 4, No. 3, pp. 9–23.

Kruger, Anne O. (1993) Political economy of policy reform in developing countries. Cambridge MA: MIT Press.

Kruger, Anne O. (1995) Policy Lessons from Development Experience since the Second World War, in: Behrman Jere and Srinivasan, T. N. (eds.) Handbook of Development Economics Vol. 3B, Amsterdam: Elsevier, pp. 2497–2550.

Kruger, Anne O. (1998) Why Trade Liberalisation is Good for Growth, in: The Economic Journal, pp. 1513–1522.

Ku, Yeun-wen / Jones, Finer Catherine (2007) Developments in East Asian Welfare Studies, in: Social Policy and Administration Vol. 41, No. 2, pp. 115–131.

Kwon, Huck-Ju (1999) The East Asian Welfare States in Transition: Challenges and opportunities, in: IDS Bulletin Vol. 30, No. 4, pp. 82–93.

Kwon, Huck-Ju (2007) Transforming the developmental welfare states in East Asia. DESA Working Paper No. 40, ST/ESA/2007/DWP/40.

Kwon, Huck-Ju (2010) Welfare Developmentalism, in: Fitzpatrick, Tony (ed. in Chief) International Encyclopedia of Social Policy Vol. 3, London & NY: Routledge, 2010, pp. 1523–1525.

Kwon, Soonma (2008) Future of long-term care financing for the elderly in Korea, in: Journal of Aging and Social Policy Vol. 20, No.1, pp. 119–136.

Kwon, Soonman / Holliday, Ian (2007) The Korean welfare state: a paradox of expansion in an era of globalisation and economic crisis, in: International Journal of Social Welfare Vol. 16, No. 3, pp. 242–248.

Kwon, Soonman / Kim, Soo-Jung / Jung, Youn (2009) Introduction of Long-term Care Insurance in Korea, in: Asian Social Protection in Comparative Perspective, Baltimore: University of Maryland, January 8–9, online: http://www.umd cipe.org/conferences/policy_exchanges/conf_papers/Papers/1661.pdf.

Lall, Sanjaya (1994) The East Asian Miracle: Does the Bell Toll for Industrial Strategy, in: World Development Vol. 22, No. 4, pp. 645–654.

Lam, Newman M. K. (2000) Government Intervention in the Economy: A Comparative Analysis of Singapore and Hong Kong, in: Public Administration and Development Vol. 20, pp. 397–421.

Lee, Chung H. (2002) The State and Institutions in East Asian Economic Development: The Past and the Future, in: The Journal of the Korean Economy Vol. 3, No. 1, pp. 1–17.

Lee, Hyun-Hoon / Minsoo Lee / Donghyun Park (2011) Growth policy and inequality in developing Asia: Lessons from Korea, Forum on Equalizing Opportunities for Inclusive Growth, held at the Asian Development Bank, Manila, on 7–8 December 2011, online: http://cc.kangwon.ac.kr/~hhlee/paper/Lee_Lee_Park_120426_final.pdf.

Lee, Yih-Jiunn / Ku Yeun-wen (2007) East Asian Welfare Regimes: Testing the Hypothesis of the Developmental Welfare State, in: Social Policy & Administration Vol. 41, No. 2, pp. 197–212.

Leftwich, Adrian (1995) Bringing Politics Back In: Towards a Model of the Developmental State, in: Journal of Development Studies Vol. 31, No. 3, pp. 400–427.

Leftwich, Adrian (1996) Two Cheers for Democracy? Democracy and the Developmental State, in: Leftwich, (ed.) Democracy and Development, Cambridge: Polity Press, pp. 279–95.

Leftwich, Adrian (2001) Keeping Politics Right In: A Reply to Huff, Dewit and Oughton, in: Journal of Development Studies Vol. 38, No. 1, pp. 152–155.

Lie, John (1990) South Korean Development: The Elusive Reality of Conflicts and Contradiction, in: Pacific Affairs Vol. 63, No. 3, pp. 367–372.

Lim, Linda (1999) An Overview of the Asian Financial Crisis, in: Journal of Asian Business Vol. 15, No. 1, pp. 79–81.

Lipset, Seymour Martin (1959) Some social requisites of democracy: economic development and political legitimacy, in: The American Political Science Review Vol . 53, No. 1, pp. 69–105.

List, Friedrich (1885 [1996]) The National System of Political Economy. NY: A.M. Kelley.

McDonnell, L. / Elmore, R. (1987) Getting the Job Done: Alternative Policy Instruments, in: Educational Evaluation and Policy Analysis Vol. 9, No. 2, pp. 133–152.

Natsios, Andrew S. (2012) The Secret Success of U.S. Aid to Korea, in: Part III – Korea's Role in Economic Development, Korea's Economy 2012, Economic Institute of America, pp. 43–44, online: http://www.keia.org/sites/default/files/publications/kei_koreaseconomy_section03.pdf.

Nolan, Marcus / Pack, Howard (2003) Industrial Policy in an Era of Globalization: Lessons from Asia. Washington DC: Institute for International Economics.

Offe, Claus (1984) Contraditions of the Welfare State, Keane, John (Ed). London: Hutchinson.

OECD (2012) Economic Surveys KOREA, Paris: OECD.

Page, John M. (1994**a**) The East Asian Miracle: An Introduction, in: World Development Vol. 22, No. 4, pp. 615–625.

Page, John M. (1994**b**) The East Asian Miracle: Four Lessons for Development Policy, in: Stanley Fischer and Julio J. Rotemberg (eds.) NBER Macroeconomics Annual 1994 Vol. 9, Cambridge MA: MIT Press, pp. 119–269.

Pack, Howard / Saggi, Kamal (2006) Is There a Case for Industrial Policy? A Critical Survey, in: The World Bank Research Observer Vol. 21, No. 2, pp. 267–297.

Pallack, Andrew (1997) Korea Says I.M.F. Has Agreed to Huge Bailout, The New York Times, December 1.

Park, Yung Chul / Choong, Yong Ahn / Yunjong, Wang (2004) In Search of a New East Asian Development Paradigm: Governance, Markets and Institutions, in: Jan Joost Teunissen and Age Akkerman (eds.) Diversity in Development. Reconsidering the Washington Consensus, The Hague: FONDAD, 2004, pp. 150–169.

Pempel, T. J (1999) The Developmental Regime in a Changing World Economy, in: Meredith Woo-Cumings (ed.) The Developmental State, Ithaca and London: Cornell University Press, pp. 137–181.

Peng, Ito (2008) Welfare Policy Reforms in Japan and Korea: Cultural and Institutional Factors, in: Wim van Oorschot , Michael Opiekla, Birgit Pfau-Effinger (Eds.) Culture And Welfare State. Values and Social Policy in Comparative Perspective, Cheltenham UK & Northampton US: Edward Elgar, pp. 162–182.

Peng, Ito / Wong, Joseph (2008) Institutions and Institutional Purpose: Continuity and Change in East Asian Social Policy, in: Politics and Society Vol. 36, No. 1, pp. 61–88.

Perkins, Dwight H. (1994) There Are At Least Three Models of East Asian Development, in: World Development Vol. 22, No. 4, pp. 655–661.

Pierson, Chris (2006) Welfare Capitalism, in: Fitzpatrick, Tony (Ed. in Chief) International Encyclopaedia of Social Policy Vol. 3, London & NY: Routledge, pp. 1518–1523.

Pirie, Iain (2008) The Korean Developmental State. From dirigisme to neo-liberalism. London: Routledge.

Polanyi, Karl (1944) The Great Transformation. Boston: Beacon Press.

Ramesh, Mishra (2004) Social Policy in East and Southeast Asia: Education, Health, Housing, and Income Maintenance, London: Routledge.

Ramesh, Mishra / Stein Kuhnle / Neil Gilbert et al. (2004) (eds.) Modernizing the Korean Welfare State: Towards the Productive Welfare Model, New Brunswick: Transaction Publications.

Rodrik, Dani (1994) King Kong Meets Godzilla: The World Bank and The East Asian Miracle, in: Albert Fishlow et al. (eds.) Miracle or design? Lessons from East Asia. Washington DC: Overseas Development Council, Policy Essay No. 11, pp. 13–38.

Rodrik, Dani (1995a) Getting interventions right: how Korea and Taiwan grew rich, in: Economic Policy Vol. 10, No. 20, pp. 55–107.

Rodrik, Dani (1995b) Trade and industrial policy reform, in: Jere Behrman and T.N. Srinivasan (eds.) Handbook of Development Economics Vol. IIIB. North Holland, Amsterdam, pp. 2925–2982.

Rodrik, Dani (1996a) Understanding Economic Policy Reform, in: Journal of Economic Literature Vol. 34, No. 1, pp. 9–41.

Rodrik, Dani (1996b) Coordination Failures and Government Policy: A Model with Applications to East Asia and Eastern Europe, in: Journal of International Economics Vol. 40, No. 1–2, pp. 1–22.

Rodrik, Dani (1998) Why Do More Open Economies Have Bigger Governments?, in: Journal of Political Economy Vol. 106, No. 5, pp. 997–1032.

Room, Graham (2002) Education and Welfare: Recalibrating the European Debate, Policy Studies Vol. 23, No. 1, pp. 37–50.

Rostow, Walt Whitman (1960) The Stages of Economic Growth: A Non-Communist Manifesto. Cambridge: Cambridge University Press.

Roy, Kartik / Blomqvist, Hans / Clark, Cal (2012) Economic Development in China, India and East Asia: Managing Change in the Twenty First Century. Cheltenham, Northampton: Edward Elgar.

Shapiro, Helen (2007) Industrial Policy and Growth, DESA Working Paper No. 53, ST/ESA/2007/DWP/53, NY: United Nations, Department of Economic and Social Affairs, online: http://www.un.org/esa/desa/papers/2007/wp53_2007.pdf.

Shapiro, Helen / Lance Taylor (1990) The state and industrial strategy, in: World Development Vol. 18, No.6, pp. 861–878.

Shin, Jang-Sup (2005) Globalization and Challenges to the Developmental State: A Comparison between Korea and Singapore, in: Global Economic Review Vol. 34, No. 4, pp. 379–395.

Shleifer, Andrei (2002) The New Comparative Economics, NBER Reporter, online: http://www.nber.org/reporter/fall02/newEconomics.html.

Shonfield, Andrew (1965) Modern capitalism: the changing balance of public and private power. Oxford: Oxford University Press.

Son, Hyun H. / San, Andres Emmanuel A. (2009) How Has Asia Fared in the Global Crisis? A Tale of Three Countries: Republic of Korea, Philippines, and Thailand. Asian Development Bank Working Paper Series, No. 174.

Soskice, David (2007) Macroeconomics and Varieties of Capitalism, in: Robert Hancké, Martin Rhodes and Mark Thatcher (eds.) Beyond Varieties of Capitalism. Conflict, Contradictions, and Complementarities in the European Economy, Oxford: Oxford University Press, pp. 89–121.

Srinivasan, Thirukodikaval Nilakanta (1985) Neoclassical Political Economy, the State and Economic Development, in: Asian Development Review, Vol. 3, No. 2, pp. 38–58.

Stiglitz, Joseph E. (1988) Economic Organization, Information, and Development, in: H. Chenery and T.N.Srinivasan (Eds.) Handbook of Development Economics Vol. I, Amsterdam: North Holland, 1988, pp. 93–160.

Stiglitz, Joseph E. (1989) Markets, Market Failures, and the Development, in: American Economic Review Vol. 79, No. 2, pp. 197–203.

Stiglitz, Joseph E. (2001) *Whither Reform?: Ten Years* of the *Transition*, in: Chang, Ha-Joon (ed.) Joseph Stiglitz and the World Bank: The Rebel Within. London: Anthem Press, pp. 127–171.

Stiglitz, Joseph E. / Yusuf, Shahid (2001) (eds.) Rethinking the East Asia Miracle, NY: Oxford University Press.

Syrquin, Moshe (1988) Patterns of Structural Change, in: H. Chenery and T.N.Srinivasan (eds.) Handbook of Development Economics, Vol. I, Amsterdam: North Holland, pp. 203–273.

Tang, Kwong-leung (2000) Social Welfare Development in East Asia, Basingstoke: Palgrave.

Thompson, Mark R. (1996) Late industrialisers, late democratisers: developmental states in the Asia-Pacific, in: Third World Quarterly Vol. 17, No. 4, pp. 625–647.

Titmuss, Richard M. (1972) Developing social policy in a time of rapid change, in: Brian M. Abel-Smith, Kay Titmuss, Kathleen (eds.) The philosophy of welfare: selected writings of Richard M. Titmuss, Allen & Unwin, pp. 254–268.

Waelbroeck, Jean (1988a) Half a Century of Development Economics: A Review Based on the Handbook of Development Economics. Working Paper 1925. Research Advisory Staff, World Bank, Washington, D.C., online: http://elibrary.worldbank.org/content/workingpaper/10.1596/1813-9450-1925.

Waelbroeck, Jean (1998b) Half a Century of Development Economics: A Review Based on the Handbook of Development Economics, in: World Bank Economic Review Vol. 12, No. 2, pp. 323–352.

Wade, Robert (1988) The Role of Government in Overcoming Market Failure: Taiwan, Republic of Korea and Japan, in: Helen Hughes (ed.) Achieving Industrialization in East Asia. Cambridge: Cambridge University Press, pp. 129–163.

Wade, Robert (1990) Industrial Policy in East Asia: Does It Lead or Follow the Market?, in: Gary Gereffi and Donald Wyman (eds.) Manufactured Miracles: Patterns of Development in Latin America and East Asia. Princeton: Princeton University Press, pp. 231–265.

Wallerstein, Immanuel (1996) Open the Social Sciences. Report of the Gulbenkian Commission on the Restructuring of the Social Sciences. Stanford: Stanford University Press.

Wallerstein, Immanuel (2000) From Sociology to Historical Social Science: Prospects and Obstacles, British Journal of Sociology Vol. 51, No. 1, pp. 25–35.

Webster, Edward / Lambert, Rob / Bezuidenhout, Andries (2009) The Polanyi Problem and the Problem with Polanyi, in: Grounding Globalization: Labour in the Age of Insecurity. Oxford: Blackwell, pp. 1–21.

Westphal, Larry E. (1990) Industrial Policy in an Export-Propelled Economy: Lessons from South Korea's Experience, in: Journal of Economic Perspectives Vol. 4, No. 5, pp. 41–59.

White, Gordon (1984) Developmental States and Socialist Industrialization in the Third World, in: The Journal of Development Studies Vol. 21, No. 1, pp. 97–120.

White, Gordon / Goodman, Roger (1998) Welfare Orientalism and the search for an East Asian welfare model, in: Robert Goodman, Gordon White and Huck-ju Kwon (eds.) The East Asian Welfare Model: Welfare Orientalism and the State. London: Routledge, pp. 3–24.

Williamson, John (1990) What Washington Means by Policy Reform, in: John Williamson (ed.) Latin American Adjustment: How Much Has Happened? Washington DC: Institute for International Economics, pp. 7–19.

Wilding, Paul Is the East Asian welfare model still productive? Journal of Asian Public Policy Vol. 1, No. 1, pp. 18–31.

Woo, Jung-en (1991) Race to the Swift: State and Finance in Korean Industrialization. NY: Columbia University Press.

Woo, Wing Thye (2004) Serious Inadequacies of the Washington Consensus: Misunderstanding the Poor by the Brightest, in: Jan Joost Teunissen and Age Akkerman (eds.) Diversity in Development. Reconsidering the Washington Consensus. The Hague: FONDAD, pp. 9–43.

Woo-Cumings, Meredith (1999a) Preface, in: Meredith Woo-Cumings (Ed.) The Developmental State, Ithaca and London: Cornell University Press, pp. ix–xiii.

Woo-Cumings, Meredith (1999b) Introduction: Chalmers Johnson and the Politics of Nationalism and Development, in: Woo-Cumings (ed.) The Developmental State, Ithaca and London: Cornell University Press, pp. 1–31.

Woo-Cumings, Meredith (2001) Miracle as Prologue: The State and the Reform of the Corporate Sector in Korea, in: Joseph E. Stiglitz and Shahid Yusuf (eds.) Rethinking the East Asia Miracle, NY: Oxford University Press, pp. 343–377.

Wood, Geof (1985) The Politics of Development Policy Labelling, Development and Change Vol. 16, No. 3, pp. 347–373.

Wood, Geof / Gough Ian (2006) A Comparative Welfare Regime Approach to Global Social Policy, in: World Development Vol. 34, No. 10, pp. 1696–1712.

World Bank (1993a) The East Asian Miracle: Economic Growth and Public Policy. NY: Oxford University Press.

World Bank (1993b) The making of the East Asia miracle, World Bank Policy Research Bulletin Vol. 4, No. 4, pp. 2–5.

Yanagihara, Toru (1994) Anything New in the Miracle Report? Yes and No, in: World Development Vol. 22, No. 4, pp. 663–670.

Zhang, Yumei (2003) Pacific Asia: The Politics of Development, London: Routledge.

Joachim Ahrens, Manuel Stark

Independent Organizations in Authoritarian Regimes: contradiction in terms or an effective instrument of developmental states?[1]

1. Introduction

Politically independent organizations which assume specific tasks in public policymaking have played important roles in advanced democratic market economies. Despite the possible issue of lacking democratic legitimation, independent organizations such as central banks, courts, regulatory and anti-trust agencies among others are considered essential actors which operate autonomously and help to depoliticize the fulfillment of distinct public tasks. This implies that these agencies maybe relatively effectively shielded against opportunistic behavior of politicians, political parties or factions in the government. In addition, they are usually also well protected against the influence of pressure groups and private interests. Political independence helps to reduce rent seeking and lobbying and may enhance the credibility of authorities because unexpected and sudden policy shifts serving narrow interests or according to changing political fads and fashions are avoided.[2] This, in turn, makes public policymaking more predictable and transparent, helps to stabilize the expectations of households and companies, and eventually improves the institutional foundation of economic growth and development.

Politically independent organizations would be also conducive to policy reform in less developed countries, transition or emerging market economies all of which rely on sustained and broad-based economic growth and development in order to overcome severe problems associated with under-development. Remarkably, many of these countries possess non-democratic, i.e. authoritarian, regimes ranging from defect democracies to fully institutionalized autocracies. Authoritarian regimes are usually characterized by the restriction or suppression of political

---

1   This article is a slightly modified and translated reprint from our contribution in Theurl (ed.) (2013).

2   See Kruse (2012) as well as Heine/Mause (2012) for a comprehensive discussion of these aspects.

participation, the closed and non-competitive recruitment of the executive elite as well as a lack of institutionalized control of the exercise of power.[3]

At first sight, the notion of independent organizations which influence or monitor *economic* policymaking in authoritarian regimes may appear as a contradiction in terms. Moustafa/Ginsburg (2009: 12) however, argue with respect to judicial organizations that "(t)he decision to accord autonomy to courts depends on the particular configuration of challenges faced by authoritarian regimes, but in an astonishing array of circumstances, limited autonomy makes sense [from the authorities' perspective; JA and MS]". One may add that this observation also holds for non-judicial organizations if the granted degree of independence is in the interest of the ruling elite.[4]

While some authoritarian governments may delegate particular policy tasks to (relatively) autonomous agencies simply in order to improve their domestic or international image as modern political leaders or to build up democratic facades to conceal the actual nature of their regime, other political leaders may in fact do so in order to make their genuine commitment to economic growth and development more credible. This relates to the central questions of this paper: Why do political elites in authoritarian regimes craft, or accept the emergence of, (relatively) independent organizations? Which specific forms and functions of these organizations can be identified? The main observation of this paper is that authoritarian governments of so-called *developmental states* have effectively used (relatively) independent organizations in order to implement market-oriented reforms, to improve private-sector coordination, and to foster economic growth and development in the long run.

The following considerations aim at explaining and illustrating this finding. The next section introduces the notion of the developmental state, its characteristics and institutional foundation. Section 3 suggests various realms in which independent organizations may exert essential functions and illustrates the arguments with distinct country examples. Section 4 concludes.

---

3   See Albrecht/Frankenberger (2011) who also discuss different definitions types of
    authoritarian regimes and various approaches to measure the extent of autocracy.
4   See e.g. North et al. (2009); Li/Lian (1999) and Stark (2012).

2. Characteristics and institutional underpinnings of developmental states

The emergence of the developmental-state concept

Effective market-oriented policy reform and sustained economic growth-cum-development require a government which is strong, i.e. capable of formulating and implementing reform policies, protect property rights, and enforce the rules of market exchange.[5] Within a non-democratic context, such "capable states" (World Bank 1997) do not frequently occur. In the political-economy literature, the notion of a non-democratic, though capable state is often associated with the concept of the so- called *capitalist developmental state*. The term is due to Johnson (1982), who distinguished a developmental state from both classical market-type economies on the one hand and centrally planned economies on the other. While he conceived the Socialist command economies to act in a plan-ideological way and the Western (regulatory) market economies to act market-rational, he suggested that a developmental state is best described as plan-rational (Johnson 1982: 18).

The developmental-state concept was inductively developed reflecting the experiences of the fast-growing economies of Japan (especially since the post-war era) as well as South Korea and Taiwan (since the 1960s) in order to emphasize the differences between the market economies in the West, in particular the United States and the United Kingdom, and those in North East Asia (Johnson 1999). At later stages, countries such as Singapore, Malaysia, Indonesia, Thailand, and more recently, China have been considered developmental states.[6] This classification reflects the overall growth performance of these and other countries in the second half of the twentieth century.

---

5   This Section draws from Ahrens (2012).
6   See e.g. Sasada (2013); Song (2009) and Beeson (2009). Note however, that the concept of the developmental state has not been exclusively applied to North East Asia. See e.g. Bardhan (2010) for an application to India, Meyns/Musamba (2010) with a view on Africa, the contributions in Woo-Cumings (1999) for applications to India as well as to Latin American and European countries as well as a more recent survey by Beeson (2007).

Table 1: Ranking of countries by real GDP per capita growth (PPP) 1950–2000

Rank	Country	Compound annual real growth rate 1950–2000 [%]	Cumulated real growth 1950–2000 [%]
1	Taiwan	6.00	1742.4
2	South Korea	5.81	1583.4
3	Equatorial Guinea	5.45	1322.2
4	Botswana	5.05	1071.9
5	Oman	4.99	1041.5
6	Japan	4.87	979.5
7	Hong Kong	4.82	951.7
8	Singapore	4.74	914.8
9	Thailand	4.20	683.0
10	China	4.15	663.5

Source: Own calculations based on Maddison (2010). Data available for 172 countries and political
    entities.

It showed that seven of the ten fastest growing countries belonged to the group
of high-performing Asian economies which had been labeled developmental states (Table 1). Malaysia and Indonesia had been ranked 20th and 28th,
respectively.

Remarkably, these East Asian economies did not only outperform most other
countries in terms of economic growth, they also realized declining poverty rates
over time, improved income distribution, and achieved social progress. What is
more, most growth processes appeared to be steady with relatively weak volatilities
and quick recoveries after recessions. Finally, policiespursued in these countries
were non-orthodox and contradicted those recommendations which later should
become known as the so-called Washington Consensus.

Developmental states and authoritarian regimes

Not by definition, but by actual politico-economic records, most developmental
states have been (at least initially) authoritarian regimes.[7] South Korea was under the control of different regimes with a varying degree of legitimacy from the
end of the Korean War in 1953 until its democratization in 1987. Essentially, the
dictatorial regimes of Syngman Rhee (1950–1960) and General Park Chung- Hee
(1962–1979) dominated this period. The rule of Park Chung-Hee marked the

---

7   The following arguments are essentially taken from Stark (2010).

beginning of the fast economic growth period. The Park era is usually portrayed as the crucial developmental-state period in South Korea (Minns 2001). In Taiwan, the Kuomintang (KMT), which was disposed from mainland China in the Chinese civil war against the Communist Party in 1949, ruled in a single-party system until the 1980s. Until his death in 1975, the KMT and Taiwan were controlled by Generalissimo Chiang Kai-Shek. Thereafter, the most prominent political figure was his son Chiang Ching-Kuo who died in office in 1988 (Wade 1990: 70–71). As in South Korea, the unions and the labor movement in general were repressed by the regime (Thompson 1996: 632–633).

While democratization took place in both Taiwan and South Korea at the end of the 1980s, other high performing East Asian economies like Singapore, Malaysia, and the People's Republic of China are still governed by authoritarian regimes today. In contrast, the archetype of the developmental state, Japan, stands out in several ways. Japan had an authoritarian regime from the beginning of its industrialization in 1868 until the end of the World War II, but it has been a democracy since the post-war period. However, it should be noted that all prime ministers of Japan have been members the LDP (Liberal-Democratic Party) since the foundation of this party in 1955, with the sole exception of a short period from 1993–1996.

The prevalence of authoritarian regimes in developmental states had fueled the debate on the relationship between regime-type and growth (for a discussion of this topic see, e.g., Thompson (1996). There is no common agreement on this question. Nevertheless, it is widely accepted that a developmental state has to be 'strong' in order to avoid the rent-seeking pressures typical for less developed countries (Cheng et al. 1998: 88). Furthermore, Haggard (2004: 60) argued that the ability to make credible commitments concerning economic and particularly industrial policy objectives was an important success factor for the East Asian economies. Such long-term commitments are hardly possible in an environment of frequent government changes. In the Japanese democracy, continuity in economic policy was not only guaranteed by the dominant role of a single party but also by the powerful role of bureaucrats, who have been employees of the ministries and thus not directly affected by political elections.

Characteristics of developmental states

Chang (1999: 192) calls a state developmental if it "can create and regulate the economic and political relationships that can support sustained indus-trialization (…) [and if it; JA and MS] takes the goals of long-term growth and structural change seriously, 'politically' manages the economy to ease the conflicts inevitable during the process of such change (but with a firm eye on the long-term goals), and engages in institutional adaptation and innovation to achieve those goals."

The concrete features of developmental states differ across countries and change through time. But essentially the main characteristics include[8]:

(1) a political leadership with a firm commitment to foster sustained and broad-based economic growth;
(2) stable political rule ensured by a sufficiently autonomous political-administrative elite that is staffed with the best available managerial talent and that does not accede to political pressures which could impede economic growth;
(3) cooperation between the public and the private sector that is guided by a pilot economic planning agency;
(4) continuous investment in universal education and policies aiming at a more equitable distribution of opportunities and wealth; and
(5) a government, whose members understand the need for market-conforming policies and interventions.

Autonomy of the economic bureaucracy

A key aspect of an ideal-type developmental state is to ensure autonomy of the economic bureaucracy as well as the political elite who are in charge of strategy formulation, actual decision making, and policy implementation. The challenge is to avoid a situation in which policy makers become captured by organizations or individuals who represent influential private business. In order to prevent vested interests from colluding with state officials, institutional arrangements, policy makers' access to financial means, as well as the sources of their political power may play an important role. The fewer funds are provided to the public sector by private actors, the easier it is to ensure the autonomy of policy makers from private interests. The independence of the *economic* bureaucracy is at least equally important. In order to achieve sustainable market-based growth, economic policy must be consistent, show a long-term focus, and exhibit complementary policy instruments. While this holds true for public policy making in general; it is even more essential if a government intends to implement more selective industrial policies. For that reason, authorities with the vision to implement a long-term development strategy need to depoliticize economic decision making. That is why adherents to the idea of the developmental state consider bureaucratic autonomy from social entanglements as a constituent characteristic of developmental states.

---

8   See e.g. Chang (1999); Johnson (1987/99) and Stark (2012).

In these states, depoliticization is facilitated through a separation of reigning and ruling actors. While politicians determine broad policy goals and protect the public administration from vested interests, the bureaucrats are in charge of planning and implementing policies and guiding the economy. Moreover, as Pempel (1999: 160) notes, "technocrats and bureaucrats enjoy disproportionately high levels of power and wield a variety of tools to enforce their will. State actors are also relatively free from major populist pressures, most especially from organized labor and organized peasants."

The organization of, and the incentives for civil servants within, the public sector crucially affect the developmental outcomes of public policies.[9] To varying degrees across countries and through time, economic, institutional, and policy reforms in East Asian developmental states relied on the establishment of an economic administration which exhibited key characteristics of a Weberian-type bureaucracy and was able to implement overall macroeconomic policies, enforce private property rights, and autonomously conduct industrial policy measures. Max Weber (1921/1972) proposed a powerful approach to strengthen a state's internal organization, i.e. is capacity to foster market development and economic growth. He suggested that efficient market operations require high degrees of calculability driven by legal rationality. In this framework, the public administration is a central and powerful tool in order to craft a functioning, modern market economy. Such an economic bureaucracy is characterized by duties which are defined according to functions. Civil servants are exclusively devoted to administrative tasks, and they are relatively independent of societal pressures. According to Weber, a government's capability of strengthening and complementing market exchange is enhanced if the administration represents a coherent entity and if bureaucrats perceive the pursuit of public-policy objectives as the most appropriate way to improve their individual well-being. An administration showing a corporate identity, which aligns the individual objectives of civil servants with those of the political leadership, must be able to act autonomously, i.e. it needs to be shielded against the pressures of vested (business) interests.

Bureaucratic professionalism is necessary, but it is not sufficient in order to ensure development-enhancing consequences of economic policies. Further key institutions constituting a Weberian-type bureaucracy comprise the replacement of political appointments or dismissals by performance-based standards in both recruitment and promotion. These standards should be based on impartial and competitive examinations. In addition, civil servants should

---

9   See Campos/Root (1996); Evans (1995); Qian/Weingast (1997) and World Bank (1997).

be provided with adequate opportunities to gain long-term career rewards, and transparent hiring-and-firing rules need to be established. Taken together, all this can improve the expertise in the public administration, help to create commitment, and enhance the effectiveness of administrative action. However, authorities have to give a high priority to education policies in order to generate large numbers of qualified bureaucrats, who will perform well in a meritocratic environment.[10]

Credible developmental commitment

These arguments highlight the importance of crafting a strong state with distinct bureaucratic capabilities. However, even an effective economic bureaucracy will produce developmental improvements only if public announcements, political promises, and administrative actions of civil servants and policy makers are conceived to be credible. This insight reveals a weak point in the concept of a strong developmental state. In order to enhance its political credibility, a reform- oriented government of such a developmental state needs to show and document its commitment to long-term economic development, e.g., through particular public investments in the public education or health sector. Moreover, it can open up the economy and expose itself to the international competition between governments for mobile resources, or it may join international organizations (like the WTO or the IMF) and thereby constrain its available policy options at least in distinct realms of policy making. Such policy decisions, in combination with a relatively autonomous and competent economic bureaucracy, can help to enhance the government's ability to deliver according to its prior policy announcements. But if there is a lack of such institutional safeguards, which bind the government to its promises, a convincing credible commitment will not be achieved. Development-enhancing consequences of economic reform policies are unlikely if the political leadership lacks legitimacy and does not show an encompassing interest in economic and social development. In such a case, the structural features of a so-called developmental state can be easily abused through arbitrary and discretionary government action. Then, a would-be- developmental state may become a predatory state.

Government-business interface

Besides a meritocratic economic administration, distinct government-business interfaces have been typical for developmental states. Relations between government

---

10 See e.g. Root (1996/98); Ahrens (2002) and Stark (2012).

and the economic bureaucracy on the one hand and the private sector on the other hand differed across countries, but in almost all countries these relations were formally or informally institutionalized and linked a relatively autonomous public administration to the private sector. This allowed for channels to exchange information and to better plan, communicate, and implement economic policies. This institutional fabric, which Evans (1995/98) dubbed *embedded autonomy*, established a participatory mechanism for major private businesses in policymaking processes (World Bank 1993; Evans 1998). The institutionalized exchange of information between private sector representatives and public agencies enabled the bureaucracy and the political leadership to gather information on the condition of the economy, the situation of private businesses, and new trends in technology. Moreover, feedback on the effects of existing regulations and previously implemented economic policies could be gathered (Root 1998; World Bank 1993). This way, businesses had notable influence on the formulation of new policies. Furthermore, the flow of information also goes from the state to the private sector. This was crucial for the effective implementation of policies (Evans 1998) and increased the credibility of the state's commitment to these policies (Root 1996; Stiglitz 1996). In the East Asian developmental states, the continuous interaction between economic bureaucracy and private business was a precondition for the implementation of what Evans (1998: 75) has called the "support/performance bargain". This means that the state apparatus on the one hand supported specific companies and industries through subsidies and similar measures. On the other hand, the impact of these measures and the performance of supported companies was closely monitored (Amsden 1995: 795).

The actual organization of government-business ties has varied among the high-performing Asian economies (Evans 1998: 76). An essential mechanism in the state-business interface of several developmental states were credible intermediary organizations such as autonomous business associations which served to share information between companies and the state and mediated in case of conflicts (Root 1998: 69). In addition, deliberation councils, which brought together bureaucrats of specific agencies and private industry, were frequently emphasized in the research on East Asian institutions.[11] These councils were of major importance in Japan and South Korea and were also emulated to a certain degree in Malaysia beginning in the mid-1980s (World Bank 1993: 181–184). Taiwan and Singapore used different channels of communication. In Singapore, private citizens reviewed government policies and commented on them by serving as directors of government statutory boards and as members of ad hoc advisory

---

11 See e.g. Root (1998: 69–70); Stiglitz (1996: 164) and Evans (1998: 75–76).

boards (World Bank 1993: 184). In contrast to other countries, formal connections between government and business were much less prominent in Taiwan (World Bank 1993; Evans 1998). However, the high importance of state- owned companies in the Taiwanese economy resulted in a considerable influence of the state on the smaller companies of the private sector (World Bank 1993). Furthermore, periodic large-scale conferences that brought together economic policy makers, business leaders and academics had been held (Evans 1998). Proponents of the *market-enhancing view* stressed the importance of banks and credit markets as intermediaries between East Asian governments and the private sector. According to Aoki et al. (1997: 8–11), state interventions in the financial sector that credibly signaled government's commitment to sustainable economic growth fostered banks' long-term orientation. This increased their willingness to invest in information-gathering, give long-term credits and to carefully monitor their debtors.

The capability and organization of the bureaucracy, as well as the functioning of the state- business interface, differed between the East Asian developmental states and their less successful counterparts in Southeast Asia. As summarized by Doner et al. (2005: 334–336), elements of the ideal-type of a meritocratic bureaucracy, which had close ties to the private sector and whose economic policies were coordinated by a pilot agency, were largely present in South Korea, Taiwan, and Singapore, but only to a limited degree in Malaysia and Thailand and even less in Indonesia. Similar differences were found in the sphere of the state-business nexus. While public- private collaboration was governed by transparent rules in South Korea, Taiwan, and Singapore, the transparency of rules was much lower in the other Southeast Asian economies (Doner et al. 2005: 335).

In the course of time, bureaucratic agencies of developmental states did not always act entirely independently of other interest groups. Private companies striving for less state control over the economy found allies within the bureaucracy, as did politicians willing to respond to foreign pressures for more liberalization. As a consequence of bureaucratic competition for influence, agencies faced a constant need to justify their actions and policies. This need for justification was an important reason why state action was overall rational, as argued by Johnson (1982: 18), and adaptive, as stressed by Root (1996: 15–16). The presence of agencies in favor of a more liberal approach to economic policy represented a potential threat to the power of economic planners and, therefore, increased their incentive to prove the viability of state interventions.[12]

---

12 One instructive example is the case of Taiwan, where the interventionist Industrial Development Board (IDB) competed for influence with the more liberal Council for

*Strong but limited states due to institution building
and exogenous constraints*

Many accounts on the developmental state characterize it as autonomous or strong, meaning that a developmental state is supposedly able to act largely independently of special interest groups and override the power of such groups to act in the national interest (Leftwich 1995: 408). Root (1996) complemented this notion by arguing that East Asian developmental states were not only strong, but also limited, which distinguished them from most other states in the developing world. The East Asian states were strong in the sense that they possessed institutional arrangements that enabled them to resist the pressures of narrow interests, to reduce rent seeking, lobbying, and corruption. They were limited in the sense that the power of governments and the bureaucracy was constrained by exogenous factors, binding rules, and credible commitments (Root 1996: 141–143). A meritocratic, autonomous, public bureaucracy along with close and transparent ties between the state and private companies were important institutional foundations of such a state. From this perspective, the stability and transparency of the consultative mechanisms involved in the process of policy making in East Asia also served to tie the regime's hands to policies once they had been chosen (Root 1998: 69).

But why did authoritarian rulers themselves decide to tie their own hands and to develop a firm, long-term commitment to pursue a broad-based growth strategy with an encompassing national interest? Moustafa/Ginsburg (2009: 9) argue that shared economic growth could threaten the coalition of ruling elites in many regimes. Particularly, authoritarian leaderships in resource-rich countries such as Saudi Arabia may not see the necessity to establish legal norms or other institutional mechanisms to attract investment and to foster growth. Instead, authorities may prefer narrow bases to finance the regime. In such cases, the perceived costs of granting autonomy to organizations in the administrative or judicial realm may outweigh the expected benefits. Therefore, authorities would be better off if they apply other mechanisms in order secure their regime.

In so-called developmental states, the cost-benefit ratio of pursuing long-term and broad-based growth and granting some independence to judicial, administrative, or economic organizations may have been just the opposite. A crucial reason for this lies in *exogenous constraints* for the ruling elites which shaped the incentives of the political leadership, limited the set of feasible policy choices

---

Economic Planning and Development (CEPD).

and eventually the power of political and bureaucratic actors in East Asia (Doner et al. 2005; Woo-Cumings 1998).[13]

The abolishment of the feudal regime of the Shogun and the beginning of rapid modernization in Japan occurred to a large degree as a reaction to the perceived threat to become colonized or at least economically exploited by Western powers. In a country that had been sealing itself from foreign influences for centuries, it was this eminent external threat that lead to a fast adaptation of western technology, laws and customs. Even in the post-war period, it was a perceived backwardness vis-à-vis the western countries that drove the majority of Japanese politicians and bureaucrats to give a clear priority to economic development (Stark 2012).

Notably, most other East Asian developmental states had been subject to similar threats or constraints at the beginning of their economic development (Haggard 2004: 60; Ahrens 2002: 210). In the case of South Korea, North Korea had been a permanent and serious threat to the autonomy and existence of the country. For Taiwan and, to a lesser degree, for Hong Kong, a similar threat came from the People's Republic of China, which never dropped its claims to either of these de facto sovereign entities. The resource-poor city state of Singapore had been part of Malaysia prior to its independence in 1965. In addition to the external threats, the fact that neither Japan nor the other early developmental states had noteworthy natural resources forced their governments to pursue market-based reform and economic development.

The prevalence of serious external threats in combination with the lack of easily disposable revenues can be considered a major reason why industrialization and catching up with the advanced economies were considered the only feasible option by East Asian authorities. Both conditions can be interpreted as constraints which limited the options available to the relevant authorities. The external threats also made the commitment of the government to economic development credible for the private sector, which was a precondition for the willingness of companies to undertake entrepreneurial risks (Root 1996; Stark 2010).

On the positive side, Taiwan and South Korea, in the immediate post-war period also Japan, received substantial financial aid from the United States. This gave the authorities in those countries free access to noteworthy financial resources; however, there was always an eminent danger that these resources could have been

---

13 Moreover, political leaderships face increasingly long time horizons of their regime, e.g. due to external protection through the United States, but also in the course of time due to continuous economic success, initiated through state activism and political stability which strengthened the regimes' legitimacy and authorities' commitment to further economic development.

withdrawn quickly in the case of obvious unjustified enrichment by the political elite. Furthermore, and probably even more important, the high performing East Asian nations had free access to important western markets, which proved to be a key factor for the success of their export-led economic strategy. In addition, the specific political circumstances of the Cold War and the privileged relationship that South Korea, Taiwan and Japan enjoyed with the United States in the post-war period enabled them to export to foreign markets while protecting domestic companies in infant industries from foreign competition and hostile takeovers (Amsden 1991).

Another exogenous factor which contributed to the emergence of developmental states in South Korea and Taiwan was Japan's colonial legacy in both countries. While Japanese colonial rule in Korea was oppressive and ruthless, it was also credited for boosting agricultural production, starting industrialization, building a cohesive bureaucracy and constructing centralized, coercive institutions. Furthermore, the colonial rule left both countries with a significantly improved infrastructure and a major accumulation of physical and human capital (Kohli 1999/2004).

3. The role of (relatively) independent organizations in developmental states

Political economists use to emphasize the importance of political independence of certain public agencies which are delegated to pursue distinct tasks. The foregoing considerations emphasized that independent organizations can and have played important roles even in authoritarian developmental states. The subsequent sections identify the realms in which independent organizations have existed in these states and give country-specific examples.

3.1 Forms and realms of independence in developmental states

Political independence of public agencies usually implies (i) the absence of any authority of an individual politician, government factions or other political bodies to give directives to these agencies and (ii) incentive structures of members of these independent organizations which are not influenced by the interests of politicians or political bodies (Kruse 2012). In our context of developmental states, we extend the notion of independence and also include two further categories: economic independence and business independence. *Economic independence* implies that distinct public organizations are not only independent of political influence, but that they are neither subject to rent seeking and lobbying from business associations or private pressure groups. Finally, *business independence* entails that private sector organizations are not subject to arbitrary political interference and that private businesses can freely thrive within the given legal and regulatory environment. All three forms of independence deserve particular attention in the institutional setup of developmental states: political independence, because the political leadership is basically strong enough to influence or directly steer (parts of) the economic bureaucracy or other public agencies; business independence, because authorities are usually strong enough to transgress against private actors' rights; and economic independence, because interventionist and selective government policies usually create numerous opportunities for lobbying and rent seeking which, if pursued excessively and uncontrolled, would undermine authorities efforts to foster overall growth and development.

Why may authoritarian governments be actually willing to grant (some) independence to public agencies, courts, or other organizations? Moustafa/Ginsburg (2009) provide some arguments with respect to the establishment of relatively independent courts. Considering the experiences of developmental states, some of their considerations may also hold for granting different degrees of autonomy to other organizations.

At first sight, one may reckon that authoritarian governments would prefer possibly opaque institutions which allow elites to amass rents and increase their private wealth through the exploitation of domestic or foreign investors who would depend on officials and other members of the political elite for protecting their investments (Root/May 2009). In cases, in which such governments grant or maintain independence of judicial or other organizations, this may simply serve as a de jure (not de facto) act to enhance the regime's legitimacy and to create an image that they seek to constrain arbitrary rule. In reality, numerous authoritarian governments have pursued exactly such an approach. However, the empirical reality also provides examples which contradict that conventional wisdom (Moustafa/Ginsburg 2009).

In fact, authoritarian government may have an interest in crafting predictable, transparent, and even accountable public organizations, procedures, and policies in order to foster economic growth and development. The precondition for that is that the political leadership relies on, and has developed a commitment to, these economic objectives, and the side condition is that the leadership's political power is not being compromised. Root/May (2009) e.g. argue that an automatic connection between strengthening the independence of courts and liberalizing the political order does not necessarily exist. They add that crafting independent rule-based organizations including a court system helps to restrict executive discretion. This, however, will not necessarily weaken the political regime, but rather contribute to craft a stable institutional framework that ensures the longevity of the regime.

A nexus of relatively independent organizations helps to build a rule of law for elites which may become an effective, accepted, and low-cost tool for intra-elite conflict resolution. This also holds for business elites, on which governments rely for investments and the support of economic growth policies. Governments can make their promise credible not to interfere arbitrarily into private business by establishing a neutral and autonomous organization which monitors and punishes transgressions against private property rights.

Furthermore, Root/May (2009: 307) identify three managerial dilemmas of authoritarian leaders which could be effectively dealt with through the establishment of a relatively independent system of courts and possibly other organizations. In their words:

> "Authoritarians face three peculiar managerial dilemmas by virtue of the status of the head of state as 'above the law.' That status limits the effectiveness of the state and its institutions because it implies the primacy of discretion over rules. Building a court system (…) can actually help establish a stable framework for regime longevity. First, autocrats require investment and therefore must create a legal system to facilitate transactions. Second, they need to enhance revenue collection and credit; therefore, they need a legal framework that holds financial intermediaries accountable for their private debts and for dealing equitably with citizens. Third, they need to ferret out disobedience and noncompliance by subordinates; a legal system that discloses the abuses of officials enhances the leader's renown and ensures greater compliance from citizens. Administrative courts can make the state's administrative apparatus work more smoothly to ensure that information about performance and malfeasance is uncovered. Improved loyalty of administrative personnel is thereby attained as well as a more contented populace."

Crafting independent organizations has been an effective strategy in authoritarian regimes in order to ensure enduring and credible economic policies. Autonomous central banks, courts, or securities regulation agencies represent important elements of such an approach. Independence in those realms helps to ensure that government's promises are credible and also that it will not renege on its promise at a later stage. Autonomous courts e.g. provide the possibility that private investors challenge public policy measures and government decisions, thereby making it more costly for government to interfere with economic transactions. In addition, 'autonomous' judicial organizations, if they are in charge of addressing controversial economic reform issue, may serve as effective devices, e.g., for a reform-minded and growth-oriented government to promote, legitimize, and enforce badly needed institutional and policy reforms in formerly populist regimes. As Moustafa/Ginsburg (2009: 10) argue: "Authoritarian rules in these contexts are sensitive to the risks of retreating from prior state commitments to subsidized goods and services, state-owned enterprises, commitments to full employment, and broad pledges to labor rights generally. They rightly fear popular backlash or elite-level splits if they renege on policies that previously formed the ideological basis of their rule."

The incentive for authorities to grant important functions to (relatively) independents courts may be strengthened and reinforced if the country is exposed to, and dependent on, international trade and capital flows and if it is a member of international organizations. "The WTO regime explicitly requires states to provide judicial or quasi-judicial institutions in trade-related arenas; a network of bilateral investment treaties promises neutral dispute resolution to reassure investors; and multilateral institutions such as the World Bank (…) expend vast resources to promote judicial reform designed to make legal institutions more effective, efficient, and predictable" (Moustafa/Ginsburg 2009: 9).

Last but not least, (relatively) independent organizations can help to strengthen the regime's legitimacy through tying the government's hands. If governments comply with these self-imposed limits on their power, they may develop a reputation for delivering on their promises and thereby strengthen their credibility and societal acceptance.

Given their exogenous constraints and their firm commitment to long-term, broad-based economic growth and development, political leaderships in developmental states faced distinct incentives to craft relatively independent public organizations, at times to accept the emergence of comparatively autonomous political jurisdictions, and increasingly to tolerate the emergence of autonomous business actors. Independent economic actors were seen as an unalterable prerequisite for a flourishing market economy and for private businesses which were willing to invest in long- term projects thereby laying the basis for economic growth. Long-term and broad-based growth had been seen in all countries as a foundation for regime survival and (in the absence of democratic input legitimation) as a justification of the leaderships continual rule through the accomplishment of economic and social objectives such as growth, a more equal income distribution, less poverty, and generally improving living standards.

Relatively independent organizations can be identified in the public as well as in the private realms of developmental states. As will be illustrated in the following section, forms of relatively independent organizations have existed in the economic administration, in economic pilot agencies and individual ministries, in subnational governments, and in courts. In some developmental states, the organizations of the government-business interface such as deliberation councils and business associations have played crucial roles and proved to operate relatively autonomously. In the private sector, (relatively) autonomous organizations have included private businesses and private intermediary organizations.

As a consequence, governments needed to accept limits on their own power in order to make their commitment to long-term economic growth credible. These limits were strengthened by granting increasing economic freedom and autonomy to private business, opening up the economy and expose domestic businesses to international competition, and granting a certain degree of independence to public agencies. Hence, independent organizations and competition limited political and economic power and helped to establish strong but limited states; strong in the sense that states could resist pressures of narrow interests; limited because government and bureaucratic powers were constrained by binding rules and credible commitment giving the private sector economic independence.

3.2 Country examples

The following mini-case studies provide snapshot-like examples which illustrate the role of relatively independent organizations and autonomous decision-making in the public realm and the private business sector and their importance for the overall economic performance of individual countries. Thereby, these cases seek to illustrate the context (along general lines) in which these organizations and institutions became effective.

3.2.1 The original developmental states: Japan, South Korea, Taiwan, and Singapore[14]

The economic bureaucracy

An important precondition for the emergence of a capable bureaucracy in the East Asian developmental states was that a strict meritocracy in the recruitment and promotion process for public officials was implemented and enforced. In addition to a transparent recruitment process through highly competitive exams, the generally high prestige of working for the state in East Asia contributed to attracting highly qualified graduates from the best universities. Once hired, these high potentials received an attractive remuneration much closer to salaries of the private sector than in other countries (Root 1996) and usually stayed in public service for most of their professional life, rising through the different ranks and acquiring detailed knowledge about the activities of ministries and agencies. Thus,

---

14 This section draws from Ahrens (2002) and Stark (2012).

a significant amount of expert knowledge was accumulated within the bureaucracy (Akyüz et al. 1998; Root 1996).

Another important characteristic of the bureaucracy of East Asian developmental states was their relative freedom from the influence of vested interests. As the World Bank notes in its study on the "East Asian Miracle", economic technocrats in East Asia were able to formulate and implement policies with a minimum of lobbying for special favors from politicians and interest groups (World Bank 1993: 167). In Japan, the Ministry of International Trade and Industry (MITI) is generally believed to have been the most important agency in this respect. MITI had the primary responsibility for economic planning and industrial policy in the catch-up phase of the Japanese economy (Johnson 1982). In the democratic setting of post-war Japan, the powerful position of the bureaucracy was also strengthened because vice-ministers – bureaucrats who had successfully risen in the ranks of a certain ministry up to the highest possible position – often possessed both more support from the lower levels of the hierarchy and more detailed expert knowledge than the minister who officially headed the respective ministry (Johnson 1982). Consequently, it was hard if not impossible for the frequently changing elected governments of Japan and their ministers to induce significant policy changes without the cooperation of the long established high-ranking bureaucrats.

The situation in Taiwan, South Korea and Singapore was different because these countries were ruled by authoritarian regimes for most of their high-growth period. In spite of the authoritarian nature of these regimes, their economic bureaucracies enjoyed a considerable degree of autonomy and influence. Powerful economic agencies similar to MITI existed in Taiwan and South Korea (Cheng et al. 1998: 88–89). In Korea, the most important agency during the rule of Park was the Economic Planning Board (EPB), which accumulated considerable power over other ministries in a process of centralization (Cheng et al. 1998). The importance of the EPB for the Korean developmental state is further evidenced by the fact that its head was awarded the rank of a Deputy Prime Minister, the second highest position in the government hierarchy (Minns 2001). In Taiwan, the Council for Economic Planning and Development (CEPD) and its predecessors, while less powerful than MITI in Japan, were responsible for tasks such as formulating the macroeconomic development plans and administering the substantial financial aid from the USA that the country received in the first years of its high growth (Wade 1990). In Singapore, the autonomy of the bureaucracy was enhanced by codifying its independence from politics. The commitment to keep politics out of the public service went so far that being a member of the dominant People's Action Party (PAP) reduced the likelihood of a bureaucratic appointment (Root,

1996). This strict separation distinguished Singapore even from other East Asian countries such as Taiwan, were KMT membership was rather a benefit for pursuing a career in ministries (Root 1996).

While it is virtually undisputed that meritocracy and bureaucratic autonomy were necessary conditions for the emergence of a public service that supported a developmental state, there is considerable evidence that these conditions were not sufficient. This becomes clear through an analysis of India, which has been characterized as a "failed developmental state" (Herring 1999). The recruitment process for the Indian civil service was via nationwide examinations which were at least as competitive as in the successful East Asian developmental States (Evans 1992) and the bureaucracy was powerful enough to lead at least some scholars to the notion that it was actually running the country (Herring 1999: 315). Nevertheless, India's economic performance for most of the 20th century had been far less successful than the rapid growth experienced by Japan, the Asian Tigers or other countries such as Malaysia, Indonesia and Thailand.

One key difference between the bureaucracy in India and its counterparts in East Asia was that entry exams had a very different focus and therefore attracted different applicants to the bureaucracy: While Indian entry exams focused on general knowledge and English skills and therefore attracted humanistically oriented graduates (Evans 1992), the recruitment process in East Asia was rather oriented towards technical and specialized skills. The second key difference is the relationship between the bureaucracy and the society. Evans (1992) argued that while the autonomy of the bureaucracy was necessary to keep its decisions free from vested interests, a solely insulated bureaucracy would lack the capability of relying on decentralized private information and implementation. Therefore, it was necessary that a close connection existed between state and society that enabled the state to stimulate, complement and reinforce entrepreneurship. While states such as South Korea had close ties to parts of the society, which shared their interest in economic development, they were largely absent in India (Evans 1992).

The government-business interface

The ties between the state and society – and in the case of the East Asian developmental states in particular between the state and private businesses – served several closely related purposes. On the one hand, they enabled political authorities to guide private companies towards the national goal of economic catch-up and the chosen development path. On the other hand, they served as a mechanism for the mutual exchange of information. In this way, private businesses had the opportunity to provide feedback on the economic policy determined and implemented by governments and economic bureaucracies. Only the existence of such a feedback cycle enabled developmental states to constantly revise their economic policies and to identify further reform needs (Root 1996).

The degree of the institutionalization of the state-business interface varied even among the most evident examples of East Asian developmental states. Japan's institutions were the most widely recognized and most thorough. Deliberation councils between the government and private industry that were organized along the lines of both different industries and different general economic topics played an important role since the beginning of the postwar period (World Bank 1993). Furthermore, informal institutions existed that improved the mutual understanding between state and business actors and, thus, promoted consensus building. Probably the most apparent of these informal institutions had been the common practice that high-ranking bureaucrats commonly assumed powerful positions in private companies after their retirement (Johnson 1982).

In South Korea, a similar mechanism of deliberation councils was implemented by the Park government. Frequent and regular meetings between the government and business leaders were carried out; in particular the monthly export promotion meetings provided an important communication channel (World Bank 1993). These encounters were based on a set of publicly known rules: it was, e.g., assured that areas of disagreement could be addressed openly and that problems would be discussed in front of all relevant players. In order to assure firms that favoritism for a particular competitor would not take place, the president never held face-to-face meetings with representatives of individual companies (Root 1996).

An important difference between the state-business relations in Japan and South Korea was the degree of state intervention in the economy. In the democratic setting of Japan, the degree of government control over the private sector varied over time and developed into what Johnson called "administrative guidance" (1982: 318), meaning that the state had a coordinating influence on private companies without exercising coercive power on their strategies. Since the Japanese economy is characterized by large business groups which are each organized around one main bank (the *keiretsu*), the bureaucracy only needed to influence a limited number of decision makers in order to have a significant impact on the economy.

In South Korea, the government was generally perceived to be "more strong handed and dictatorial" (World Bank 1993). One mechanism that enabled the government to exercise control over the private sector was the nationalization of the banking sector, which took place shortly after Park came into power (Minns 2001). In this way, the state was able to direct investment to the designated target industries. In Korea, the centralized structure of the political regime in combination with the prevalence of the *chaebol* (large, diversified and commonly family owned business groups) enabled the state to exercise more control over the business sector and to pursue more ambitious industrial policies than in Japan or Taiwan (Akyüz et al. 1998).

The state-business interface in Taiwan differed significantly from both Japan and Korea and is generally considered to have been weaker. Formal mechanisms for the exchange of information were almost entirely lacking (World Bank 1993). In general, the Taiwanese government kept business in a much more subservient position than in Japan or Korea (Root 1996). This may have been motivated by the fact that the government prior to the democratization in the late 1980s was made up by members of the KMT, who had fled from mainland China. In contrast, the business sector was dominated by native Taiwanese. The lack of personal ties and trust between these groups caused the Kuomintang government to rely more on public enterprises than was the case in either Korea or Japan (Cheng et al. 1998). As a consequence, one of the largest state-owned sectors of the non-communist world emerged (Wade 1990; Evans 1995). Instead of guiding the private sector through subsidies for specific target industries, new industries were generally established by state-owned companies in Taiwan (Wade 1990). In contrast to South Korea and Japan, the private sector of the economy was not characterized by large diversified business groups but by a large number of small private companies similar to the German *Mittelstand* (Thompson 1996). The investments of public enterprises into new industries set incentives for complimentary investments by the smaller private companies through signaling the commitment of the political decision makers to economic diversification (Wade 1990).

Concerning public-private consultation mechanisms, Singapore shared more similarities with Japan and Korea than with Taiwan. Statutory boards that were responsible for monitoring the bureaucrats' performance as well as government advisory committees had private citizens as directors (World Bank 1993), in spite of the strictly authoritarian, single-party political system. The National Wages Council played a very important role for the economy and fulfilled several functions. While its main responsibility was to facilitate bargaining between labor and employers (Root 1996), it also furthered the government's guidance of both business and labor (World Bank 1993). This council was comprised by two secretaries of the concerned ministries as representatives for the government, trade union representatives and business representatives. Interestingly, not only Singaporean companies but also foreign investors from Japan, the USA and Germany were represented in the National Wages Council (Root 1996). This clearly shows one key difference that distinguishes the city-state of Singapore from other developmental states: While the economies of Japan, South Korea and Taiwan relied primarily on domestic companies in their catch-up process, Singapore's economy has been characterized by a significant amount of foreign direct investment of multinational companies since the beginning of its fast growth process (Shin 2005). Silverstein (2009) points to yet another noteworthy aspect by arguing that Singapore appears to prove that an authoritarian government is able to establish an effective system based on the rule of law, which essentially meets the standards of a globalized economy, but does not undermine the authorities' power. Silverstein's (2009: 83) explanation is telling:

> "Lee Kuan Yew told Parliament in 1995 that when the government is taken to court by a private individual, 'the court must adjudicate upon the issues strictly on their merits and in accordance with the law. To have it otherwise is to lose (…) our standing and … our status as an investment and financial centre. The interpretation of documents, of contracts in accordance with the law is crucial. Our reputation for the rule of law has been and is a valuable economic asset, part of our capital, although an intangible one' (Singapore Parliamentary Debates, Nov. 2, 1995: col. 236). (…) Singapore therefore presents countries like China with the possibility of an alternative model: while economic reform and prosperity demand the rule of law, the rule of law does not necessarily mean that judicialization – and the expansion of individual rights – necessarily will follow."[15]

3.2.2 A new developmental state? Capitalism, Chinese-style

Chinese transition has been taking place without political democratization. But even in China, a gradual, though far-reaching change of institutions has taken place – a market-induced transformation of the Leninist state (Heilmann 1998) and hence the emergence of a post-socialist transition order. This change entailed substantial alterations of the country's governance structure.

So far, two major phases of economic transition can be distinguished: The first phase (1978–1993) was characterized by gradual reforms which aimed to realize efficiency gains through reforms of the planned economy. The second phase started with the decision of the Third Plenum of the 14th Party Congress in September 1993 to transform China's economy into a *socialist market economy*. Since then building market institutions and creating a rule-based market economy have become key objectives of transition policymaking.[16]

---

15 But note in this context the statement by Root/May (2009: 308–309): "The institutions that give Singapore a reputation for clean business practices also enable its leaders to intimidate political opponents."

16 See Qian (1999). This section draws from Ahrens/Jünemann (2011).

Political feasibility and legitimacy

From the perspective of Chinese authorities, policy reform and institution building had to yield material benefits for large parts of the population. Even more important than in other developmental states, economic growth and modernization were conceived as the foundation of political power, that gave legitimacy for, and support of, the political monopoly of the Chinese Communist Party (CCP) and its leadership (Gilley 2008). Through the implementation of comprehensive economic reforms, "China's politicized capitalism has evolved a strategy of transition aimed at balancing the interest of reformers to safeguard the power and privileges of the political elite even while instituting reforms that both reduce the scope of state managerial controls over production and distribution and expand the role of the market as a mechanism to motivate and guide economic growth" (Nee and Opper 2006: 3).

Hussain et al. (2000) and Qian (2003) convincingly argued that unorthodox *transitional institutions* turned out to be more effective than presumably best-practice institutional arrangements in a period of economic transition. Especially in China's authoritarian regime, they made market- oriented reforms a viable policy choice, because they helped political authorities maintain power and control and, additionally, opened up ways to make political elites winners of reform. Finally, specific transitional institutions tailored to society's needs, capacities, and capabilities could be much faster developed than best-practice institutions – the latter usually need a long period of time to be crafted and enforced, and in an underdeveloped authoritarian transition economy, there would be a lack of human capital to operate them. In China, new transitional institutions took advantage of the existing social capital and helped to preserve basic practices and codes of behavior. Evidence shows that transitional institutions served as functional equivalents to first-best institutions, e.g. with respect to creating incentives for doing business, to introduce competition, or to establish control rights over the means of production.

Competition, adaptive efficiency, and institutional innovation

During the first phase of economic transition, reform-minded political authorities developed and maintained their capacity to foster policy and institutional measures promoting market exchange despite increasing corruption and cleavages within the CCP. In the course of time, the central government managed to credibly limit its own power through decentralization, anonymous banking, and increasing openness vis-à-vis other economies. In this context, the incentive compatibility of policymakers at the national and the subnational levels had been of particular importance.

In the absence of the rule of law and private property rights, economic growth could be propelled via increasing competition and distinct *transitional institutions* which proved viable in this particular environment. These institutions were not influenced by theoretical models, but relied rather on innovation and experimentation resulting from and reinforcing the adaptive efficiency of the country's institutional matrix (Qian 1999).

An important step in the early phase of transition was the gradual reform of the agricultural sector through the introduction of the household responsibility system (i.e. a shift from collective to individual production and ownership) and a partial liberalization of certain goods markets. This helped to restore economic incentives, to yield quickly substantial productivity gains, and to develop a nascent, but increasingly flourishing independent private sector at a time when a restructuring of the state sector was off limits especially for ideological reasons. It also increased confidence in market forces and strengthened the support of further reforms at later stages (Lee 1997). Regarding industrial restructuring, China adopted a dual-track approach which allowed to maintain parts of the planned economy for a transition period, until a possibly emerging private sector would have gained sufficient economic strength so that it can absorb surplus labor from heavy industry (Qian 2003). This approach helped to enhance economic efficiency of state-owned enterprises (SOEs), to minimize opposition to economic reforms *ex ante* (due to temporarily protected status-quo rents) and to increase the opposition to reform reversal *ex post* (due to an increasing number of people benefiting from reforms) (Lau et al. 2000). This approach was clearly compatible with a prevailing, potentially market-skeptical political ideology, and it was consistent with a gradual strategy of opening up vis-à-vis the rest of the world.

The household responsibility system and the dual-track approach to industry shifted the focus away from distributional activities and provided incentives for myriads of Chinese to engage in productive activities. As a response, numerous small economic actors emerged as independent dynamic economic entrepreneurs who (in concert) could exert effective influence on market- oriented institution building.

Decentralization, hard budget constraints, and competition

Competition on domestic markets was further strengthened and the power of the central government limited through decentralization and the emergence of a so-called system of market-preserving federalism (MPF), Chinese-style (Montinola et al. 1995). This system provided regional and local governments with relatively hard budget constraints, but also with incentives and means to conduct, largely independently of the central government, their own economic policies and to claim the residuals of so-called Township-Village Enterprises (TVEs), while the central government sought to hinder subnational governments to erect trade barriers and to preserve the common market.

Moreover, decision-making over market entry had been decentralized. This gave a considerable impetus to sub-central governments to foster the emergence of new collectively-owned and rural companies, the transactions of which were market-based, with output planning fading away. Jurisdictional autonomy in a system of MPF made territorial governments behave as entrepreneurs searching investment opportunities, taking risks, and providing capital at a time when risk markets had been largely underdeveloped (Hussain et al. 2000).

In the 1990s, when genuine private companies still played an insignificant role, TVEs contributed substantially to economic growth. Local governments were capable of protecting TVEs against ideologically motivated anti-private-property programs[17], and it was easier for TVEs to receive bank credits.[18] As TVEs were publicly owned, managers could be monitored and sanctioned by the local government, thus reducing principal-agent problems. But a major precondition for the emergence and success of TVEs was decentralization leading to market-preserving federalism.

This system established a high degree of independence from the central government because it provided local governments with authority over local economic development and gave them the right to retain most of the local tax revenues.[19] But

---

17 Che/Qian (1998a/b) argue that local governments were less likely to be expropriated than private owners as the local government used TVE rents for improving the provision of local goods. Thus, the interests between central and local governments were better aligned than the interests between the central government and private owners.

18 First, banks were exposed to less risk when lending to TVE's as the local government could bear some of the banks'risk due to cross-subsidization among its various TVEs. In addition, the fact that local governments protected the TVE's property reduced default risk. Second, local governments capitalized on their personal relationships to state-owned bank managers, see Qian (1999).

19 Qian (1999) argues that the local government founded their own business rather than taxed private businesses as it was cheaper to extract rents from the own business. Following the same argument, the central government faced difficulties to take away proceeds from TVEs; in addition, Krug/Hendrischke (2004) argue that a high amount of social capital might have facilitated the emergence of entrepeneurship in China and the absence of secure property rights.

as the ideology against private property rights became less restrictive over time, the advantages of local government ownership were reduced. Consequently, local governments transformed more and more TVEs into individual shareholdings (Che 2002).

Decentralization provided incentives and opportunities for experimentation and economic change without triggering major dislocation (Hussain et al. 2000). Thus, decentralized decision- making units facilitated the quest for development enhancing institutions and solutions to problems of transition and underdevelopment (which differed across regions). To some degree, MPF in combination with TVEs served as functional equivalent to (weak) private property rights and the missing privatization of SOEs. Competition among TVEs, between them and other companies, and between different jurisdictions fostered the emergence of market-oriented business practices, facilitated market exchange, and yielded efficiency gains in different branches of industry.

External opening up and competition

Another key characteristic of the Chinese transition process has been the gradual opening up of the economy. This did not only relate to foreign trade flows, but also to the attraction of foreign direct investment (FDI) in special economic zones (SEZs), which were considered as a core component of the overall approach to economic reform already in the late 1970s (Nee and Opper 2006). SEZs represented a transitional institution in the sense that a free-trade area or a customs union with third countries may have appeared to be more efficient from a theoretical viewpoint. Since, however, these options were politically not feasible, SEZs served as a feasible way to open up the economy and, in addition, signal the government's commitment to market-oriented reform. This was reinforced, e.g., through public infrastructure investment, low tax rates, and liberal institutions and market rules governing SEZs (Khan 2002). Eventually, SEZs proved to be an appropriate institutional innovation which allowed for economic and institutional experimentation, yet helped authorities to maintain control over the economy and provided them with feedback on the efficacy of public policy measures.

Finally, the gradual opening up of the Chinese economy, increasing its exposure to foreign competition and membership in international organizations helped to incrementally and credibly enhance reform commitment. Particularly WTO accession confirmed the government's commitment to gradually invigorate the rule of law as an additional limiting factor to its power. Moving closer to a rule-based economy, economic institutions have been more consistently enforced during the second period of transition (particularly through the privatization of SOEs and the restructuring of the financial sector). This helped to enhance authorities' credibility and reliability from the viewpoint of economic actors including foreign investors, governments, and international organizations (Ahrens/Mengeringhaus 2006).

Stock-market development

China had performed better than most other transition countries when standard measures for stock market performance are analyzed, even though the country has only slowly developed a legal framework for stock markets and showed a weak law enforcement record (Pistor and Xu 2005). Given this seeming contradiction, there must have been other governance institutions that served as a substitute for the lack of formal law (enforcement) and that were thus complementary to the wider institutional transition context in which the stock market had been embedded. Initially, China had primarily relied on an administrative governance system built around a quota system that relied on the decentralized structure of the Chinese administration (Qian/Xu 1993). This system served two important functions: It helped mitigate serious information problems that investors and regulators faced in China, and it helped local bureaucrats to select viable companies at the IPO stage. Quotas had been the basic feature of economic management and regulation in China before and during the transition period. The system was designed to allocate critical resources across regions, such as credits or energy (Pistor/Xu 2005). The annual quota for a region, i.e. the amount of shares firms were allowed to issue to the public, was set in an intense bargaining process between central and regional authorities.

The primary purpose of the central government to adapt the quota system to the stock market was to gain and maintain control over its size and stability. In practical application, however, it went far beyond that: Due to regional competition, it fostered a selection and information collection process that facilitated market development during the start-up period, because the quotas were set by the central authority drawing on the quality of the companies selected and handed in for assessment by regional governments. Regions, which performed well, were rewarded by the China Securities Regulatory Commission (CSRC) and those whose companies failed or underperformed were punished. Regions thus had an incentive to collect and reveal critical information about the real quality of companies in their area. Based on their assessment, the CSRC pre-selected companies that were allowed to enter the formal approval process. The quota system has significantly raised disclosure levels and transparency – critical factors for a functioning stock market. Of course, the system with its inherent institutions has not been built for the long-run, but must be seen as a transitional institution. Today, China has already started to abandon the system and to "grow out of" the quota system.[20] China is now strengthening its legal infrastructure and enforcement mechanisms (Lu and Yao 2003).

Towards a rule of law for elites?

While judicial institutions had been almost fully undermined and rendered ineffective under Mao Zedong, authorities in post-Mao China have sought to enhance the status of the legal system in order to strengthen the central government's legitimacy (Moustafa/Ginsburg 2009). In fact, it appears as if judicial institutions can actually enjoy some real independence from political influence. The incremental shift towards an elementary rule-based form of governance may help the political leaders to distance themselves from failures and excesses in the past, but also to more effectively institutionalize government's rule and to establish commonly agreed mechanisms of conflict resolution at relatively low transaction costs. As Landry (2009: 234) explains:

"The party facilitates the diffusion of legal knowledge among its members, as well as access to the courts. Party membership and to a lesser extent Youth League membership have a direct and positive impact on the likelihood of going to court in civil and economic cases. To the extent that one of the key goals of Chinese legal reformers is to shift the transitional burden of dispute adjudication away from the party and government agencies to more autonomous courts, party and CYL members seem to be a positive force for change. (…) the CCP enhances access to legal institutions among its members. (…) if party members receive selective benefits from these institutions, they are more likely to support them in the long run."

4. Conclusion

Developmental states constitute a distinct subgroup of emerging markets or in the terminology of North/Wallis/Weingast (2009), of mature limited access orders (LAOs). Subject to path- dependent institutional developments, confronted with country-specific exogenous constraints, and based on particular formal and informal institutional underpinnings, their political elites have faced strong incentives to credibly pursue long-term and broad based economic growth and development

---

20 See Naughton (1996), who describes China's economic reform process as an approach of "growing out of the plan". The quota system serves as one example for the pattern of Chinese reform in general. It was put in place in 1993 and officially abandoned in 2000.

strategies. In this context, (relatively) independent organizations as well as competition in the public as well as in the private sphere have often played subtle, but essential roles for formulating and implementing policies. The institutional setup and the incentives for business and political leaders have helped to mutually balance interests and thereby contributed to avoid both business capture by the state and state capture by big business.[21] Developmental states have been relatively close to the threshold to become an open access order (OAO). But this transition will not automatically occur. South Korea and Taiwan are examples for a successful transition. Singapore appears to be a case which shows that open access in many business areas may go hand in hand with persistent limited access in political realms without allowing for excessive rent creation at the expense of society.

Relatively independent economic and administrative organizations in combination with various forms and degrees of competition plus government guidance implied a country-specific nexus of transitional institutions which fulfilled functional equivalents in order to accomplish political legitimacy, to establish strong but limited states and to enhance political leaderships credible commitment to economic growth and development.

The relative autonomy of administrative organizations and private businesses in East Asia in general, and of provincial governments in China, allowed the emergence of competitive processes within the public sector for alternative policy solutions and within the private sector for innovative business solutions. Thus, decentralized searches for new or revised policies and business practices occurred, which allowed an effective exchange of information between the public and the private sector and thus yielded relatively fast feedback mechanisms on specific policy measures. This supported governments' pragmatic flexibility in policymaking and enhanced policy adaptability.

This paper argued that relatively independent institutions and organizations may exist in authoritarian regimes, because their existence serves the interests of the ruling elites. In non- democratic *developmental states*, relatively independent organizations also exist for the same reason, but they fulfill yet another function: they effectively contribute to craft relatively secure institutional foundation for long-term and broad-based economic growth and development.

---

21 See Zweynert (2010) for a discussion of state and business capture in Russia, which illustrates that Russia currently does not show the preconditions to become a developmental state.

References

Ahrens, J. (2002) Governance and Economic Development: A Comparative Institutional Approach. Cheltenham: Edward Elgar.

Ahrens, J. / Jünemann, P. (2011) Adaptive efficiency and pragmatic flexibility: characteristics of institutional change in capitalism, Chinese-style, in: W. Pascha et al. (eds.)., Institutional Variety in East Asia. Formal and Informal Patterns of Coordination, Cheltenham, UK and Northampton, MA: Edward Elgar.

Ahrens, J. / Mengeringhaus, P. (2006) Institutional Change and Economic Transition: Market-Enhancing Governance, Chinese-Style, in: European Journal of Comparative Economics Vol. 3, No. 1, pp. 75–102.

Akyüz, Y. / Chang, H.-J. / Kozul-Wright, R. (1998) New perspectives on East Asian development. Journal of Development Studies, 34 (6), 4–36.

Albrecht, H. / Frankenberger, R. (2011). Die 'dunkle Seite' der Macht: Stabilität und Wandel autoritärer Regime, in: H. Albrecht, R. Frankenberger, S. Frech (eds.), Autoritäre Regime. Herrschaftsmechanismen, Legitimationsstrategien, Persistenz und Wandel. Schwalbach/Ts.: Wochenschau Verlag.

Amsden, A.H. (1995) Like the Rest: Southeast Asia's 'late' industrialization, in: Journal of International Development Vol. 7, No. 5, pp. 791–799.

Aoki, M. / Murdock, K. / Okuno-Fujiwara, M. (1997) Beyond the East Asian miracle: Introducing the market-enhancing view, in: M. Aoki, H.-K. Kim and M. Okuno-Fujiwara (eds.). The role of government in East Asian economic development: Comparative institutional analysis. Oxford: Oxford University Press, pp. 1–37.

Bardhan, P.K. (2010) The paradigm of capitalism under a developmental state: does it fit China and India?, in: Singapore Economic Review Vol. 55, No. 2, pp. 243–251.

Beeson, M. (2009) Developmental States in East Asia: A Comparison of the Japanese and Chinese Experiences, in: Asian Perspective Vol. 33, No. 2, pp. 5–39.

Beeson, M. (2007) Regionalism, Globalization and East Asia: Politics, Security and Economic Development. Basingstoke: Palgrave.

Campos, J.E. / Root, H. (1996) The Key to the Asian Miracle: Making Shared Growth Credible, Washington, DC.

Che, J. (2002) Rent Seeking and Government Ownership of Firms: An Application to China's Township-Village Enterprises, William Davidson Working Paper Number 497, online: http://www.bus.umich.edu/KresgeLibrary/Collections/Workingpapers/wdi/wp497.pdf, retrieved January 10, 2006.

Che, J. / Qian, Y. (1998a) Insecure Property Rights and Government Ownership of Firms, in: Quarterly Journal of Economics Vol. 113, No.2, pp. 467–496.

Che, J. / Qian, Y. (1998b) Institutional Environment, Community Government, and Corporate Governance: Understanding China's Township-Village Enterprises, in: Journal of Law, Economics, and Organization Vol. 14, No.1, pp. 1–23.

Chang, H.-J. (1999) The Economic Theory of the Developmental State, in: M. Woo-Cumings (ed.), The Developmental State (pp. 182–199), Ithaca and London: Cornell University Press.

Cheng, T.-J. / Haggard, S. / Kang, D. (1998) Institutions and growth in Korea and Taiwan: the Bureaucracy. Journal of Development Studies Vol. 34, No. 6, pp. 87–111.

Doner, R.F. / Bryan, K. / Slater, D. (2005) Systemic Vulnerability and the Origins of Developmental States: Northeast and Southeast Asia in comparative perspective, in: International Organization Vol. 59, pp. 327–361.

Evans, P. (1998) Transferable lessons? Re-examining the institutional prerequisites of East Asian economic policies, in: Journal of Development Studies Vol. 34(6), pp. 66–86.

Evans, P. (1995) Embedded Autonomy: States & Industrial Transformation, Princeton, NJ: Princeton University Press.

Evans, P. (1992) The State as Problem and Solution: Predation, Embedded Autonomy, and Structural Change, in: S. Haggard and R.R. Kaufman (eds.) (1992), The Politics of Economic Adjustment. International Constraints, Distributive Conflicts, and the State. Princeton, NJ: Princeton University Press.

Gilley, B. (2008) Legitimacy and Institutional Change: The Case of China, Comparative Political Studies Vol. 41, No. 3, pp. 259–284.

Haggard, S. (2004) Institutions and Growth in East Asia, Studies in Comparative International Development Vol. 38, No. 4.

Heilmann, S. (1998) Die marktinduzierte Transformation eines leninistischen Staates, in: W. Merkel and E. Sandschneider (eds.). Systemwechsel IV: Die Rolle von Verbänden im Transformationsprozeß. Opladen: Leske Budrich, pp. 279–328.

Heine, K. / Mause, K. (2012) Delegation und demokratische Kontrolle: Können Behörden politisch zu unabhängig sein? Manuskript vorgetragen auf der Jahrestagung des Ausschusses für Wirtschaftssysteme und Institutionenökonomik, Jena, 23.–25. September 2012.

Herring, R.J. (1999) Embedded Particularism: India's Failed Developmental State, in: M. Woo-Cumings (ed.): The Developmental State, Ithaca and London: Cornell University Press

Hussain, A. / Stern, N. / Stiglitz, J. (2000) Chinese reforms from a comparative perspective, in: P.J. Hammond and G.D. Miles (eds.). Incentives, organization, and public economics: papers in honour of Sir James Mirrlees. Oxford: Oxford University Press, pp. 243–277.

Johnson, C. (1982) MITI and the Japanese Miracle. The Growth of Industrial Policy, 1925–75, Stanford.

Johnson, C. (1986) The nonsocialist NICs: East Asia. International Organization, 40 (2) Spring, pp. 557–565.

Johnson, C. (1987) Political institutions and economic performance: the government–business relationship in Japan, South Korea, and Taiwan, in: F.C. Doyo (ed.), The Political Economy of the New Asian Industrialism (pp. 136–164), Ithaca.

Johnson, C. (1999) The Developmental State: Odyssey of a Concept. In: M. Woo-Cumings (ed.), The Developmental State. Ithaca and London: Cornell University Press, pp. 32–60.

Khan, M.H. (2002) State Failure in Developing Countries and Strategies of Institutional Reform. Paper presented at the ABCDE Conference Europe, Oslo 2002.

Kohli, A. (1999) Where Do High-Growth Policies Come From? The Japanese Lineage of Korea's "Developmental State", in: M. Woo-Cumings (ed.) The Developmental State, Cornell University Press.

Kohli, A. (2004) State-Directed Development. New York: Cambridge University Press.

Krug, B. / Hendrischke, H. (2004) Entrepreneurship in Transition: Searching for Governance in China's New Private Sector, Discussion Paper ERS-2004–008-ORG. Rotterdam, Erasmus Research Institute for Management.

Kruse, J. (2012) Unabhängige staatliche Institutionen: Funktionalität und demokratische Legitimation. Manuskript vorgetragen auf der Jahrestagung des Ausschusses für Wirtschaftssysteme und Institutionenökonomik, Jena, 23.–25. September 2012.

Landry, P. (2009) The Institutional Diffusion of Courts in China: Evidence from Survey Data, in: T. Ginsburg and T. Moustafa (eds.) Rule by Law. The Politics of Courts in Authoritarian Regime, Cambridge, UK: Cambridge University Press, pp. 207–234.

Lau, L.J. / Qian, Y. / Roland, G. (2000) Reform without Losers: An Interpretation of China's Dual-Track Approach to Transition, in: Journal of Political Economy Vol. 108, No. 1, pp. 120–143.

Lee, D. (1997) Lessons of Transition Economies' Reform for North Korea, in: D. Lee (ed.) The System Transformation of the Transition Economies. Europe, Asia and North Korea, Seoul: Yonsei University Press, pp. 183–232.

Leftwich, A. (1995) Bringing politics back in: Toward a model of the developmental state, in: The Journal of Development Studies Vol. 31, No. 3, pp. 400–427.

Li, S. / Lian, P. (1999) Decentralization and coordination: China's credible commitment to preserve the market under authoritarianism, China Economic Review Vol. 10, pp. 161–190.

Lu, S.F. / Yao, Y. (2003) The Effectiveness of the Law, Financial Development, and Economic Growth in an Economy of Financial Depression: Evidence from China, Stanford Center for Research on Economic Development and Policy Reform, Working Paper No. 179, online: http://scid.stanford.edu/pdf/credpr179.pdf, retrieved January 14, 2006.

Meyns, P. / Musamba, C. (eds.) (2010) The developmental state in Africa: problems and prospects. Duisburg: Institute for Development and Peace: INEF Report 101.

Minns, J. (2001) Of Miracles and Models: The Rise and Decline of the Developmental State in South Korea. Third World Quarterly Vol. 22, No. 6, pp. 1025–1043.

Montinola, G. / Qian, Y. / Weingast, B.R. (1995) Federalism Chinese Style – The Political Basis for Economic Success in China, in: World Politics Vol. 48, No. 1, pp. 50–81.

Naughton, B. (1996) Growing Out of the Plan – Chinese Economic Reform 1978 – 1993, Cambridge, UK.

Nee, V. / Opper, S. (2006) On Politicized Capitalism. Paper presented at the Annual Conference of the International Society of New Institutional Economics in Boulder, CO, 21–24 September 2006; online: www.isnie.org/ISNIE06/06.3/opper.pdf, retrieved February 15, 2009.

Maddison, A. (2010) Statistics on world population, GDP and per capita GDP, 1–2008 AD, online: http://www.ggdc.net/MADDISON/oriindex.htm, retrieved July 19, 2011.

Moustafa, T. / Ginsburg, T. (2009) Introduction: The Functions of Courts in Authoritarian Politics, in: T. Ginsburg and T. Moustafa (eds.) Rule by Law. The Politics of Courts in Authoritarian Regime, Cambridge, UK: Cambridge University Press, pp. 1–22.

North, D.C. / Wallis, J.J. / Weingast, B.R. (2009) Violence and Social Orders. A Conceptual Framework for Interpreting Recorded Human History. New York, NY: Cambridge University Press.

Pempel, T. J. (1999) The Developmental Regime in a Changing World Economy, in: M. Woo-Cumings (ed.): The Developmental State. Ithaca and London: Cornell University Press, pp. 137–181.

Pistor, K. / Xu, C. (2005) Governing Stock Markets in Transition Economies: Lessons from China, in: American Law and Economics Review Vol. 7, No. 1, pp. 184–210.

Qian, Yingyi (1999) The Institutional Foundations of China's Market Transition, Stanford University, online: http://www.econ.stanford.edu/faculty/workp/swp99011.pdf, retrieved January 5, 2006.

Qian, Y. (2003) How Reform Worked in China, in: D. Rodrik et al. (eds.) In Search of Prosperity, Analytical Narratives on Economic Growth, New Jersey, pp. 297–333.

Qian, Y. / Weingast, B.R. (1997) Institutions, State Activism, and Economic Development: A Comparison of State-Owned and Township-Village Enterprises in China, in: M. Aoki, H.-K. Kim and M. Okuno-Fujiwara (eds.) The Role of Government in East Asian Economic Development. Comparative Institutional Analysis (pp. 254–275), Oxford.

Qian, Y. / Xu, C. (1993) Why China's Economic Reforms Differ: The M-form Hierarchy and Entry/Expansion of the Non–State Sector, Economics of Transition, 1(2), pp. 135–170.

Root, H.L. (1998) Distinctive institutions in the rise of industrial Asia, in: H.S. Rowen (ed.) Behind East Asian growth: the political and social foundations of prosperity. London and New York: Routledge, pp. 60–77.

Root, H.L. (1996) Small Countries, Big Lessons. Governance and the Rise of East Asia, Hong Kong: Oxford University Press.

Root, H.L. / May, K. (2009) Judicial Systems and Economic Development, in: T. Ginsburg and T. Moustafa (eds.) Rule by Law. The Politics of Courts in Authoritarian Regime, Cambridge, UK: Cambridge University Press, pp. 304–325.

Sasada, H. (2013) The evolution of the Japanese developmental state: institutions locked in by ideas. London: Routledge.

Shin, J.S. (2005) Globalization and Challenges to the Developmental State: A Comparison between South Korea and Singapore. Global Economic Review, 34, pp. 379–395.

Silverstein, G. (2009) Singapore: The Exception That Proves Rules Matter, in: T. Ginsburg and T. Moustafa (eds.), Rule by Law. The Politics of Courts in Authoritarian Regime, Cambridge, UK: Cambridge University Press, pp.73–101.

Song, H.-Y. (2011) The Korean developmental state and its neoliberal transition in the world system, in: P. Manning and B.K. Gills (eds.), Andrew Gunder Frank and global development: visions, remembrances, and explorations. London: Routledge, pp. 211–231.

Stark, M. (2012) The Emergence of Developmental States from a New Institutionalist Perspective: A Comparative Analysis of East Asia and Central Asia. Frankfurt/Main: Peter Lang Verlag (in press).

Stark, M. (2010) The East Asian developmental state as a reference model for transition economies in Central Asia – an analysis of institutional arrangements and exogeneous constraints, Economic and Environmental Studies Vol. 10, No. 2.

Stiglitz, J.E. (1996) Some lessons from the East Asian miracle, The World Bank Research Observer Vol. 11, No. 2, pp. 151–177.

Theurl, T. (ed.) (2013) Unabhängige Staatliche Institutionen in der Demokratie, Schriften des Vereins für Socialpolitik Bd. 337, Berlin: Duncker&Humblot.

Thompson, M. (1996) Late industrialisers, late democratisers: developmental states in the Asia-Pacific. Third World Quarterly Vol. 17, No. 4, pp. 625–647.

Wade, R. (1990) Governing the Market: Economic Theory and the Role of Government in East Asian Industrialization, Princeton and Oxford.

Weber, M. (1921/1972) Wirtschaft und Gesellschaft. Grundriss der verstehenden Soziologie, Tübingen.

Woo-Cumings, M. (ed.) (1999) The Developmental State, Ithaca and London: Cornell University Press.

World Bank (1993) The East Asian Miracle: Economic Growth and Public Policy, Oxford et al.

World Bank (1997) World Development Report 1997. The State in a Changing World, Oxford et al.

Zweynert, J. (2010) Business Capture und die Finanz- und Wirtschaftskrise in Russland, in: T. Theurl et al. (ed.), Institutionelle Hintergründe von Krisen, Schriften des Vereinsfür Socialpolitik N.F. 332, Berlin: Duncker & Humblot, pp. 69–87.

Erik Terk

Practicing Catching-up: a Comparison of Development Models of East Asian and Central-Eastern European Countries

1. Introduction

This article makes an attempt to compare the development patterns of the economies of the East Asian and Central and Eastern European (CEE) regions, which have been the fastest in catching up on the global arena. It observes both the internal features of the economies and economic policies and the parameters characterising their relation with the international background (openness, integration). he statistical materials used have been taken mostly from the World Economic Forum competitiveness reports and from the WB and IMF sources, while the descriptions of economic policy and its dynamic are based on materials concerning the regions under discussion and their individual countries. The goal of the article is not to reach conclusions characterising the behaviour of the economies of the entire East Asian or CEE regions, but the economic development models, specific features, development and performing of countries, which have displayed top performance in either region and have reached the level of developed economies.

There is no reason to presume that such definition of goal would allow for the determination of the features of a common model of success; there can be several successful models. Yet both the similarities and differences should provide materials for discussions on the economic policies of individual countries and contribute to further development of the general theoretical background of the treatment of catching up. A considerable problem in the detailing of the task of study was caused by the fact that the economic growth cycles of the countries under observation do not coincide in time.

In case of some East Asian countries we can speak of rapid growth lasting even more than 50 years with only minor setbacks (the beginning of sustainable economic growth in Taiwan dates back to 1958, in South Korea to 1978/79 and in Singapore to 1965) (Hermes 997). In case of the CEE countries a change of political and economic regime occurred at the turn of the 1980s-1990s with significant setbacks in the volume of GDP; in their case we can speak of a growth cycle not longer than 20 years. Therefore the selection of the CEE regional champions was not based exclusively on economic growth rate, but also considered the index of quality of economic transition (containing economic, social political and governance-related components) and the economic competitiveness rankings in the latter years of the period under observation.

The article has been structured as follows. It opens with a description of the general catching-up situation. This is followed by a brief review of theoretical backgrounds related to the catching up subject. Further we present a general scheme for carrying out the comparison, dwell briefly on either region's special features, and then analyse the individual countries according to common criteria. Among the selected criteria especial attention is these considered crucial for success in the innovation-based economic development stage. (see Porter 1990)

The article is concluded by a summary outlining the common features and differences of the economic development models of the two groups of countries analysed.

2. The Catching-Up Phenomenon and its Treatment

Although the present time is characterised by an increasing internationalisation/globalisation of economy and great opportunities are predicted to countries participating in international economy, including those initially less wealthy (the latecomer advantage), the number of countries, which have actually succeeded in reaching high development levels from modest starting positions, is quite limited, especially if we exclude the oil based economies. When observing the entire period since the end of WW2 until present day, the latecomers making it to the developed economies certainly include the so-called minor Asian tigers, which have been riding on Japan's coattails: Taiwan, South Korea, Singapore and Hong Kong. Whether Japan itself can be included in this group is questionable – its economy was in a miserable state after the war, but the same cannot be said about the 1930s. The People's Republic of China, although it has seen rapid economic growth in the past decades, cannot be described a developed economy as yet when considering the country as a whole rather than some of its coastal regions. If we conditionally consider as developed economies those with GDP per capita adjusted with PPP approaching at least 20.000 USD – roughly the economies among the world's 50–60 wealthiest – the "tigers" like Thailand and Malaysia cannot be included among developed economies. No suitable example of growth can be found in the American continent. Chile stands out as to its economic growth against the general background, yet its level of economic development does not meet the above criterion for the time being. In Europe, Ireland, Finland and Spain can be viewed as newcomers among the highly developed economies, but these countries launched their rising trajectory from a higher starting position. The final region, where highly developed economies can be looked for, is the post-socialist economies of central and Eastern Europe (CEE). Candidates for such economies could be the countries, which more than doubled their GDP during the decade and half preceding the latest international economic (financial) crisis: Slovenia, the Czech Republic, Poland, Slovakia, Hungary, Estonia, and Lithuania. (Russia, whose economic growth has been relatively fast as well, should be included among the oil based economies). With the exception of Slovenia they have narrowly crossed the lower bar of the "league of wealthy economies".

Accordingly, only some 10–15 economies of the world can be considered catching-up champions, dependent on the strictness of criteria, with a clear majority belonging to East Asia and CEE. While extensive literature covers the growth economies of either region, East Asia and CEE separately, there is a dearth of studies attempting to generalize the success experience of both regions. Even in cases where this has been done, the authors are rather careful in recommending one region's development experience to the other[1]. The reason is obviously the difference of development contexts in these regions, while at least a partial cause is also the peculiarity of the corresponding general theoretical framework. The mainstream economists have been generally having trouble interpreting the East Asian economic success. They tried to interpret it for a long time as a triumph of market ideology and export orientation, while turning a blind eye to the peculiar features of the region's practice compared to the traditional economic theories and economic policy postulates. When it was no longer possible after researchers like Amsden (Amsden 1989) and Wade (Wade 1990) clearly outlined the region's economic models' specific characteristics, they tended to interpret the peculiarity as a temporary deviation due to culture and path dependence, which would be eliminated in time (the so-called Asian crisis of the second half of the 1990s provided some basis for such beliefs).

However, often there were honest admissions as in the article by the IMF economist M. Sarel: "Everyone agrees that the economies of the East Asia, and particularly the Four Tigers, have grown spectacularly over the past generation, but nobody seems to agree on why." (Sarel 1996).

The theoretical concepts for the treatment of the CEE economic development after their leaving behind the communist past and the corresponding recommendations, the economic transition theory, were drafted in the end of the 1980s and the beginning of the 1990s. It was based on mainstream economics and

---

1   They are bolder in recommending the East Asian experience to central Asian countries (e.g. see Stark 2010).

considering the experience of macroeconomic regulation gained in Latin America in the 1980s. However, the theory gave setbacks in its practical implementation, especially regarding Russia, and needed ongoing regulation, especially towards greater significance of the development of institutions. One could stare about the more successful transition economies that by the turn of the century at the latest they had already completed the standard tasks required by the treatment of transition – i.e. the compulsory programme. The 2000s are also characterised by attempts to apply the treatment of varieties of capitalism (Hall/Soskice 2001) to the CEE economies, within which it was claimed that at least some more extreme examples like Slovenia and Estonia have adopted principally different paths in developing mature market economy (see Norkus 2012).

A common framework for understanding the problems of different regions' economies in catching up with the developed economies and the options for solving them could be provided in principle by the theory of development economics. However, there is the difficulty that although the basics of development economics were created during WW2 specifically in consideration of the expected requirements of the CEE countries after the war, it was later further elaborated, considering particularly the specifics and needs of developing countries (high share of rural population, low education level, needs for industrialisation etc.). While this situation could have been typical of, for example, South Korea of the late 1950s and early 1960s, it certainly does not characterise the advanced East Asian economies of the present period nor the CEE countries under discussion. It seems that instead of further elaboration of development economics in relation to the needs of more highly advanced growth economies, we should rather discuss new institutional economics as a branch of science, which today attempts to interpret the situations and challenges of "tiger economies".

3. Constructing the Sample of 3+3

Out of the East Asian growth champions we have selected three countries for further detailed study: Taiwan, South Korea and Singapore. The inclusion of Japan in the sample would not have been practical as its economic growth period began significantly earlier than that of the others while Japan has not displayed spectacular growth recently. Hong Kong, after its transfer to China, can be viewed, despite the continuing economic and political special regime, not as a country leading traditional economic policy but rather as a specific connecting element between the People's Republic of China and world economy. Therefore it cannot be easily compared to other countries on the same basis. The remaining East Asian countries cannot claim inclusion in the sample due to their too low per capita

GDP. It can be argued that they have not yet reached the same stage of economic development where either region's countries included in the sample have been for the past couple of decades.

Picking the CEE economies for the sample, however, was more difficult that the selection of the East Asian trio, since the region contains a significantly larger number of countries with relatively high growth rate during the past two decades and the differences between their success indicators are not large. The volatility of macroeconomic indicators caused by the latest economic crisis further complicates the task. Considering, as mentioned above, three indicators, namely the rate of economic growth, the index of success in accomplishing transformation and the competitiveness index of the period's final years, three countries made the grade: Slovenia, the Czech Republic and Estonia. The comparison of the success indicators of these three countries and the East Asian countries can be found in Table 1. The omission of the countries was determined, in Lithuania's case, by the slightly lower economic growth rate, in Slovakia's case the low competitiveness index, while in Hungary's case both the growth rate and competitiveness index were lower, although the gap was not too wide. As for the complex index of accomplishing transformation, it was significantly higher in Slovenia, the Czech Republic and Estonia as compared to their rivals. This became decisive in the selection of Slovenia. Although Slovenia displayed higher per capita GDP level than the others and had enjoyed success for most of the past couple of decades, it faced a macro-economically difficult situation at the end of the period, which also lowered its competitiveness ratings.

Table 1: Basic parameters of development background, state of economy and dynamism of the analysed countries

	South Korea	Taiwan	Singapore	Slovenia	Czech Rep.	Estonia
Population (mio.)	48	23	4.6	2	10	1.3
Ethnic diversity	Extremely low	Majority han Chinese, but arrivals from mainland (1949) differ somewhat	Very high, different large ethnic groups	Relatively low	Moderate	Quite high share of non-ethnic Estonian residents due to Soviet regime

	South Korea	Taiwan	Singapore	Slovenia	Czech Rep.	Estonia
Statehood	Emerged as result of the Korean war (1950–1953) in the southern part of the country	Emerged in 1949 as a result of the civil war in China (officially Republic of China, not recognised by most countries)	Became independent of the Malaysian Federation in 1965	Became independent of former Yugoslavia in 1991	Emerged with the break-up of Czechoslo-vakia in the beginning of 1993	Independence restored in 1991
Start of sustainnable growth cycle in economy	1978–1979	1958	1965	1993–1994	1995	1993–1994
Participation in intl. economic blocks and trading agreements	WTO from 1995; FTA with USA from 2011	WTO from 2002; FTA negotations with USA	ASEAN from 1965; FTA with USA from 2004	WTO from 1995; EU from 2004; Eurozone from 2007	WTO from 1995; EU from 2004	WTO from 1999; EU from 2004; Eurozone from 2011
Per capita GDP in 2012 (PPP) (thousands of USD)	32.0	38.6	60.8	27.9	27.0	21.7
Per capita GDP growth 1993–2007	2.8X	2.5X	2.6X	2.7X	2.4X	3.1X
Coping with inter-national cri-sis starting from year 2008	Zero growth 2009, moderate growth restored in next years	Small decline in 2009, fast restoration of growth, but slowing down later	Minor decline of growth in 2009, fast restoration, but slowing down later	Steep fall 2009, followed by zero and low negative growth	Moderate fall in 2009, followed by low growth or small decline	Very steep fall in 2008–2009; followed by fast restoration of growth, later unstable growth

	South Korea	Taiwan	Singapore	Slovenia	Czech Rep.	Estonia
Share of industry in GDP	Very high (40%)	Moderate (30%)	Moderate (27%)	Moderate (27–28%)	High (38%)	Moderate (30%)
Dynamics of competitiveness index ranking of countries 2004–2012	positive: 29 => 25	negative: 4 => 12	positive: 7 => 2	highly negative: 33 => 62	negative: 40 => 46	negative: 20 => 32

All the countries in the sample were dealing with not only achieving economic growth, but also with developing their statehood, albeit in diverse conditions and during different periods. Significant changes in the political environment concerned all these countries as well. It is true that the political dynamic has been different in the CEE and East Asian countries. The first group saw at the end of the 1990s a rapid transition to multi-party democracy, while the East Asian countries during their first development period were characterised by authoritarian political regimes, yet the political regions of these countries has significantly democratised by the early 1990s. The building and reinforcement of statehood, in case of some countries in somewhat hazardous international environment, must also have been an important background factor for the national/social mobilisation necessary for economic development.

When interpreting the indicators in the table we should keep in mind that the initial level of the Singaporean economy as of 1993 was significantly higher than that of the others. The growth rates of all six countries in the 1993–2007 period can be considered relatively similar. Estonia's higher indicator can be partly explained by the fact that the country experienced a very steep fall of GDP in 1990–1993 due to the regime change, much steeper than Slovenia or the Czech Republic, and the following growth began from a lower starting level compared to the other countries. More significant differences could be found in the dynamics of competitiveness

4. Market Competition-based Approach and its Limitations

The subject of latecomer catching-up is by its nature interdisciplinary. It uses treatment schemes of economics, political science and sociology, while different emphases have dominated in different periods. Sociological approaches were quite popular on that subject in the 1960s and early 1970s. The concepts of integrative

society and functional elites were developed. Many debates were held on the opportunities of development planning. The attention was focused, in the development planning and broader contexts, on the replacement of the traditional
elites (in developing countries the large landowners as a rule) by responsible bureaucracy, representatives of modern spheres of entrepreneurship, managers and
experts, assuming that these would be more capable of representing the national
interests. It was presumed that the new elite would be able to choose between the
various strategies for economic development; a classical example was the debate
over whether a country should concentrate on narrower breakthrough areas in
order to succeed in the international economy, or attempt to advance on a wide
front. The predominant paradigm of theoretical treatment changed starting from
the end of the 1970s and in the 1980s. In connection with globalisation the approach became significantly more economy- and especially market-centred with
the problem being viewed predominantly through the prism of adjusting to the
international market environment. Other factors were moved to background. If
the political aspects of the issue were addressed, besides the economic ones, these
were viewed as the paradigm of egoistic competition between various stakeholders rather than that of realisation of national interests. This approach has been
practiced for more than 30 years by now and a number of empirical studies have
been carried out under it.

Seeking to comprehend the behaviour of states (economies) in the increasingly globalising environment, economists have carried out comparative studies
focusing specifically on the categories of openness and mobility, which attempt to
observe the response to changes by private actors and the public sector (the state)
and the ties between these responses. Such studies usually attempt to operate with
a rather limited number of factors and expect to find some clear patterns in their
interplay. The approach is usually emphatically market-centred. The central issues
of these studies are, primarily, the response of firms, especially those operating
internationally, to the tax situation of one country or another; secondly, the response of less dynamic factor of labour to the wage differences between countries.
In case of the states the studies primarily observe their reaction to the flight of
capital due to excessive taxation, their rapidity of receiving the disciplining signals
of the market and responding to those (response is in most cases perceived as
the curbing of the public sector spending, reduction of red tape and the lowering
of taxes), as well as the implementation of active tax policy, i.e. inventing tax
manipulations so as to attract desirable capital. Despite the general principle that
labour as a whole is less mobile than capital, there is an increasing recognition
of the need for measures allowing to win over the more mobile part of labour,

the global common, by salary, taxation of the individual or other means, to buy its loyalty. For example, economists have concluded that the higher the concentration if power in a state, the faster and more efficient is the feedback between investments and politics. The high share of backward sectors in the state is seen as a major obstacle; their significance (possible social and political risks related to such sectors) prevents the politicians from responding to the market signals with the necessary flexibility.[2]

If the combination of factors described above were actually predominant in the world, it would mean a "race to the bottom" regarding the administrative and social expenses and a global levelling of economic conditions, where the only differences would be the rapidity and success of adjustment of individual countries.

It is true that economists admit the existence of some factors complicating the situation. They accept that in case of investing in a country capital is interested in the level of the corresponding technical infrastructure, the education level of labour (at least basic education) and the efficiency of the institutions important for business environment. Improving these conditions is largely the task of the state. Economists have to accept that for example the taxation level of a state and the development standards of the institutions tend to have positive correlation. It is also argued that some peculiarities of the target market or the agglomeration effect may be so influential that they could outweigh for the capital the simple arguments based on tax competition. In some cases when analysing the impact of globalisation attempts were made to extend the composition of markets under observation by covering both the economic and political markets (in the public choice theory sense) and by differentiating in both cases between the domestic and foreign markets (for details see Libman 2007: 17–18). In such a case we would discuss, besides the domestic and foreign market of goods and production factors (commodities, investments and labour market) the domestic political market and the international market of harmonisation and integration projects. In the domestic political market the central issues are those of taxes, protectionism and support to various groups of the population. Traditionally the influence of the conflicts and negotiations between the social-democratic and liberal parties is emphasised here as the central mechanism, which helps to create a certain balance between the business efficiency motives on the one hand and the attempts

---

2   Among the countries observed in our article, the then agrarian South Korea and Taiwan faced that problem in the initial stage of their growth cycle, but both were able to solve it by introducing agrarian reforms. The problem of the European post-socialist countries was rather the excessive industrialisation as they needed to get rid of a large share of outdated industry of the state socialist era.

to protect certain groups of population against market impacts considered too destructive on the other hand. It is also admitted, however, that the weakening of this balancing mechanism can be observed recently as the major parties' positions have drawn closer over the above issues and the parties tend to display cartel-type behaviour.

Some authors supporting emphatically market economy positions have also expressed the opinion that great powers can still possess some strategic manoeuvring space in the environment of globalisation; they are able to develop some specific infrastructural and institutional structure of preparing for economic growth, while smaller nations with population below 20 million lack such opportunities (Gaidar 1997: 317–318). If their existing traditions favour the emergence of national entrepreneurial sector and their citizens manage to spare and invest their income instead of spending it all on consumption, they would be able to exploit the opportunities emerging in the international markets and possess a chance of reaching decent economic growth; otherwise they would be doomed to the misery of "stagnation poverty". Y. Gaidar tries to cheer up the smaller countries by claiming that their choices are straightforward. The great powers' space for strategic choices is wider, but they are also facing greater opportunities for making fatal errors and get bogged down in market restriction and excessive state activism. However, it can be stated by now that although the approach based on adjustment to international markets brought new important aspects to the theory, the explanation capacity had been lower than expected. It is being increasingly emphasised, especially based on the East Asian experience, that besides the ability to adjust to markets, coordination of long-term policy efforts towards development is also significant. Proceeding from more advanced ideas of the social premises of economic development and the potential of institutional regulation, a search for the opportunities for creating such coordination mechanisms is going on.

Since this article discusses small relatively open economies, which are located in two highly different geographical regions and are quite diverse, but have all managed to adjust rather successfully to the conditions of international market, we can presume that the results of comparative analysis can shed new light on issues like the mobility of industrial factors, mechanisms of adjustment of economies and the accompanying dynamics of competitiveness.

5. Theories Describing Development Planning, Coordination and State Activism

Theories, which consider the adjustment to market strategy insufficient in the interpretation of the catching up phenomenon, have operated with keywords like social mobilisation/collective mobilisation, modernisation management, developmental state, neo-corporatism, varieties of capitalism. A. Gerschenkron, one of the classics of economics theory, comparatively studied the countries, which could be considered early industrialisers or latecomers to industrialisation and found out that the latecomers must make specific efforts and use specific solutions in order to successfully catch up with the already launched and ongoing process (Gerschenkron 1962). Paying the costs of development thus calls the actual collective mobilisation, which in turn requires greater central coordination. Such collective mobilisation primarily presumes the very setting of the (imperative) goal of catching up, advancing a concept necessary for its realisation, the concentration of resources, which presumes the forming of the facilitating mechanism, paying attention to the building of infrastructure and the training of labour and creating the political and social conditions allowing for accumulation (Palan et al. 1999).

Viewed from the position of methodological individualism prevailing in mainstream economics approach, introducing the category **of social mobilisation** to development economics is a move not readily accepted. Achieving quite long-term agreement between a large number of actors with individual interests seems barely credible from that viewpoint. This contradiction can be explained to some extent by the fact that social mobilisation often occurs as a national-level mobilisation involving the entire ethnos. "Belonging to a definite nation can /.../ be regarded as a factor cementing the relationship between what is and what should be", as M. C. Botez and M. Celac define it (1986). Within a nation-state, the political will can be mobilized for attaining collective goals derived from abstract societal images of the future. The impetus can be provided by the gaining of independence by a state, the related surge of motivation, as well as an outward challenge to the nation/ethnos or any other realisation of the criticality of the situation. All that may contribute to the curbing of excessive domination of particular interests and acceptance of the state's coordinating role (developmental state, the competition state). In order to the motivation effect and mobilisation effect to emerge there must exist a sufficiently attractive desirable image of national development, formulated by the elite, which then can be detailed and perpetuated in a more or less democratic national dialogue.

Botez and Celac underline that this process cannot be treated proceeding from the primitive design-oriented approach: a) to imagine the desired state (not merely at the mechanisms level, but as a desirable objective state), b) to design and implement the necessary means in order to attain the given goals. Such approach may be suitable for performing some narrower goals, but in case of the economy or the society as a whole there will inevitably emerge a need for adjusting the goals or transitioning from performing the tasks of one development stage to those of the next. These transitions are always crucial as they reveal, whether the continuation of the catching-up policy can be ensured or the success would remain only temporary.

Although the use of the term "social mobilisation" in connection with the modernisation of economy has a rather long history, modern social scientists treat it with considerable caution, especially when emphatically national mobilisation is concerned. This attitude is caused by the fear that models of government and power structures emerging that way could mean the emergence of authoritarian and totalitarian regimes, the spreading of chauvinistic attitudes etc. It is true that the industrialisation latecomers studied by Gerschenkron, Germany, Japan and Russia, became troublemakers in the international stage. Yet social mobilisation on national basis in the reconstruction of post-war economy can be observed in highly pro-democratic countries like in Scandinavia and in a highly positive sense. Without discussing this phenomenon we would find it hard to understand the Irish so-called economic miracle, which began in the 1960s, or the economic rise of the East Asian countries.

It must be emphasised that although development planning from the viewpoint of the state as a whole is more topical in case of the East Asian countries compared to "regular capitalist economies", such activity should not be equated to state planning previously practices in the communist countries or the long-term economic development plans used in some developing countries like India of the 1950s–1960s. The East Asian threesome's case was rather one of focused policy for forming breakthrough sectors, which could compete in the international economy and creating necessary conditions for these sectors within the country (or outside, e.g. the development of the country's brand). Such approach requires visionary strategic thinking, the development of corresponding policies and implements and capability in their realisation. At the same time it must be quite flexible, able to adjust to the changes of foreign markets as well as the needs of different stages of development.

When discussing the role of the state in the preparation and realisation of an economic growth leap, we cannot ignore the term of **developmental state.** This term was brought to scientific use in respect to Japan by Chalmers Johnson (Johnson 1982). The term designates not just state interference with economy, but a type of policy directed to the contribution to the emergence of economic growth and new perspective economic sectors or clusters, e.g. high-tech sectors, by using corresponding policy instruments. (Woo-Cumings 1999). In this sense the developmental state is contrasted not only to the predatory state, or the weak state, but also to the regulatory state, which does focus on various types of economic regulation via its agencies, but does not possess the ambition to accelerate specifically economic growth and to make corresponding choices.

It is especially the East Asian countries, which are described in literature as typical developmental states, although elements of this type of state have been identified also in countries on other continents: Ireland, some African and Latin American countries. It is theoretically an extremely intriguing question whether the developmental state will remain only a regional phenomenon or whether this model or its close variation would become a development economic alternative of broader significance. A restrictive factor is that this model requires from those preparing for its implementation both high qualification and motivation to act in the interests of the country as a whole, rather than individual stakeholders, as well as the presence of strong political support and determination from those implementing the policy.

The above is closely related to the issue of **industrial policy** as a tool for developing economy. Economic development implies structural transformation. Productivity varies across activities, a country's development potential and accordingly the potential to catch up are largely dependent on what it produces and sells in the world market. Market fundamental approaches proceed from the idea that such choices should be made exclusively by the entrepreneurs based on market signals. But there exists another point of view arguing that the countries keen on rising in the value chain need selective policies intended to promote specific industries. Part of the process of the structural transformation and technological improvement is autonomous and may be facilitated and promoted by the market as investors seek out profitable opportunities. But this may be too slow a process in relation to a country's own growth aspirations or in relation to technological improvements occurring elsewhere. Government intervention becomes necessary when competition alone does not propel business firms to innovate and undertake productivity enhancing investments (Irfan ul Haque 2007). The success of Japan and the subsequent growth tigers is one of the basic arguments of the champions of the latter position, and, in a somewhat simplified manner, the developmental state has been defined as a state implementing industrial policy.

The popularity and acceptance of industrial policy in the toolbox of economic policies has greatly varied over time. It used to be a quite prestigious field of policy in the post-war years, but the situation changed with the beginning of the 1980s. As Rodrik (2004) points out: "The reality is that industrial policies run rampant during the last two decades – and nowhere more than in those economies that have steadfastly adopted the agenda of orthodox reform." Authors promoting industrial policy like Rodrik and Chang consider this situation strange, since in their opinion industrial policy had given positive results in East Asian and several other countries, and, furthermore, it would be hard to find any country in the practice of latest decades, which has achieved notable success in economic development without its government leading active development policy and promoting industry (Rodrik 2004; Chang, H.-J. 2002).

It seems that a new turn, this time towards the recognition of industrial policy, has occurred in the years 2004–2005. This included the change of the European Union's official position towards that policy (Török et al. 2013: 2). On the one hand this was caused by the return of the understanding that manufacturing and manufacturing jobs are highly significant even in today's economy and employment and require, due to their complexity, special and selective attention.[3] On the other hand, it is typical of the present-day world that industrial policy principles are applied outside its traditional sphere of implementation – manufacturing (e.g. in relation to keywords like cultural industries, creative industries, green growth etc.). Yet we probably cannot hail the rebirth of industrial policy in its previous form and extent. It has to be admitted that the international context of industrial policy implementation has significantly changed: new rules governing international trade, the ban on export subsidies and quantitative restrictions (WTO, EU internal regulations), the rise of global value chains and marketing networks. The governments' freedom of manoeuvre ("policy space") has therefore become more restricted. The methods of industrial policy have changed as well. Policymakers also frequently emphasise the unwillingness to return to the so-called state-dirigisme approach and the "picking of winners" ideology of the previous industrial policy. They are seeking for new and more flexible methods allowing for cooperation with various stakeholders: experimental economics, providing acceleration "nudge" for some sector etc. However, despite their novelty, these approaches nevertheless remain more or lessselective instruments in the shaping of economic structure.

A somewhat broader construction for the discussion of the impact of the state on economy and the development policies used for this is the **varieties of**

---

3   Discussions on industrial policy should differentiate between the developmental direction, promotion of the development of new sectors and supra-sectoral spheres contributing to economic growth as a whole, and between the defensive (shield-type) industrial policies, e.g. several countries' attempts to preserve by state interference their automobile industries, hit by the latest economic crisis. In some countries, e.g. in Scandinavia, the combined use of these policies can be observed (Palan et al. 1999: 103–120). This article focuses on the developmental type of industrial policy.

capitalism concept, which has won considerable popularity in the last decade. Hall and Soskice (Hall/Soskice 2001), some of the founders of this approach, differentiate between two "ideal types" of capitalism: liberal market economies and coordinated market economies. In the former case firms operate through competitive markets in all areas of economic life (including the labour market), with price signals, supply and demand being crucial. In the second form of economy firms are coordinated through many non-market relationships, both in the relations between enterprises and between the firms and the state. Other authors have later added further elements to this coordination-centred model, e.g. differences in corporate governance and the extent and structure of welfare systems.

The treatment of Hall/Soskice developed from comparative studies of the developed Western countries, where a clear difference could be noted between the working of economy in the "Anglo-Saxon" societies on the one hand and continental Europe (Germany, France) on the other hand. Later, further groups were identified among the latter: e.g. the Scandinavian-type capitalism (with social-democratic influence) and the South European capitalism. For example, studies concerned the development of innovation in such groups of countries or the advantages granted to the specialisation on particular sectors of industry by one type of capitalism or the other.

It appears that liberal market economy with its dynamism and market-centred nature is a favourable environment for information technology business, while coordinated market economy is suitable for automobile industry.

There have been considerable difficulties with the fitting of Asian and Central and Eastern European economies in the above groups. Hall /Soskice initially placed Japan in the same group as the continental European capitalism, although Japanese capitalism differed from that of e.g. Germany by various important features. East Asian countries have been later grouped separately as the Asian capitalism or Asian corporative capitalism, emphasising such features of the group as developmental orientation or low level of welfare spending.

In numerous cases regarding Central and Eastern Europe it is not yet possible to talk about clearly developed models of capitalism, yet some differences can already be identified. The greatest tendency towards the coordinated market economic model has been observed in Slovenia and to a somewhat lesser degree in the Czech Republic. The Baltic states, especially Estonia, are considered to tend towards liberal market economy. Slovenia and Estonia are in fact considered the most extreme examples of these two orientations in the region (Damian/ Knell 2005; Buchen 2007).

Z. Norkus in his book (Norkus 2012: 268) does not yet classify any CEE countries in the coordinated or liberal capitalism groups. He treats these countries as different varieties of post-communist capitalism. He describes the variety including the Baltic states as Weberian-Friedmanian capitalism, designating by that term a combination of so-called constructive bureaucracy on the one hand and market and financial fundamentalism on the other. He designates the group including Slovenia and the Visegrad countries as Weberian-Porterian capitalism, emphasising with the latter the competitiveness development ideology promoted by M. Porter.

6. Development Indicators and the Countries' Scores

The different aspects of development and the related factors could be measured by an extremely large number of indicators. For the sake of clarity we have selected for the following analysis a limited number of more significant indicators and grouped them in four blocks, each of which performs its definite role in ensuring the development process. (The RES abbreviation in the figure designates result). The first block in the figure depicts the connection of the country's economy with the global environment. We concentrated in this block the connections occurring at the international level as well as the indicators of actual internationalisation level of business organisations. The second block displays the progress in achieving a favourable and well-operating domestic business environment. The third block concentrates the mechanisms enabling the country's economy to modernise itself and, figuratively speaking, to launch itself on a new and higher trajectory. We are not arguing that primarily the state agencies develop economy, but the elevation to a new level of development can occur only in cooperation of entrepreneurs, universities, state representatives and other actors. And the state can play an important role as the organiser of this cooperation. An important aspect of our treatment is the issue of the mutual links and balance between two blocks, the ones covering development policies and social welfare policies. Both blocks are largely financed from the state budget and they are often lumped together as public expenditures. Yet essentially these are two different, although partly overlapping functions. The overlapping part includes, for example, education, which is a factor influencing economic development on the one hand, but a public benefit on the other hand. The same applies to health-related services. An important issue is striking the right balance between the financing of developmental and welfare functions. But it must also be kept in mind that the welfare block plays an important role in ensuring the continuity of development by supporting the coherence and stability of the society.

The landscape of development determinants of the leader countries of the CEE region is dominated by a pair of elements. These are firstly INTEGRATION and secondly MACROECONOMIC & BUSINESS ENVIRONMENT. As for integration the dominating factors are the EU, where all three countries belong, and the European Monetary Union, which joins two of the three. There is a clear interconnection between the elements – the desire to belong to the EU or the eurozone created the need to observe the set rules quite closely and strongly disciplined the macroeconomic policy of the countries (the MACROECONOMIC component).

Figure 1: Conceptual framework for the classification of development indicators.

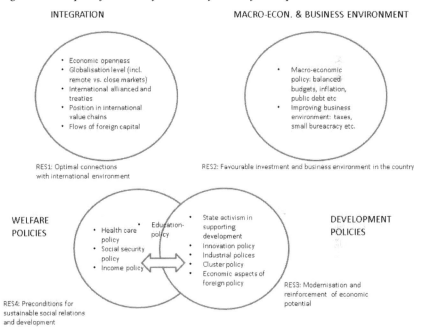

The EU membership significantly boosted the economic growth of the countries under observation, while the prospect of accession, which increased their reliability and attractiveness among foreign business partners, began to have its effect even several years before the accession. The INTEGRATION (with EU) component is highly significant for all three countries due to the opportunity to make use of the EU structural measures in development (especially in the building of technical infrastructure, as well as in research and innovation policy etc. (the

DEVELOPMENT POLICIES component). Integration with countries outside EU is not well developed.

Although access to the EU markets and the expansion of this opportunity in the future (the services market) is important for the CEE-3 countries, the use of this opportunity is limited not by the entry barriers but the scarcity of strong domestic firms and limited control over international marketing channels. As a result, their companies work for mediators rather than the end consumers of the target markets and the domestic firms' investments in the integration partners' markets are small (especially in comparison with the rather large investments received as the host country). The realisation of export capability is also obstructed by the low clustering level of domestic enterprises, often including the capable ones. There are attempts to overcome these drawbacks to some extent by using development policies (DEVELOPMENT component).

Macroeconomic policy (MACROECONOMIC) is generally of the type allowing all three countries to be viewed as a reliable, predictable and stable economic environment (positive contrast with some South European EU member countries). This is viewed as important in the economic policies of Estonia and the Czech Republic as for the aspect of attracting foreign investments. The general image is marred by deviations caused by the impact of the latest international economic crisis, which led to corrections in the regular macroeconomic policy, e.g. by influencing the balance of budget. In Slovenia's case the situation has been influenced in recent years by a complex mix of economic difficulties and domestic policy problems

In case of the East Asian countries we can notice a different (sequential) logic between the blocks depicted in the figure. In Asia regional integration has been driven more by markets than by governments. Economic integration has been largely driven by the development of increasingly sophisticated production networks that span the region and enable companies to benefit each country's comparative advantages (Capanelli 2009: 2). It is possible here to identify the starting push for transition to economic growth trajectory the move the individual countries to export promotion policy in the 1960s. Admittedly, this was accompanied by a need for greater adjustment to international trade regulations, but it did not mean formal integration into any economic association, adoption of its rules or even rapid opening of one's domestic market. The opening of the market to foreign goods and investments in Taiwan and South Korea occurred gradually and these countries use moderately high import tariffs even now. Export promotion policy in the East Asian countries led, either immediately or with a brief delay, to serious efforts in the DEVELOPMENT POLICIES block, so as to develop preconditions and capability for producing goods demanded in the world markets and characterised by as high value added as possible. The scale of dependence on domestic resources or the attraction of foreign capital depended on the individual countries. The latter option meant major efforts in creating positive branding to the country. The gradually rising cost of economy confronted the development policies with new tasks (transition to high technologies etc.). As for the MACROECONOMICS (and business environment block), gradualism can be observed here as well. Important moves within that block had to be made even in the period preceding economic growth, e.g. the suppression of inflation. Approaching the ideas defined in the Washington consensus has taken place during a relatively long period and not necessarily by accepting all requirements at once. Yet it can be argued that the Asian threesome has presently reached well-balanced and business-friendly economies.

By using the above conceptual scheme, we have derived a number of indicators for measuring the various aspects of development and attempted to use them for rating the development models of different countries. Generalisations about the various East Asian region's and CEE region's models can be found in the next chapter.

One might ask, whether 20 years is not too long a period to claim that a country has lasted throughout it on account of a single strategy or development model. However, a more detailed analysis allows claiming that strategies and methods changed together with circumstances, these changes occurred within the framework of the existing model rather than representing its radical replacement. Only the change of course of the Czech Republic in 1995 can be cited as an exception, during which Premier Vaclav Klaus' Czech-type (domestic) construction of capitalism was replaced by a strategy mainly oriented at foreign investments. As Drahokoupil (Drahokoupil 2007) claims, it marked a principal change of the market economic model, a transition to the competition state paradigm, which meant significant curbing of welfare spending in order to turn the business environment acceptable to foreign investors. Whether this change of direction can be described as a radical U-turn, remains nevertheless questionable, since there are other views. It seems that changes in other countries under observation, including those occurring in Korea with the large concerns (chaebols) due to the Asian crisis, can be interpreted as a radical change of development model to an even lesser degree. As was mentioned by R. Sharma (Sharma 2012: 160): „After 1998 the big Korean corporations brought in more professional managers to oversee day-to –day operations , but with the founding families still in charge the long-term strategical decisions were no less bold".

Table 2: Basic indicators of the development models by countries[4]

	South Korea	Taiwan	Singapore	Slovenia	Czech Republic	Estonia
Index of globalisation of economy[4] (rankings)	Low ranking (86)	Index not available	Extremely globalised (ranks 1st in the world)	Moderately globalised (ranks 33)	Highly globalised (ranks 14)	Highly globalised (ranks 8)
Regional markets vs. global markets	Both regional and world markets	Both regional and world markets (share of PRC increasing)	World markets	Mainly regional markets	Mainly regional markets	Mainly regional markets
Share of foreign investment in economy	Low	Relatively low at last period (more outward than inward investments)	Very high	Low	High	High
Characterisation of economic model	Corporative type of coordinated economy. Developmental state	Developmental state. Network type of coordination (to connect resorce flows and multiple agents)	Developmental state with strong governmental level coordination (via governmental agencies)	Coordinated market economy. Welfare corporatism	Intermediate type between coordinated and liberal market economy with small shift towards the former	Liberal market economy with "competition state" ideal. Weberian-Friedmanian model (Z. Norkus)
Macroeconomic balance	Well-balanced	Satisfactory balance	Improving, generally good (except for high govt. debt)	Worsened in recent years, currently unsatisfactory (govt. debt, budget balance)	Problematic (govt. budget balance, govt. debt)	Relatively good, improved since peak of crisis
Share of taxes in GDP	Relatively low (25%)	Extremely low (17%)	Extremely low (16%)	High (43%)	High (42%)	Moderate (37%)
Index of economic freedom (rankings)	Average (34)	Relatively high (20)	Extremely high (2)	Low (76)	Average (29)	Relatively high (13)

---

4   Usually lower for large economies.

	South Korea	Taiwan	Singapore	Slovenia	Czech Republic	Estonia
Strategic export sectors	Electronics, telecom, automobile, shipbuilding	Electronics, ICT, instruments	High-tech products as electronics and telecom, pharmaceuticals. Financial services, entrepôt services	Machinery and equipment, automotive, chemicals	Machinery and equipment, automotive, chemicals	Diversified profile. IT and some services have on important position
Use of industrial policy instruments	Strong	Strong	Strong	Moderate	Moderate	Weak
Innovation policy and innovation capability(rankings)	Well-developed (16)	Well-developed (14)	Well-developed (8)	Average (32)	Average (34)	Average (30)
Level of education	Very high	Very high	Very high	High	Moderate	High
Business sophistication index (rankings)	High (24)	Very high (15)	Very high (17)	Low (58)	Moderate (38)	Low (51)
Level of unemployment in the past decade	Low (below 5%)	Low (below 5%)	Very low (approx. 2%)	High (above 10%)	Moderate (6–7%)	Relatively high, fluctuating (approx. 10%)
Population income level differences (Gini)	High (42%)	Moderate (34%)	High (47–48%)	Low (24%)	Moderate (31%)	Moderate (31%)

At the same time, especially when observing a longer time period, a gradual "shifting" of the development models' individual parameters, including those of key importance, can be noticed. While a low level of income differences in the society was considered one of the typical features of Taiwan and South Korea in the 1970s–1980s, it is no longer so at present. It is nevertheless remarkable that all three East Asian countries have managed to keep their unemployment levels very low in the latter period, despite changes like giving up life-time contracts in South Korean large firms and Taiwan's loss of a significant share of jobs to mainland China.

6. Region vs Region: Similarities and Differences Between Development Models

Similarities

Both groups of countries represent strongly export-oriented economies. Although these are typical modern service economies, the share of industry in GDP is actually higher in comparison with other developed economies, especially in case of South Korea and the Czech Republic. With the exception of South Korea, which could be considered a medium-size economy, the rest are small economies with highly limited capability of domestic markets to balance the disturbances caused by foreign markets. When observing the period as a whole one could argue that all economies involved in the study have managed to create a balanced macro-environment necessary for investments and normal economic development; the ratings of its quality are quite close in all cases. Yet as export-oriented economies they are strongly dependent on the state of foreign markets. Its deterioration, especially in case the negative effect of some further factor should be added, can deteriorate the economic environment quite suddenly. However, as the experience of the Asian crisis and the latest global economic crisis show, they have nevertheless managed to overcome such situations relatively rapidly.

Although the economic growth rate of the countries under observation has been closely linked to the international market situation and growth in their primary export markets, their growth rate throughout the period as a whole has outpaced the international background. Fastest economic growth in that period was displayed by Estonia, while the growth rate of Slovenia could also compete with those of the East Asian threesome. It has to be admitted, however, that the EU support financing played some role in their economic growth during the second half of the period.

Both the CEE and East Asian countries included in the sample are characterised by high education level of the working population and high assessments of education quality. This applies, with some nuances and differences as to the countries, to basic, secondary and university education. It is worth reminding that at the time when the East Asian countries started their economic success story, their education indicators were not at all high. While the education level in the CEE countries has been historically high, it has been growing in the East Asian countries parallel with the economic growth process.

When comparing the situation in the first and second half of the study period, a convergence of some features of both groups' development models can be observed. While the economic models of two East Asian countries,

South Korea and Taiwan, could be considered strongly state-centred at the beginning of the period, these countries have undergone some liberalisation during the period. As of now, according to the summary indicator of the Index of Economic Freedom, rather than any individual indicator, all the East Asian countries covered by the study (together with Estonia and the Czech Republic, but not Slovenia, whose corresponding index has deteriorated lately) can be clearly included in liberal economies, enjoying greater freedom than majority of the EU countries.

While the countries of the East Asian region under observation clearly stood out at the beginning of the period as to their greater deposits and investments in fixed assets as share of GDP, such wide gap no longer exists. While one could state regarding the beginning of the period that the export of the CEE countries in the study was greatly directed at neighbouring markets and that of the East Asian countries in the sample mainly at the remote markets, the present analysis of those countries' dominant export partners no longer displays a noticeable difference. Yet the reason for the vanishing of the difference is not the expanding export geography of the CEE countries, but the increasing share of the PRC as the target market of East Asian countries' export, especially since the beginning of the international economic crisis. The export of all countries under observation basically depends very strongly on one or two dominating target markets. In case of the Czech Republic and Slovenia this is Germany, in Estonia's case Sweden and Finland and in the East Asian export tigers' case the PRC (especially if the latter is viewed together with Hong Kong).

Differences

On the other hand, there are quite noticeable differences, which do not allow discussing a common success model of the East Asian and CEE countries.

An inevitable collateral effect of catching up is the economies becoming more costly. Continuing successful exporting at more expensive production input requires elevation to a higher value added level, production of more sophisticated, innovative and expensive output and selling it directly to the end user whenever possible. The East Asian countries are clearly more successful than the CEE trio in that respect and have also created greater potential for further development of these activities in the future. International comparative studies use as the assessing instruments two synthetic indicators: the innovation potential index and the business sophistication index. The latter essentially reflects the positioning of the country's firms in the international value creation chains: focusing on unique operations, sophistication of business models and processes, existence of local

supplier networks, control over distribution channels, the establishment of local clusters. The countries of the East Asian trio are, judging by the innovation
potential index, usually among the top ten of the world. Small countries find it
hard to compete with large ones in business sophistication. The world's leading
nations in that respect are the great economies like the USA, Japan and Germany,
although the positions of our East Asian threesome in these rankings are not at all
bad. The innovation potential ratings of the Czech Republic, Slovenia and Estonia
are better than those of the other CEE region countries, but remain significantly
below those of the leading nations. The situation with business sophistication is
worse still. The indicators are low all over the CEE countries and show no sign
of improving. The low position in the value chain obstructs the actual implementation and effect of both educational and research levels and the innovation
potential (Terk et al. 2013).

The higher level a country's economy occupies, the greater is the role of the
universities' potential in continued economic growth. Although the universities
of the CEE threesome hold relatively strong positions to the region's general background, their level is significantly lower in comparison with the top universities
of the East Asian trio, which can compete with the world's leading players. This
holds especially true regarding technological higher education.

Although, as we pointed out above, the three East Asian countries display a
tendency towards liberalisation, movement towards greater consideration of mar-
ker regulation, their economies nevertheless differ from the CEE countries' ones
as to the greater role of the state in the direction and regulation of long-term
economic development as well as the general aspiration to coordinate the actions
of economic agents in advance rather than to rely on ex-post regulation working
via the market. The East Asian countries correspond even now to the definition
of developmental state (see …) Yet the mechanisms implementing the developmental functions are quite different in all three East Asian countries.

The above is closely related to the issue of the grade of "strategicity" of sta-
te-level development planning. It is characteristic of the East Asian countries
to base their development policy on ambitious strategic visions, which aim at
strengthening the country's geopolitical positions and /or creating new competitive advantages in the international business environment, For instance,
the APROC programme (APROC- Asia-Pacific Regional Operations Centre)
developed in Taiwan in the late 1990s, which involved not simply plans for
strengthening Taiwan's positions as a high-tech manufacturing centre (Taiwan as a "science and technology island"), but turning it simultaneously into
maritime and air transport, off-shore banking, telecommunication and media

centre and creating leverage between these different functions. The key issues of the "Singapore 21" programme included "knocking at global and regional firms' doors" for finding new capital, technologies, ideas and markets and attracting the HQs of international business leaders to Singapore, but also further development of the existing value chains and promoting the globalisation of business based on domestic capital. It is clear that the realisation of such ambitions goals requires the championing activity by the state, cooperation between firms and their close cooperation with the state institutions. The development of such visions and development planning as a whole need not remain within the framework of state bureaucratic practice; it has involved the launching of broader discussions of socially and culturally sensitive issues like, in Singapore, the extent of desirable immigration, the balance of domestic and foreign entrepreneurship, the need for "creativity import" or conflicts over values between generations and the opportunities for considering these values.

In case of the three CEE countries we can discuss significantly less visionary and more technical development planning, which involves no ambitions or visions for major development leaps, strategic shifts and changes in the positioning of the country's economy; instead the plans concern the development of individual aspects of economy along the traditional established lines of the European Union: balancing the macroeconomic environment, developing infrastructures, supporting small business etc. The limiting factors are, on the one hand, the shortage of budget resources for carrying out major strategic manoeuvres (the lion's share of the budget is tied up in funding the tasks set by legislation, including social spending), and on the other hand, the need to consider the possible financing from the EU structural funds, its goals and rules. As it is, the structural funds have become for the new member countries a main source for making major strategic investments. As a result, the strategic development materials no longer reflect the country's development vision, its specifics, but rather development goals forced into a standardised format, which have prospects for finding EU financing during any given period.[5]

---

5 The above obviously does not mean a total absence of more radical visions related to economic development in the CEE countries. For example, in the first half of the period under observation discussions in Estonia involved a vision of the country as an international transit gateway and the "Test site Estonia" idea, advanced by technical scientists and entrepreneurs. Yet in either case we can talk only about a "one-idea vision" rather than a complex development vision for the country as a whole and neither proposal turned into a central idea for national development strategy.

It can also be argued that the concept of the role of the state in the CEE countries predominantly remains in the limits of an eliminator or compensator of market failures, while developmental functions transcending these limits are rarely accepted. It is true that the concept of a market failure eliminator contains the state's activities in supporting R&D and the vertical-type innovation policy, e.g. in distributing development grants among high-tech small firms regardless their field of activity. On the other hand, horizontal innovation policy for the development of certain new business sectors or supporting some kind of export are "grey areas" at best, where involvement could result in accusations of violating market economy dogmas or even the competition regulations established by the EU. Thus industrial policy, at least in the more openly liberal CEE countries, has not become one of economic policy keywords, unlike the East Asian countries.

A central parameter of the development model – the share of GDP redistributed via taxes – is cardinally different in the East Asian and CEE threesomes. While the indicator remains between 16–17 percent in Taiwan and Singapore (true, it has reached 25 percent in South Korea), it amounts to more than 40 percent of GDP in the Czech Republic and Slovenia. Since the East Asian countries do not spare budget resources for economic development, it is obvious that supporting economic development in the countries of the region largely occurs on account of welfare spending. Whether the gap in the welfare systems is actually as wide as the statistics show is of course arguable. As Kim (Kim, Pil Ho, 2010) shows in his article, a part of the welfare spending in East Asian countries is met not only by individuals or their families, but also by firms or the state provides disguised forms of subsidies to the population. In any case the financing of welfare costs by the state in the East Asian countries has been shifted to the orphan's role compared to other priorities. If their priority should significantly increase, this could strongly influence the whole situation in these countries.

What could be said about the **future prospects** of either region's development models, which have so far brought success to them? Regarding the East Asian three, it can be claimed that besides achieving remarkable economic growth, they have also created a very strong potential for further progress in the shape of high-level universities, high innovation capability and remarkable level of business sophistication. Problems could arise with long-term retention of the developmental state features favouring economic growth in an environment of political rivalry between political parties, typical of a pluralistic society, and in a situation, where social (welfare) spending must inevitably increase (partly due to the fact that the share of compensating mechanisms not entirely suitable to market economy is declining). Nor is it clear whether the national social mobilisation tools, aimed at long-term goals and favouring corresponding compromises, will keep operating as efficiently as previously. Since the successful development models of the CEE countries are more heterogeneous than the East Asian ones, it is more difficult to advance a generalising hypothesis about their future. It seems that the main problem will be the issue of whether they can rise in the international economy to performing higher value added functions in an environment of probably rising costs. There are certain premises regarding the education and innovation potential, although these cannot be compared with the East Asian ones, but the relatively weak position of the leading CEE countries in the international value chains gives reasons for concern. The situation has shown no signs of improvement in recent years. It is not certain that Slovenia and the Czech Republic, which have created expensive welfare systems, will be able to retain them. Considering the more individualistic mentality compared to East Asia, the CEE countries various elite groups will certainly find it more difficult to agree on long-term development strategies and priority fields of investment necessary for promoting future economic growth.

Whether the rapid economic growth of the CEE three or its individual countries could continue after the exhaustion of its initial factors – the initial effect of entering open market economy from the basis of low production costs and the impact from EU accession – or whether they can create economic growth engines required for continued success, remains open for the time being.

When attempting to guess the direction of development of the governance model in the countries under observation, we can use the classification proposed by Claus Offe (Offe 1975), which differentiates between three forms of public policymaking: rule-based bureaucratic decision making, goal-oriented public planning and participatory governance. Let us try to adjust this classification to the situation of the catching-up countries. As experience has shown: bureaucratic routines are unsuited for complex public programmes requiring the mobilisation of diverse resources and commitments. Purposive actions require acceptance of goals as well as social and fiscal costs. Democratic participation tends to generate demands that are inconsistent with capital accumulation and is prone to politicise the process of administration. Which combination of these three variants is possible and preferable in a country strongly depends on cultural background and path dependence. If we presume that the first option would be insufficient for the CEE countries for maintaining high economic growth and narrow focusing on the development of competitiveness elements specific to an individual country would be needed, we should find ways and suitable forms for linking goal-oriented approach to greater involvement of various stakeholders and the public. This need not be easy, but it is necessary. Considering the peculiarities of history and culture, the options of development models suitable for the CEE countries should probably contain a larger share of horizontal rather than vertical coordination when compared to the East Asian countries. This was at least shown by the results of a survey of economic, political and cultural elite carried put in Estonia in early 2013; it appeared that the respondents wanted significantly more focused and goal-oriented governance, yet not the corporatist or state-centred version, but the option involving the wider public (Estonia in the world 2013)

References

Alesina A. A. / La Ferrara E. (2005) Etnic Diversity and Economic Performance, in: Journal of Economic Literature, Vol. XLIII, September, pp. 762–800.

Amable, B. (2003) The Diversity of Capitalism. Oxford: Oxford University Press.

Amsden, A.H. (1989) Asia's Next Giant: South Korea and Late Industrialization. New York and Oxford, Oxford University Press.

Botez, M. C. / Celac, M. (1986) Undesirable Versus Desirable Societies, in: Technological Forecasting and Social Change Vol. 30, pp. 50–91.

Buchen, C. (2007) Estonia and Slovenia as Antipodes, in: Varieties of Capitalism in post-communist countries.

Chang, H-J. (2001) Kicking Away the Ladder. Development Strategy in Historical Perspective. Anthem.

Capannelli C. (2008) Asian regionalism: How does it compare to Europe`s? East Asia Forum Papers.

Comisso, E. (1998) Implicit Development Strategies in Central East Europe.

Damian and Knell (2005) How important is Trade and foreign ownership in closing the Technology Gap. Evidence from Estonia and Slovenia, in: Review of World Economics No. 141, pp. 271–295.

Drahokoupil, J. (2007) Political support of competition state, in: the Visegrad Four: The comprador service sector and its allies. Garnet Working Paper No. 22/07.

Estonia in the world (2013) Estonian Human Development Report 2012/2013. Tallinn.

Gerschenkron, A. (1962) Economic Backwardness in Historical Perspective: A Book of Essays, Cambridge, MA, Belknap Press of Harvard University Press.

Hall, P. A. / Soskice, D. (2001) Varieties of Capitalism. Oxford: Oxford University Press.

Hermes, N. (1997) New explanations of the economic success of East Asia. Lessons for developing and Eastern European countries. Thorbecke, Erik & Henry Wan: Revisiting East and South Asias Development Model.

Index of Economic Freedom 2013, The Heritage Foundation.

Irfan ul Haque (2007) Rethinking industrial policy, UNCTAD.

Gaidar, J. (1997) Anatomija ekonomitseskogo rosta, Moscow, Yevraziya.

Johnson, C. (1982) MITI and the Japanese Miracle. The growth of Industrial Policy, 1925–1975, Stanford, CA, Stanford University Press.

Kim, Pil Ho (2010) The East Asian welfare state debate and surrogate social policy: an exploratory study on Japan and South Korea, in: Socio-Economic Review No. 8, pp. 411–435.

Kuusk, K. (2012) Eksperimenteeriv majanduspoliitika. Tallinn: Estonian Development Fund.

Lane, D. / Myant, M. (2007) Varieties of capitalism in post-communist countries. Palgrave.

Либман А. М. (2007) Фискальная политика в условиях глобализации. Информационное-аналитический бюллетень ЦПГИ ИЭ РВН No. 4.

Molitor, G.T.T. (2008) Visionary National Economic Planning. Plans, Potentials and Progress. Journal of Futures Studies Vol. 12, No. 4, pp. 93–108. Singapore, Coherent and integrated national planning.

Myant, M. The Czech Republic. From "Czech" Capitalism to "European" Capitalism.

Norkus, Z. (2012) On Baltic Slovenia and Adriatic Lithuania. A qualitative comparative analysis of patterns in post-communist transformation. Apostrofa & CEU Press, Vilnius, 375 p.

Offe, C. (1995) Berufsbildungreform. Eine Fallstudie über Reformpolitik. Frankfurt: Suhrkamp.

Palan, R. / Abbot, J. / Deans, P. (1999) State Strategies in the Global Political Economy. London & NY: Pinter.

Pascha, W. (2004) Economic integration in East Asia and Europe. A Comparison.

Pinto, H. / Tiago Santos Pereira (2013) Efficiency of innovation Systems in Europe: An Institutional Approach in the Diversity of National Profiles. European Planning Studies Vol. 21, No 6, pp. 755–779.

Porter, M. (1990) The Competitive Advantage of Nations. London: acmillan.

Rodrik, D. (2004) Industrial Policy for the Twenty-first Century. EPR discussion paper 4767.

Sarel, M. (1996) Growth in East Asia. What we can and what we cannot infer. IMF.

Sharma, R. (2012) Breakout Nations. In Pursuit oft he Next Economic Miracles. W.W. Norton, NY, London

Sorensen, G. (2004) The Transformation of the State. Beyond the Myth of Retreat. Palgrave.

Stark, M. (2010) The East Asian development state as a reference model for transition economies in Central Asia.

Terk, E. / Männik, K. / Lassur, S. (2013) Innovation, in: Estonia in the world. Estonian Human Development Report 2012/2013. Tallinn.

The Slovenia Times (2012) We Need Coherent Vision of our Future. Interview with Dr. Peter Kraljic, Vol. 10, pp. 8–9.

Török, A. et al. (2013) The "resurrection" of industrial policy in the European Union and its impact on industrial policy in the New Member Countries. European Commission Working Paper No. 26.

Wade, R. (1990) Governing the Market: Economic Theory and the Role of Government in East Asian Industrialization. Princeton, NJ: Princeton University Press.

Woo-Cumings, M. (1999) The Developmental State, Cornell University Press.

Appendix 1. Openness, social cohesion and the ghost of state activism – the dilemmas of Estonian elite anno 2013

Estonia's economy already has turned into an example of liberal capitalism, which is attracting even some international interest. Yet the outcomes of this Weberian-Friedmanian model as designated by the Lithuanian researcher Z. Norkus, are contradictory. As shown by a survey (Estonia in the world 2013) carried out in the beginning of 2013 among different groups of Estonia's elite (economic, political, cultural, scientific elite), these groups, which generally rated Estonia's development of the past 20 years as successful, are concerned, among other problems, about the declining competitiveness of economy, insufficient rate of technological development, vague focusing of state policies on the solving of priority problems, but also the increasing income difference gap. Are the representatives of the Estonian elite looking for the developmental state model known from East Asia and would that mean turning away from economic openness?

In order to understand better the mental world of the respondents, sociologists have constructed on the base of answers to various questions two general indices – an index of satisfaction with the preceding trends and an index of openness.

Figure 2: Links between important development parameters (based on estimations of elite groups' members).

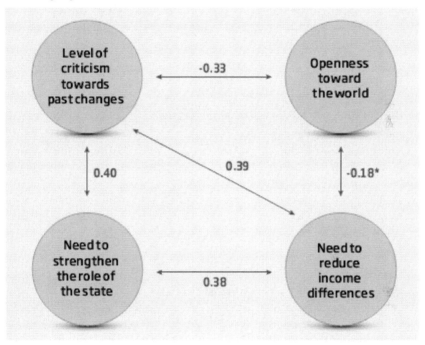

Fig. 2 shows how these two composite indicators relate – firstly, to the idea of reduction of income differences as a precondition for successfully coping with globalisation, and secondly, to the respondent's wishes to strengthen the role of the state in various spheres of activity.

Do the correlations of Fig. 2 confirm the cliché about the contradiction between the people who are rejecting global trends, disappointed in market economy developments to date and supportive of an increased role for the state; and, on the other hand, the people with open views who are satisfied with the market economy reforms and supportive of the strengthening of the state's role?

Actually, they do not. Based on the figure we can conclude that the desire to strengthen the role of the state is associated with a critical attitude toward the development, which has taken place, as well as an inclination to consider the reduction of income differences to be important; but the openness index has no statistical connection to the idea of strengthening of the state's role (nor with the desire for more focused policies).

Considering the significance of the aspiration for openness and the equalisation of incomes as broader indicators, let us take a closer look as the connection between the two attitudes. When combining these two indicators, the respondents were divided in four groups:

- A – the "globalists" (support Estonia's continued integration into global economy and the EU), who support the reducing of the income gap – 37% of the respondents;
- B – the "globalists", who reject the need for reducing the income gap – 33% of the respondents;
- C – the "Estonia-centred" supporters of income gap reduction. They are critical of integration with the world and the EU, as well as support the reduction of income differences – 23% of the respondents.
- D – the "Estonia-centred" rejecters of income gap reduction. They are not happy about the policies, which promote globalisation or income equality – 11% of the respondents.

The „globalists" favouring the income gap reduction include an above-average share of scientists and below-average share of politicians, whole the group of „globalists" rejecting income equalisation has a greater representation of economic elite and especially entrepreneurs. We find a large number of cultural figures, but also politicians among this Estonia-centred group, which favours income equalisation. Yet of both cultural figures and politicians a minority (less than a third) belong to the above group. Among the economic elite this combination of attitude is clearly unpopular.

The groups A and C tend to favour increasingly the role of the state, more than the others do. Both of these groups very strongly support increasing the role of the state in regional policies and the promotion of educational activities. Group C, characteristically, places greater emphasis on the role of the state in social security, in the organisation of ethnic relations and in health care policies, but also in the development of economic structures. For this part of „globalists", who favour equalisation, the corresponding spheres of activity are the promotion of innovation, migration control and the improvement of the environment. The "globalists" who reject income equalisation also indicate less than average support for increasing the role of the state in the spheres of activity under observation. However, more than 50% of them still support the strengthening of the state's role in regional development and the organisation of education.

Jüri Sepp and Uku Varblane

The Decomposition of Productivity Gap between Estonia and Korea

1. Introduction

Estonia and the Republic of Korea (or South Korea) are both in a similar situation in terms of future economic challenges – there is a need to close the development gap between them and the world's richest. Both countries have so far been quite successful in this respect, though Korea has gained a considerable head start compared to Estonia since it began that chase more than a decade earlier[1]. Statistics reveal that over the past decade the two countries have been able to significantly reduce their backlog from the average *per capita* gross national income (GNI) of OECD countries (Figure 1). In 2002 the GNI of Estonia and Korea were 45% and 76% from OECD average respectively, whereas by the year 2011 the corresponding figures had been increased to 58% and 87% – an increase of 13 and 11 percentage points. It is noticeable that the race of catching up is taking place in somewhat different race classes as Estonia is currently trying to reach to a level where Korea was already a decade ago. However, the statistical ratios reveal that some convergence has occurred – the level of Estonian gross national income relative to Korea has risen from 59% to 67%. In absolute figures, net national income per person was 26425 USD in Korea and 17616 USD in Estonia (in PPP terms) in 2011.

However, the figure 1 shows that the process of convergence has been far from monotonous and unified nature as the global economic downturn in 2009–2010 has caused a recession only in Estonia but not in Korea. Estonia was thriving during the economic boom in 2004–2007 and reached as close to Korea as the latter is compared to the OECD average, the subsequent economic crisis, however, had in principle thrown the whole process some five years back. Moreover, the quicker growth in Estonia and the process of continuing convergence is not certain or guaranteed. During the particular period, the average absolute increment of gross national income per capita was 881 USD in OECD, 1033 USD in Korea and only

---

1   In some sense, the period of centrally planned economy in Estonia can be seen as a failed attempt to find an alternative option for accelerating the economic growth. Unfortunately, undervaluation or ignorance of market signals resulted in a dead end.

844 USD per year in Estonia. If this tendency continues, income disparities will further increase.

Figure 1: Income convergence in Estonia and Korea 2002 to 2011.

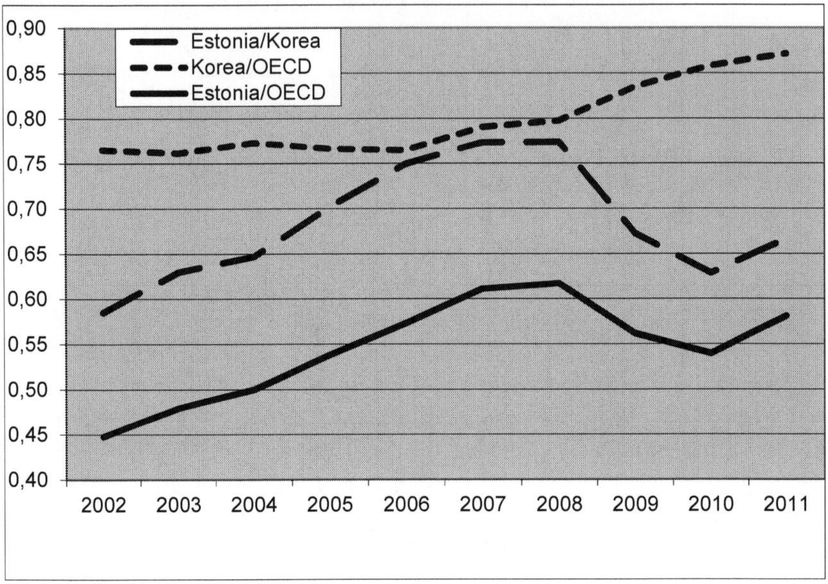

Source: OECD

In this paper we will focus on one specific aspect of convergence process and examine the structural determinants of the productivity gap between Korea and Estonia. In other words, the goal is to explain the patterns of structural transformation and decompose the productivity gap between Estonia and Korea both at the national level and in manufacturing sector in particular.

Productivity differences between countries can be decomposed into three separated effects. One of which is characterising the differences in allocation of labour between industries (the between-effect), the second measures the productivity growth caused by intra-branch productivity growth (within-effect) and the third component represent a cross (covariance) effect of both structural and productivity differences, that is positive when industries with growing labour productivity are increasing their market share. In addition to the aggregated components, the contribution of individual sectors is also of interest. The data used in this paper is from the OECD Database for Structural Analysis (STAN). The calculations of the analysis are based on the data from the year 2006. The novelty in methodology lies in a spatial comparison and the application of relative productivity indicators in explaining the productivity gap.

Spatial analysis of productivity gap is not widely used in the literature. Rodrik (2012: 38) is one of the few who has applied productivity decomposition analysis for explaining regional productivity differences. In his research, he comes to the conclusion that unification of employment structure of China and India with developed industrial countries would result in productivity increase of three and two times respectively. The decomposition of aggregate productivity has been also used in explaining the productivity gap between Australia and New-Zealand, whereas contributions of individual sectors were calculated (Yang/Stephenson 2011). Similar decomposition was applied in our earlier work (Sepp/Eerma 2009) where we found the components of manufacturing sector productivity gap between Estonia and Ireland or Finland, as well as between the EU-average. However, Rodrik's own fundamental interest is related to the decomposition of productivity dynamics of countries or regions. In contrast to the typical approach of focusing on the specific country[2], Rodrik raises the question of the fundamental roots of the international variation of productivity components. His motivation for this type of analysis lies in the peculiar patterns of productivity components of Asia, South-America and Africa. Havlik (2013), de Vries et al (2012) and Chansomphou, Ichihashi (2013) represent the other examples of large-scale cross-national comparisons of productivity decomposition in transition economies, however with the focus towards the BRIC countries.

The transformation patterns of sectoral structure of the economy have been studied both empirically using stylized facts, as well in the framework of growth theory.[3] In general, the economic structure is considered as a determinant of productivity and thereby the influencing factor of economic welfare. Timmer/ Szirmai (2000) and several follow-up papers are talking about the structural bonus hypothesis. It should be emphasized, however, that there is definitely a two-way causality. A rather classic and generally accepted notion is that tertiarization and rising share of service sector employment in the developed countries could be largely denoted to the consequence of the increased productivity of the manufacturing sector. It enables and generates both the growth in demand for services as

---

2   Particularly on the structural changes in manufacturing industry the relevant research has been done by Marczewski, Szczygielski (2007) in the Polish, by O'Donnell (2007) in the Irish, by Szalavetz (2009) in the Hungarian and by Akkemik (2006) in the Turkish manufacturing experience.

3   Fisher (1935); Clark (1940); Fourastié (1949); Kaldor (1961); Baumol (1967); Fuchs (1968); Kuznets (1971) and Madisson (1980) are the classics in this sphere.

well as releases labour for service sector, where in many branches the "internal" productivity growth opportunities are relatively limited.

In developing countries, the released labour may be exploited in low-productivity agriculture or even in black economy. In this case, the impact of structural transformation on the overall productivity is negative (de Vries et al. 2011; Rodrik 2011). Therefore, in this paper we pay special attention to the links between employment and productivity. If this link is negative, the structural burden occurs – employment shift away from relatively progressive industries towards those with lower growth of labour productivity (Baumol 1967). In the opposite case, if the positive relation emerges, there is a specialization in economy as the labour shifts from low to high productivity sectors, which amplifies the average productivity growth (structural bonus). In the latter case, to a certain extent we can also refer to the process of smart specialization. Previous studies have not, however, given an unambiguous justification for those linkages between productivity and employment shifts[4]. Rodrik (2012: 40) for instance believes that the explanation lies in the country-specific effects of globalization that depend on the framework conditions of each particular country e.g. the local policy and development strategies. McMillan et al (2011) emphasize the intensity of import competition, availability of natural resources, over-regulated labour market and the overvalued currency as the main barriers for productivity enhancing transformations. In this paper, we investigate and control the previous results with comparing Estonia and Korea. The required further work should be done on the basis of an econometric analysis of a larger sample.

2. Results of Productivity Decomposition

The most general measure in cross-country comparison of productivity levels is GDP *per capita*. However, this figure is significantly dependent on the employment rate and the average annual hours worked. Table 1 shows a comparison of Korea and Estonia with respect to U.S.

---

4   The "structural bonus and burden" hypothesis were examined on example of Asian economies by Timmer/Szirmai (2000), on a large sample of OECD and developing countries (Fagerberg 2000), and more recently by Peneder for USA, Japan and EU member states (Peneder 2003) and by Havlik (2013) for CEE countries. Based on a structural decomposition, de Vries (2011) find that for China, India and Russia reallocation of labour across sectors is contributing to aggregate productivity growth, whereas in Brazil it is not. This strengthens the findings of McMillan and Rodrik (2011).

Table 1: Productivity levels of Korea and Estonia in 2011 (U.S. = 100)

Country	GDP *per capita*	GDP per hour worked	Hours worked *per capita*
Estonia	46	43	106
Korea	63	49	128

Source: OECD

As GDP per capita accounts for 63% of the U.S. level in Korea and 46% in Estonia, the rate of GDP per hour worked is somewhat lower – 49% and 43% respectively. This indicates that the intensity of labour utilization in Estonia and Korea is higher than in the U.S. The number of hours worked per capita makes up 103% of the U.S. level in Estonia and 128% in Korea. Higher intensity of labour utilization in Estonia and especially in Korea is the basis for considerable discrepancies between the ratios of GDP per capita and GDP per hour worked compared to the U.S. With regard to the comparison between Estonia and Korea, the hourly productivity in Korea exceeds Estonian level by a narrow 15%, whereas on a *per capita* basis, the Korean advantage is around 38%. This particular feature will be the object of interest in the present work and the basis for the decomposition.

Before focusing on the results of the decomposition analysis, we will explain in a bit more detail the differences in the employment and productivity of Estonia and Korea at the relatively aggregated level of NACE classification (14 activities, which we call the economic sectors).

In both countries, the largest share of employment is in the manufacturing sector, as in Estonia the share is over 20% and in Korea a bit less (Table 2). In terms of employment share, energy and water management, construction, transportation and communications and the public sector are also of high importance in Estonia. In Korea, by contrast, the share of labour employed in finance, trade, in other services and in agriculture exceeds the corresponding levels of Estonia. To understand the relevance of these differences in employment structure on average productivity, it is relevant to briefly examine the sectoral productivity levels. At first, we consider the so-called relative productivity, which is obtained by dividing the share of the value added of the sector with the corresponding employment share. The result is the reference coefficients, which describe the productivity of the particular sector with respect to the average sector or nation's average.

Table 2: The sectoral structure of employment and value added and relative productivity indexes of Korea and Estonia in 2006 (%)

	Employment share		Share of value added		Relative productivity index	
	Korea	Estonia	Korea	Estonia	Korea	Estonia
Agriculture, hunting, forestry and fishing	7.7	5.0	3.2	3.2	41.0	63.5
Mining and quarrying	0.1	0.8	0.2	1.0	303.3	119.5
Manufacturing	18.0	21.1	27.5	17.0	152.5	80.7
Electricity, gas and water supply	0.3	1.9	2.3	3.1	692.4	159.1
Construction	7.9	9.7	7.5	8.7	95.0	89.5
Wholesale and retail trade – repairs	16.0	13.7	8.7	14.5	54.0	105.8
Hotels and restaurants	8.9	3.5	2.4	1.7	27.0	48.8
Transport, storage and communication	6.4	9.5	6.8	11.1	107.1	117.0
Financial intermediation	3.4	1.1	6.8	4.0	199.6	351.3
Real estate, renting and business activities	9.4	7.4	14.6	20.1	155.9	270.4
Public admin. and defence – compulsory social security	3.5	6.0	6.4	5.2	185.3	85.5
Education	7.2	9.1	6.3	4.2	87.5	46.8
Health and social work	3.0	5.8	3.9	3.0	131.0	51.7
Other community, social and personal services	8.3	5.3	3.5	3.3	42.7	61.9
Total	100.0	100.0	100.0	100.0	*	*

Source: OECD

Although, the relative productivity indexes of the two countries are moderately correlated (r=0.3), which refer to the rather similar general tendencies, some significant differences occur. Productivity levels in Korean electricity, gas and water supply sector and in mining significantly exceed the average levels in Korea (nearly seven and three times respectively). Financial intermediation and business services are approximately in the same role in Estonia with over 2.5 times higher productivity compared to the Estonia's average and also exceeding the corresponding levels of Korea. These are the regularities we have also observed in a previous study (Sepp et al. 2009) – in transition economies the financial sector is relatively more profitable than in older market economies. The same applies for the real estate, renting and business activities. In both countries, the share of agriculture, hotels and restaurants and other community, social and personal services in total value added is relatively small. However, in Korea these sectors are of particularly low return compared to an average. The striking difference between Korea and Estonia appears on public sector figures. Three public sector branches included in the analysis comprise 13.7% of the employment in Korea, meanwhile as much as 20.9% in Estonia. In terms of value added the share of public sector accounts for 16.8% of total economy in Korea and 12.4% in Estonia. In other words, the productivity of a single employee of the public sector of Korea exceeds the national average. In Estonia, however, the corresponding level is only about 60% of the average. As a whole, the sectoral productivity variation in Korea is considerably higher than in Estonia.

It is also remarkable that due to the higher relative productivity, manufacturing sector in Korea accounts for more than 27% of the total value added. In Estonia the relative productivity of manufacturing sector remained below the nation's average, and therefore the contribution to overall value-added was smaller compared to the employment share.

We take cognizance of these notable disparities and now focus on productivity decomposition. We use the same productivity (GDP *per capita*) gap notation, which according to the Table 1 is 38% between Korea and Estonia.

This gap could be decomposed into three components as follows:

$$t-1 = \Sigma se^*(qk-qe) + \Sigma(t^*sk-se)^*qe + \Sigma(t^*sk-se)^*(qk-qe), \qquad (1)$$

where

t – the ratio of the average productivity in Korea and Estonia;

t-1 – the average productivity gap between Korea and Estonia;

qk and qe – share of industry in total employment in Korea and Estonia (Table 2);

sk and se – the relative productivity of industry in Korea and Estonia (Table 2).

With using the multiplier t we can switch from relative productivity deviations to the actual deviations adjusted with the average productivity levels (Table 3). It appears that in as many six sectors, the productivity in Korea lags Estonian levels. The largest backlog exists in the wholesale and retail trade – around 30%. However, the real productivity in Korean electricity, gas and water supply sector exceeds the corresponding level of Estonia almost six times, the difference is 3.5 to 2.6 times in mining and manufacturing. Korea has also about three times higher productivity in the public sector. Essentially, the latter means better financing.

Table 3: *Relative and real sectoral productivity deviations and reference coefficients of Korea compared to Estonia in 2006 (%)*

	Productivity deviations		Reference coefficient
	Relative	Real	
Agriculture, hunting, forestry and fishing	-22.5	-6.8	89
Mining and quarrying	183.8	299.3	350
Manufacturing	71.8	129.9	261
Electricity, gas and water supply	533.3	797.0	601
Construction	5.5	41.7	147
Wholesale and retail trade – repairs	-51.8	-31.2	70
Hotels and restaurants	-21.8	-11.5	76
Transport, storage and communication	-9.9	30.9	126
Financial intermediation	-151.7	-75.7	78
Real estate, renting and business activities	-114.5	-55.1	80
Public admin. and defence, social security	99.8	170.4	299
Education	40.7	74.1	258
Health and social work	79.4	129.3	350
Other community, social and personal services	-19.1	-2.9	95

Source: Author's calculations

In equation 1, the first component describes the effect of the differences in the sectoral structure of employment, the second component describes differences due to the inter-industry productivity differences and the third component represents the cross effect of first two components. The formation of these individual components is shown in Table 4. Sectoral productivity differences in manufacturing clearly play the largest role in Korean-Estonian productivity gap. Assuming equal productivity levels in the other economic sectors, the productivity gap between Korea and Estonia would be 27.3% due to the manufacturing sector only. Therefore, we will explore the impact of manufacturing in more detail below. Productivity discrepancies in energy and water management sector increase the overall productivity gap by another 15.3%. However, the third component of the decomposition, the cross effect, reduces that margin by 12.7%, which means that higher productivity in Korea has concurred with lower share of employment. In terms of structural differences (between effect), the contribution of the financial intermediation to the productivity gap is the largest with 8%.

Table 4: Decomposition of productivity gap across sectors

	Structural difference	Productivity difference	Cross effect	Total
Agriculture, hunting, forestry and fishing	1.7	-0.3	-0.2	1.2
Mining and quarrying	-0.9	2.4	-2.2	-0.6
Manufacturing	-2.5	27.4	-4.0	20.9
Electricity, gas and water supply	-2.5	15.3	-12.7	0.1
Construction	-1.6	4.0	-0.7	1.7
Wholesale and retail trade – repairs	2.4	-4.3	-0.7	-2.6
Hotels and restaurants	2.6	-0.4	-0.6	1.6
Transport, storage and communication	-3.7	2.9	-1.0	-1.7
Financial intermediation	8.0	-0.9	-1.7	5.4
Real estate, renting and business activities	5.2	-4.1	-1.1	0.0
Public admin. and defence, social security	-2.2	10.3	-4.4	3.7
Education	-0.9	6.7	-1.4	4.4
Health and social work	-1.5	7.5	-3.7	2.4
Other community, social and personal services	1.8	-0.2	-0.1	1.6

Source: Author's calculations

The summary results of the decomposition analysis are presented in Table 5. The important finding of our analysis is that the discrepancies in productivity levels of individual sectors play the dominant role on productivity gap formation between Korea and Estonia as these discrepancies account for 66%. Fortunate for Estonia, the interaction or cross effect of productivity and structural differences is clearly negative (correlation coefficient about -0.4), which indicates a structural burden exist. Significantly higher productivity levels in some sectors of the Korean economy are mostly related to the smaller share of employment compared to Estonia. In this particular case, the structural and productivity difference components have the opposite signs in every single sector (Table 4). Consequently, the within-component of the productivity gap between Korea and Estonia would be 32% if the calculations are based on the structure of employment in Korea instead of Estonia.

Table 5: Components of productivity gap 2006 (%)

	Structural difference	Productivity difference	Cross effect	Total
Effect	6	66	-34	38
Percentage	16	175	-90	100

Source: Authors' calculations

The net effect of pure structural transformations is rather modest (16% of the total productivity gap), but still important. However, the between-component of the decomposition becomes negative (-28%) if we use the productivity levels of Korea as the basis of our calculations. Hence, the crowding-out hypothesis is confirmed in our analysis at the sectoral level. An interesting notion is that in Korea, alongside manufacturing and energy sector with ultra-high productivity levels, relatively large share of people are employed in low productivity agriculture, trade, hotels and restaurants.

3. Decomposition of Manufacturing Sector Productivity

Whereas the conception that positive deviations of productivity levels between countries tend to result in negative deviations in employment structure at aggregate level is generally accepted, the contributions, linkages and connections of the individual branches are not enough studied in order to talk about general knowledge, even at the empirical level. In the following paragraphs we analyse these branch-level relations taking manufacturing sector as an example. We compare Korean and Estonian manufacturing sectors using a STAN database of 12 manufacturing industries (Table 6). A number of differences, even larger than at sectoral level, occur between Korean and Estonian economy. Whereas Korea has virtually no forest and wood industry, in Estonia it is the second important manufacturing branch in terms of employment share (behind the textile industry). In contrast, Estonia has not had much of the mechanical engineering industry compared to Korea. Three branches of the mechanical engineering industry included in the analysis account for only 15.8% of total employment in Estonia, while in Korea the corresponding figure is as high as 46.4%! Korea has also relatively higher employment share in the chemical industry.

Table 6: Employment, value added and relative productivity in different branches of manu-
facturing sector of Korea and Estonia in 2006 (%)

	Employment		Productivity		Relative productivity	
	Korea	Estonia	Korea	Estonia	Korea	Estonia
Food products, beverages and tobacco	6.5	11.7	5.0	12.5	78.1	106.6
Textiles and textile products	8.8	16.9	4.3	8.3	49.6	49.2
Leather, leather products and footwear	1.0	1.5	0.5	0.6	45.2	43.2
Wood and products of wood and cork	0.9	15.8	0.5	13.8	58.2	87.2
Pulp, paper, paper products, printing and publishing	5.5	5.8	4.1	7.7	74.7	133.0
Chemical, rubber, plastics and fuel products	12.0	5.9	16.3	10.4	136.1	174.8
Other non-metallic mineral products	3.0	4.0	3.3	8.8	111.7	223.0
Basic metals and fabricated metal products	13.0	12.2	15.8	10.3	121.9	84.5
Machinery and equipment, n.e.c.	11.6	2.8	9.4	4.7	81.3	167.3
Electrical and optical equipment	21.6	8.2	24.3	11.1	112.8	134.7
Transport equipment	13.2	4.8	14.7	4.2	110.8	88.7
Manufacturing n.e.c. and recycling	3.0	10.4	1.7	7.6	54.9	72.6
Total	100.0	100.0	100.0	100.0	*	*

Source: OECD and authors' calculations

In addition to the review of employment shares, it is relevant to examine the relative productivity levels of different manufacturing branches. Interestingly, the differences within the manufacturing sector do not appear to be as large as the differences at the sectoral level. Correlations between the productivity levels of the two countries (around 0.6) are significantly stronger here, compared to correlations between the aggregated sectors. Hence, the manufacturing branches with higher and lower level of productivity coincide rather well. In both countries, productivity levels are the lowest in the textile and leather industries with relative productivity less than half the average of manufacturing sector. Chemical industry and machinery can be regarded as the branches with the highest productivity. If at the sectoral level the variability in productivity was greater in Korea, then in manufacturing industry it is larger in the context of Estonia. This is in line with the hypothesis of McMillan and Rodrik (2011) that the lower variability in productivity levels is a characteristic feature of higher level of development of the state. We should not forget that on average the Korean manufacturing sector

was 2.61 times more productive than Estonian. Taking that in account, we have
calculated the real deviations of productivity in addition to relative ones (Table 7).
It turns out that in all of the manufacturing branches, the productivity in Korea
is higher compared to Estonia. The largest discrepancies in favour of Korea stand
in metalworking industry and in the manufacturing of transport equipment, particularly the automotive industry, where the productivity exceeds Estonian level
by more than three times. The smallest gap between Korea and Estonia occurs in
the industries of non-metallic mineral products and machinery and equipment
wherein Korea has the lead of about 30%.

Table 7: Deviations of the relative and real productivity in branches of manufacturing industry in 2006 (%)

	Productivity deviations		Reference coefficient
	Relative	Real	
Food products, beverages and tobacco	-28.4	97.1	191.1
Textiles and textile products	0.4	80.0	262.6
Leather, leather products and footwear	2.0	74.7	272.8
Wood and products of wood and cork	-29.0	64.5	174.0
Pulp, paper, paper products, printing and publishing	-58.3	61.7	146.4
Chemical, rubber, plastics and fuel products	-38.6	180.1	203.1
Other non-metallic mineral products	-111.3	68.1	130.5
Basic metals and fabricated metal products	37.4	233.2	376.0
Machinery and equipment, n.e.c.	-86.0	44.6	126.7
Electrical and optical equipment	-22.0	159.3	218.2
Transport equipment	22.1	200.1	325.5
Manufacturing n.e.c. and recycling	-17.7	70.5	197.1

Source: Authors' calculations

Subsequently, the decomposition analysis is applied for examining the impact and
contribution of individual branches on the formation of manufacturing productivity gap (161%).

Table 8: Decomposition of productivity gap across manufacturing branches

	Structural difference	Productivity difference	Cross effect	Total
Food products, beverages and tobacco	-5.6	11.4	-5.1	0.6
Textiles and textile products	-4.0	13.5	-6.5	3.0
Leather, leather products and footwear	-0.2	1.1	-0.3	0.6
Wood and products of wood and cork	-13.0	10.2	-9.6	-12.4
Pulp, paper, paper products, printing and publishing	-0.4	3.6	-0.2	2.9
Chemical, rubber, plastics and fuel products	10.6	10.7	10.9	32.2
Other non-metallic mineral products	-2.2	2.7	-0.7	-0.1
Basic metals and fabricated metal products	0.6	28.6	1.7	30.9
Machinery and equipment, n.e.c.	14.7	1.2	3.9	19.9
Electrical and optical equipment	18.0	13.1	21.3	52.3
Transport equipment	7.5	9.5	16.9	34.0
Manufacturing n.e.c. and recycling	-5.3	7.3	-5.2	-3.2

Source: Authors' calculations

It is particularly noteworthy that in a number of major manufacturing branches of Korea, the structural and productivity effects are both positive and together shape a positive cross effect. The industry with the largest contribution to the manufacturing sector productivity gap is electrical equipment. It is followed by manufacturing of transport equipment, metalworking and manufacturing of chemical products with more or less equal contribution to the productivity gap. The only industry that contributes to the reduction of the productivity gap is forest and wood industry, particularly through the higher share of employment in Estonia. The summary results of industry level decomposition are represented in Table 9.

Table 9: Components of productivity gap in manufacturing sector in 2006 (%)

	Structural difference	Productivity difference	Cross effect	Total
Effect	21	113	27	161
Percentage	13	70	17	100

Source: Authors' calculations

The importance of different components in explaining the productivity gap in manufacturing sector is rather different compared to the component structure in a more aggregated sectoral level. The positive cross effect should be noted in parti-cular, which means that in the manufacturing sector, the increase in productivity does not necessarily mean a crowding out of labour, but rather the opposite – the attraction of labour. The structural bonus hypothesis finds some support in Korea – the employment has shifted towards the most successful industries. However, the within component still accounts the largest share (70%) of manufacturing sector productivity gap. About 30% of Estonia's backlog in manufacturing sector could be accounted for differences in employment structure if the calculations are based on the productivity levels of Korea. This result is consistent with our previous study, in which the structural bonus accounted for approximately 20% of the productivity gap between Estonian manufacturing compared to Finnish and EU average and as much as 40% compared to Ireland (Sepp/Eerma 2009).

4. Concluding Remarks

The decomposition of the productivity gap between Korea and Estonia lead us to the following conclusions:

The impact of the employment structure on average productivity varies on different structural levels. Whereas at more aggregated sectoral level the structural burden hypothesis was confirmed, in less aggregated level – taking manufacturing industry in our study – the structural bonus prevailed. In the first case, high level of productivity was accompanied with decreasing share of employment. In the second case, contrarily, the labour was converging to the manufacturing bran-ches with higher productivity. It needs a further research, whether it is a random structural specificity or a regular legitimacy.

At aggregated sectoral perspective, Korea lags Estonian productivity levels in several areas, particularly in traditional private sector services (trade, hotels and restaurants etc.) and the overall productivity gap (38%) is mainly related to the manufacturing industry. Significant sectoral variations in productivity can be considered as one of the weaknesses of the Korean economy.

In accordance with the previous studies, the relatively high productivity in financial intermediation and real estate sector in the young market economies was confirmed.

The situation in the public sector is substantially different in those two coun-tries. Korea is characterized by a relatively low public sector employment share, but significantly higher productivity of the funding compared to Estonia.

In manufacturing sector, the average productivity in Korea is 2.6 times higher compared to Estonia and unlike the more aggregated sectoral level, it concerns all the manufacturing branches. Electronics and manufacturing of transport equipment are playing the most important role in formation of the productivity gap. Considering both productivity, employment and their interaction, there is just one branch in Estonian manufacturing industry that somewhat mitigates the productivity gap – the wood and forest industry.

References

Akkemik, K. A. (2006) Patterns of Industrialisation, Structural Changes and Productivity in Turkish Manufacturing (1970–2000). Journal of Economic Cooperation Among Islamic Countries.

Ark, B. van / O'Mahony, M. / Timmer, M. (2012) Europe's productivity performance in comparative perspective: trends, causes and recent developments, in: Mas, M. and Stehrer, R., pp. 65–92.

Baumol, W. J. (1967) Macroeconomics of Unbalanced Growth: The Anatomy of Urban Crisis, in: The American Economic Review, Vol. 57, pp. 415–426.

Chansomphou, V. / Ichihashi, M. (2013) Structural change, labor productivity growth, and convergence of BRIC countries, Hiroshima University, Graduate School for International Development and Cooperation (IDEC).

Fagerberg, J. (2000) Technological progress, structural change and productivity growth: a comparative study, in: Structural Change and Economic Dynamics Vol. 11, No. 4, pp. 393–412.

Havlik, P. (2013) Structural Change and Economic Growth in the New EU Member States. The Vienna Institute for International Economic Studies. GRINCOH, May 2013.

Jorgenson, D. / Timmer, M.P. (2010) Structural Change in Advanced Nations. GDGC.

Kaldor, N. (1961) Capital Accumulation and Economic Growth, in: F. A. Lutz and D.C. Hague (eds.), Proceedings of a Conference Held by the International Economics Association. London: MacMillan, pp. 177–222.

Kuznets, S. (1971) Economic Growth of Nations: Total Output and Production Structure, Cambridge, MA, Harvard University Press.

Maddison, A. (1980) Economic Growth and Structural Change in Advanced Countries, Chapter 3 in: I. Levenson and J. Wheeler (eds.), Western Economies in Transition: Structural Change and Adjustment Policies in Industrial Countries, Boulder, CO, Westview Press.

Marczewski, K. / K. Szczygielski (2007) The Process of Structural Change in Polish Manufacturing in 1995–2003 and its Determinants, Industrial Competitiveness and Restructuring in Enlarged Europe. How Accession Countries Catch Up and Integrate in the European Union. Hoshi, I.; Welfens, P.J.J., Wziatek-Kubiak (eds). New York: Palgrave Macmillan, pp. 161–195.

McMillan, M. / Rodrik, D. (2011) Globalization, Structural Change, and Productivity Growth. Mimeo, Harvard University.

O'Donnell, M. (2007) Structural Change, productivity and Performance. Evidence from Irish Manufacturing, Industrial Competitiveness and Restructuring in Enlarged Europe. How Accession Countries Catch Up and Integrate in the European Union. Hoshi, I.; Welfens, P.J.J., Wziatek-Kubiak (eds). New York: Palgrave Macmillan, pp. 196–224.

Peneder, M. (2002) Industrial Structure and Aggregate Growth, WIFO Working Papers 182, WIFO.

Rodrik, D. (2012) Die Schaffung von Arbeitsplätzen und erfolgreicher Strukturwandel in Entwicklungsländern. DIW-Vierteljahrshefte zur Wirtschaftsforschung, 81. Jahrgang, 03.2012. pp. 33–43.

Sepp, J. / Eerma, D. (2009) Industry's Structure and Productivity in Estonia and in the Developed EU Countries. The Key-Factors of Business and Socio-Economic Development (207–217). Wilkes-Barre: Congress of Political Economists International.

Sepp, J. / Paas, T. / Eerma, D. (2009) Sectoral structure of the economy and the position of transition countries in European Union, in: Baltic Business and Socio-Economic Development 2008: 4th International Conference Baltic Business and Socio-Economic Development 2008; Riga, Latvia; 30.09 – 02.10.2008. (Toim.) Prause, G.; Muravska, T. Berliner Wissenschafts-Verlag, 2009, pp. 115–129.

Szalavetz, A. (2009) 'Tertiarization' of manufacturing Industry in the New Economy – Experiences in Hungarian companies, online: http://www.vki.hu/workingpapers/wp-134.pdf

Timmer, M. / Szirmai, A. (2000) Productivity growth in Asian manufacturing: the structural bonus hypothesis examined, in: Structural Change and Economic Dynamics, Elsevier, Vol. 11(4), pp. 371–392.

Vries, G. de / Erumban, A.A. / Timmer, M.P. et al. (2012) Deconstructing the BRICs: Structural transformation and aggregate productivity growth, in: Journal of Comparative Economics, Elsevier, vol. 40(2), pp. 211–227.

Yang, Q. / Stephenson, J. (2011) Industry productivity and the Australia-New Zealand income gap, NZIER public discussion document.

Jüri Sepp, Helje Kaldaru and Jürgen Joamets

The Characteristics and Position of the Economic Structures of Estonia and Korea among the OECD Countries

1. Introduction

Prior research has shown that when it comes to time and regional variation, the behaviour of the various industries of the economy tends to be contingent upon each other.[1] The variance of their relative importance is linked regardless. This in turn allows us to pose the question of not only an overarching trend of structural change but also one of economic typology and to study the placement and movement of countries within the said typology. The topic of varying economic structure between countries was brought up by Wacziarg/Imbs (2000) and from a convergence viewpoint by Wacziarg (2001) specifically. Unfortunately, not many in-depth studies on the subject have been done to date. Studies on structural convergence include Höhenberger/ Schmiedeberg (2008) and Melihovs/Kasjanovs (2011). The latter have also attempted to find a structural typology among European countries by utilising cluster analyses. Paas et al. (2009) and Sepp (2009) have combined factor and cluster analyses to show that European countries may be divided into certain groups which can be characterised by specific traits:

- The service-based welfare states of Western and Northern Europe with a strong but small core of high value-added industries,
- The countries of Southern Europe where in addition to manufacturing, tourism is in a prominent position. These countries have a small but high value social sector as well.
- The transition states of Eastern and Central Europe with a sizable but low value-added manufacturing presence. Both the business and private services sectors in these countries are on the rise. In addition, these countries have remarkable returns on mediation activities.

---

1   Fisher (1935); Clark (1940); Fourastié (1949); Kaldor (1961); Baumol (1967); Fuchs (1968); Kuznets (1971) and Madisson (1980) are the classics in this sphere. See the overview by Jorgenson/Timmer (2011).

- Similar conclusions have been drawn by Janger et al. (2011: 17), however, their typology is based on more than just the structure of the economy:
- Higher-income countries with a specialisation in knowledge-intensive sectors, including Austria, Belgium, Denmark, Finland, France, Germany, Ireland, the Netherlands, Sweden and the United Kingdom.
- Higher-income countries with a specialisation in less knowledge-intensive sectors, including Cyprus, Greece, Italy, Luxembourg, Portugal and Spain.
- Lower-income countries with a trade specialisation in technologically-progressive sectors including the Czech Republic, Hungary, Malta, Poland, Slovakia and Slovenia.
- Lower-income countries with a specialisation in less knowledge-intensive sectors, including Bulgaria, Estonia, Latvia, Lithuania and Romania.

The typology of the various economic structures may seem hidden at first glance and as such is also an intriguing subject outside of the European Union. The current article will look at the OECD countries while paying special attention to finding the positions of Estonia and Korea within this conglomeration of countries. For generalisation purposes, we will use principal component analysis while relying on the STAN database for data on employment structure in OECD countries in 2006. The following 14 sectors will be under examination:

1. Agriculture, hunting, forestry and fishing
2. Mining and quarrying
3. Manufacturing
4. Electricity, gas and water supply
5. Construction
6. Wholesale and retail trade – repairs
7. Hotels and restaurants
8. Transport, storage and communication
9. Financial intermediation
10. Real estate, renting and business activities
11. Public administration and defence – compulsory social security
12. Education
13. Health and social work
14. Other communal, social and personal services

2. Sectoral Structure of Employment

Excluding the quarrying industry, for which no data was available, our component analysis reached a structure that could be described with three or four components (the corresponding values were greater than one). It is remarkable that the first two components were not at all dependent on the specification of the following two, which speaks volumes about their robust and objective nature (Table 1). The density of correlations between first components found from two different models reached 0.99.

When interpreting the first two components (Table 1) we can see some overlapping with the components found with European Union data (Sepp 2009). Firstly, the **tertiarisation component** (F13 and F14), which has a significant positive relation to finance and business services and social and healthcare sector employment and a negative relation to the agriculture, manufacturing and energy sectors. The second component of employment structure (F24 and F23), however, is strongly connected to the transport and communication sector as well as the manufacturing and energy sectors. All of these industries share an aptitude for technology. On the other hand, a negative relation can be seen with the housing, catering and wholesale industries, and in the case of three components (F23), other personal and social services which can all be summarised as the leisure industry. This component can be called the **technology component** in accordance with its positive relation.

Table 1: The hidden components of employment structure (factor loadings in the case of a 3 or 4 dimensional specification)

Industry	Components of the 4-dimensional model				Components of the 3-dimensional model		
	F14	F24	F34	F44	F13	F23	F33
1 AGR	-0.786				-0.823		
3 MAN	-0.736	0.351			-0.718	0.397	
4 ELE	-0.586	0.647			-0.551	0.684	
5 CON			0.451	0.595			0.760
6 WHO		-0.684				-0.679	
7 HOT		-0.708	0.540			-0.767	0.484
8 TRA		0.853				0.834	
9 FIN	0.579			0.656	0.579		0.479
10 REA	0.886				0.866		
11 PUB			-0.705				-0.646
12 EDU				-0.735			-0.488
13 HEA	0.745				0.744		
14 OTH			0.787			-0.435	0.408

Note: The first three letters of the name of the economic sector will be used as an acronym. Only statistically significant factor weights are listed
Source: Authors' calculations based on OECD STAN data

The above interpretation is also confirmed when looking at the allocation of the countries on the level of factor scores (Figure 1). It is worth noting that Estonia is an outlier – it has the largest technology component. This also sets it apart from other transitional economies which without it form a cluster of six countries. One may say that Estonia is clearly the most technologically advanced out of them. On the other hand, Japan alongside Korea seems to be moving closer to the economic structure of the tourism-based countries of Southern Europe. Despite this, Korea and Japan still belong to the cluster of advanced western service-based economies, although with relatively extensive deindustrialisation (the score of the first factor is slightly negative). Their counterparts among the developed countries are Northern European countries, where the traditional retail and communal services sectors do not employ as many individuals.

Figure 1: The OECD countries according to the first two latent variables of employment in 2006 (factor scores).

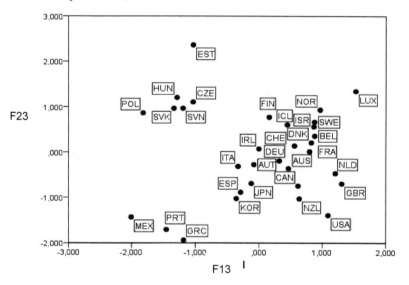

Source: Authors' calculations based on OECD STAN data

The largest contribution of the current study is the forming of a third (and fourth) component (Figure 2). These components are described by a relatively modest public sector, especially in the public services and education sense. This void in employment is filled by construction and multiple private sector services.

Figure 2: The OECD countries according to the first and third latent variables of employment in 2006 (factor scores).

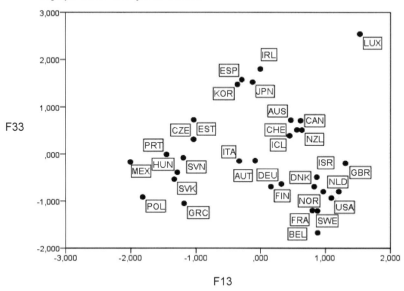

Source: Authors' calculations based on the OECD STAN data

Broadly speaking, the last two components separate large and small public sectors regarding employment. In the three dimensional model the component analysis integrates the last two components of the four dimensional model. In this case, the countries where employment in education and public services is relatively low (Japan, Korea, Ireland and Spain) have the largest positive factor scores, with the largest outlier being Luxembourg. The latter can be explained by the opportunity of using the public infrastructure, especially education systems, of its larger neighbouring countries. In place of the public sector, these countries have a large proportion of employment in construction, housing, financial services and other social and personal services in the private sector. This affinity is shared by the smaller Anglo-American countries (Australia, Canada and New Zealand), as well as Switzerland and Iceland, with the only transition state being Estonia. Larger economies like the UK and the US may not be able to afford a small public sector. Countries inclined toward a large public sector include the state-centred France and Belgium and also a majority of the Northern countries. Examples from less wealthy countries also include Poland and Greece. All in all, this component can be referred to as the **private economy component**.

Of course, in a four-dimensional world, the third and fourth components do not align. When looking at them separately (Figure 3), one can see that Luxembourg makes up the fourth component, or the **minimal education system**, almost all on its own. The opposite can be seen with Sweden and Israel. The other countries are relatively similar in this case.

Figure 3: *The OECD countries according to the third and fourth latent variables of employment in 2006 (factor scores).*

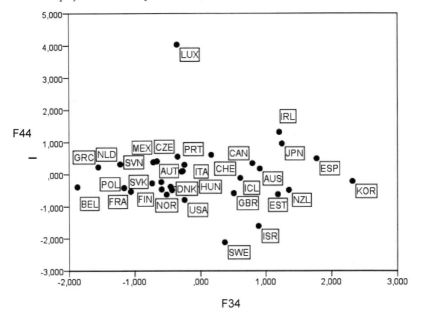

Source: Authors' calculations based on the OECD STAN data

On the contrary, Korea seems to be the most frugal when it comes to public administration employment including social protection. The scores of this component exceed one in Spain, Japan, Ireland and the Netherlands. Estonia is not far behind. The countries with the largest public administration employment are Belgium and Greece, which could be related to servicing their large national debts.

Finally, the factors are cross-checked among each other and various socioeconomic indicators (Table 2).

Table 2: *The relations of the latent variables of the employment structure with the proportion of budgetary income in the GDP of the state and national income per capita (excluding Luxembourg)*

	F14	F24	F34	F44	F13	F23	F33	Ratio of state budget to GDP
Ratio of state budget to GDP	0.45	0.34	-0.27	-0.33	0.44	0.35	-0.40	1.00
GNI per capita	**0.83**	-0.08	0.00	-0.08	**0.82**	-0.12	-0.12	0.36

Source: Authors' calculations based on the OECD STAN data

As expected, financial well-being (GNI per capita) is mostly and essentially only connected to the first so-called tertiarisation components of both specifications (F14 and F13). The other components do not describe well-being. The components are, however, moderately related to a country's monetary "thickness" (the state's proportion in GDP) – the tertiarisation and technology components have a positive relation and the private sector components a negative.

3. Relationship between Employment Structure and Relative Productivity

The latent components of employment are also connected to the relative productivity – that is to say in relation to the country's average productivity – of the various industries to a noteworthy extent (Table 3). In addition to this, we can see that the correlation between the proportion of employment and relative productivity is inverse in a number of industries. For example, in service-based economies relative productivity is lower in the service sector than in their manufacturing-based counterparts. The opposite is true when looking at the manufacturing sector. It is worth noting that the comparatively higher productivity of the service sector in less wealthy manufacturing-based countries is rather widespread, encompassing industries that do not define the first component in employment structure.

Table 3: *The links between employment components and the relative productivity of industries*

Industry	F13: Services *versus* Manufacturing		F23: Technology *versus* Tourism		F33: Private *versus* public sector	
	Employment	Productivity	Employment	Productivity	Employment	Productivity
AGR	-0.82					
MAN	-0.72	0.29	0.40			

Industry	F13: Services *versus* Manufacturing		F23: Technology *versus* Tourism		F33: Private *versus* public sector	
	Employment	Productivity	Employment	Productivity	Employment	`Productivity
ENE	-0.55		0.68	-0.61		
FIN	0.58	-0.49			0.48	0.29
HEA	0.74	-0.42		-0.51		
REA	0.87	-0.66				
TRA		-0.48	0.83	-0.48		
HOT		-0.37	-0.77		0.48	
WHO		-0.45	-0.68	0.37		-0.31
OTH		-0.29	-0.43	0.31	0.41	-0.50
CON					0.76	
PUB					-0.65	0.36
EDU				-0.49	-0.49	0.27

Source: Authors' calculations based on the OECD STAN data

A similar inverse relation between employment and relative productivity repeats itself in the case of the other components as well. The second component differentiated between countries with a higher proportion of employment in technological industries (manufacturing, energy and water management, transport and communication) and tourism-based states with a higher proportion of employment in housing, catering, retail and other personal services. Table 3 shows that employment and relative productivity are inversely related to the second component. Housing and catering is an exception in that higher employment in the sector is not coupled with lower productivity. The same can be said about the manufacturing sector. No significant differences between countries can be seen in employment in the education sector but better funding has brought with it higher productivity within the sector in the tourism-based countries.

The third component is predominantly characterised by its inverse relation with employment and productivity. This is mainly seen in education, public administration and private services. An outstanding confluent relation can be seen with both productivity and employment and financial services. No palpable difference in productivity can be seen as far as countries with a small government having a significant percentage of people employed in construction, housing and catering go.

In summary, we have confirmed the conclusion reached through the deconstruction of Estonia and Korea's average productivity (Sepp/ Varblane 2014) stating that a rise in a sector's employment brings about a dip in its productivity. We have confirmed the structural burden hypothesis. This relation is, however, not univocal. One can only assume the extent of the influence of international competition on open sectors of the economy. Globalisation forces the labour force in wealthier countries out of low value-added industries. This entails a higher proportion of employment in the service sector at a lower value-added because international competition has a lower effect. This does not, of course, mean a lower level of absolute productivity.

4. Employment Structure of the Manufacturing Industry

The following will take a detailed look at the employment structure of the OECD countries using the aforementioned principal component method. We are interested in whether the latent components that define it (Table 4) have any relation to the previously explained components of the general structure of the economy. All analysis will be based on the data of 10 industry sectors in the OECD countries in 2006.[2] In addition to this, aggregate data of low, medium, and high-technology manufacturing is included. The variants presented in the table show that the first principal component is robust regardless of the model used. For the main part, this can also be seen in the case of the second principal component. Their interpretation is aided by the aforementioned classification of low, medium, and high-tech industries. One can clearly see that the first principal component (G12 and G13) describes, or generalises, **employment in high and medium-tech sectors** and the second (G22 and G23) describes **employment in the low-tech sector.**

Table 4: The hidden components of employment structure in the manufacturing sector in the OECD countries in 2006 in the case of a 3 or 4 dimensional specification

Sector	3-dimensional model			2-dimensional model	
	G13	G23	G33	G12	G22
Food and textile industry			0.534		0.572
Textile, clothing and leather industry		0.789			0.885
Forestry		0.895			0.760

---

2   Food products, beverages and tobacco; Textiles and textile, leather, leather products and footwear; Wood and products of wood and cork; Pulp, paper, paper products, printing and publishing; Chemical, rubber, plastics and fuel products; Other non-metallic mineral products; Basic metals and fabricated metal products; Machinery and electrical and optical equipment; Transport equipment; Manufacturing n.e.c. and recycling.

Sector	3-dimensional model			2-dimensional model	
	G13	G23	G33	G12	G22
Paper and printing industry			-0.906		
Chemical and fuel industry	0.830			0.818	
Manufacturing of non-metal minerals		0.555	0.520		0.703
Metal industry	0.734			0.743	0.432
Machinery	0.930			0.935	
Transport equipment	0.617			0.618	
Manufacturing n.e.c.		0.849			0.813
Low-tech industry		0.957			0.959
Medium-tech and high-tech industry	0.938			0.940	

Source: Authors' calculations based on the OECD STAN data

Low-tech manufacturing is based on textile, forestry, partially metal and food industry as well as other industries. High-tech manufacturing includes the manufacture of various machines and gadgets as well as chemistry and a large portion of metalwork. The role of the third component (G33) is to describe the paper, cellulose and printing industries first and foremost. These industries cannot be completely categorised under a certain technological level and are not influenced by the spatial variation of other subindustries (related to Finland, Sweden and Canada's specialisation).

This interpretation is also seen when looking at the allocation of countries at the component level. We will only look at two dimensions simultaneously (Figure 4). Manufacturing-based states are clearly set apart from the other by both general employment and level of technology. Manufacturing states are the countries where the factor score of at least one component is positive. The level of technology is determined by which factor score is greater. All transition states as well as some Southern European countries have specialised in low-tech manufacturing. Estonia and Portugal are forefront performers (the score of the second component exceeds two). Most other transition states are also represented in high-tech manufacturing, performing around the average (the Czech Republic, Slovenia, Slovakia and Hungary). Italy is not far behind. Highly advanced high-tech countries are mainly represented by Germany and Korea, the latter of which we are very interested in. A similar industrial trend can also be seen in Finland, Switzerland, Sweden and Japan, although to a much lesser extent. In conclusion, it can be said that Estonia and Korea are polar opposites as far as the internal structure of industrial employment goes.

When looking at how the first two components of industrial employment are related to the third component of the general economy we can see that the only statistically significant relation is between the low-tech and the tertiarisation components. As expected, this relation is negative. It is somewhat unexpected that the tertiarisation component is also inversely related to the medium-tech and high-tech component. This can be somewhat explained by the negative correlation between industrial employment and national income per capita. The low-tech industry stands at -0.70 and the medium-tech and high-tech industry at -0.35. One can assume that the main reason is the negative relation between employment and relative productivity.

Figure 4: The OECD countries based on the first two latent components of industrial employment structure in 2006 (factor scores).

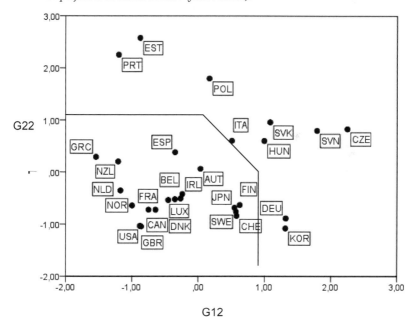

Source: Authors' calculations based on the OECD STAN data

Table 5: The relationship of manufacturing and general employment components in the economic structure

	G12: Medium- and high-tech industry	G22: Low-tech industry
F13: Tertiarisation	-0.37	**-0.79**
F23: Technology	0.39	0.27
F33: Private sector	0.05	-0.03

Source: Authors' calculations based on the OECD STAN data

The aforementioned relations can be seen in Figures 5 and 6. Low-tech manufacturing is once again represented by the transition states, headed by Estonia and Portugal. An intermediate group is made up of other Southern European countries. Medium and high-tech manufacturing employment is slightly more complicated (Figure 6). The transition states are more clearly separated. The Czech Republic, Slovenia, Slovakia and Hungary are grouped with Korea and Germany. Estonia, along with Portugal and Greece, is left behind even by countries that are in essence already service based.

Figure 5: The relation of the tertiarisation and low-tech industry employment components.

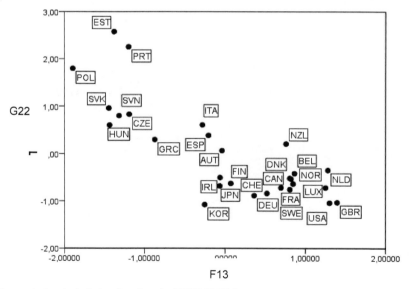

Source: Authors' calculations based on the OECD STAN data

Figure 6: The relation of the tertiarisation and medium-tech and high-tech industry employment components.

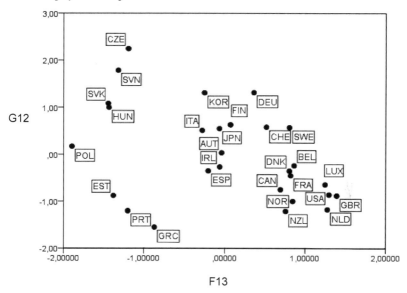

Source: Authors' calculations based on the OECD STAN data

5. Summary

The regional variations of the OECD countries and the European Union have relatively similar latent components. A clear difference can be seen starting at the third component.

The main trend of the evolution is explained by the **tertiarisation component** which expresses the outstanding growth of the service sector relative to the two first (primary and secondary) sectors. At the same, this is either accompanied or preceded by an important rise in relative productivity in manufacturing and a dip in the service sector (compared to the averages of the economy). The strongest inverse relation between the proportion of employment and relative productivity and the first structural component can be seen in the real estate sector: 0.87 and -0.66 respectively. Korea's overall lead over Estonia in the tertiarisation process is not very large (the deviation of its factor score is below one) and Korea is still around the average.

On the other hand, according to the second sectoral structure component, Estonia and Korea are polar opposites. Estonia is at the forefront of **technological**

employment, which means a relatively large proportion of employment in sectors such as transport, communication and energy. However, Korea (as well as Japan) tends to be a part of the contrasting tourism-based countries' group, where a large portion of the workforce is employed in housing, catering and retail, akin to Mediterranean countries. Unfortunately, it must be repeated that a rise in employment entails a relatively lower level or productivity, especially in the technology sector. For instance, the second principal component's relation to employment and productivity in the energy sector is 0.68 and -0.61 respectively.

The present study could, for the first time, interpret the following components in a meaningful way. Both the third and fourth component had a strong relation with differences in the **institutional sectoral structure**. In essence, countries with large and small employment in the public sector could be differentiated. Both Estonia and Korea, especially the latter, are countries with low employment in the public sector. Employment in public administration and social protection is especially minute in Korea. Countries such as these have a large portion of employment in private services and especially construction to make up for their smaller public sector. The opposite can be seen in countries like France, Belgium, the Nordic countries, Poland and Greece. A reference to structural barriers must be made, meaning that the component has an inverse relation to both employment and productivity. This can be seen mainly in public administration, at -0.65 and 0.36 respectively. This means that a public sector with low employment may not necessarily be low on funding.

An even clearer picture was seen in the structural **typology of the manufacturing**. Two principal components were found, which were based on a dominant technological level. The STAN database divides the various industries into low, medium and high-tech manufacturing and as such pre-aggregated data could be added into the component analysis. The factor score of medium and high-tech manufacturing in the first component turned out to be 0.94. The factor score of low-tech manufacturing in the second component reached 0.96. The content of the components is confirmed by the loadings of the various industries. The first component encompasses primarily machinery and the chemistry and fuel industries, while the second includes the textile, clothing and leather industries as well as forestry and manufacturing n.e.c. The third component is characterised by strong loadings in the paper and printing industry.

Korea and Estonia can both be considered manufacturing states because the factor score of at least one component exceeds one. Unfortunately, the different manufacturing specialisation of the two countries is clear as well. Estonia as well as Portugal is one of the low-tech manufacturing countries, while Korea is one of the high-tech manufacturing countries alongside Germany. Both Estonia and Korea have a very low representation of the other's level of technology (the factor score is negative). The largest industrial countries seem to be the transition states of Central Europe where industries of both technological levels are strongly represented.

As expected, the relation between the **tertiarisation and industrialisation** components is negative. General tertiarisation means deindustrialisation in employment in both the low and medium to high-tech sectors, albeit with varying intensity (-0.79 and -0.37 respectively). The difference in association coefficients hints at an inverse relation with relative productivity. Employment in manufacturing converges toward industries with higher relative productivity in times of economic upswing.

References

Baumol, W. J. (1967) Macroeconomics of Unbalanced Growth: The Anatomy of Urban Crisis, in: The American Economic Review 57, pp. 415–426.

Clark, C. (1940) The Conditions of Economic Progress. London: MacMillan & Co. Ltd.

Fisher, A.G.B. (1935) The Clash of Progress and Security. London: MacMillan & Co. Ltd.

Fourastié, J. (1949) Le Grand Espoir du XXe Siècle. Paris: Presses Universitaires de France. Reprinted as 'Moderne Techniek en Economische Ontwikkeling' (1965). Amsterdam: Het Spectrum.

Fuchs, V.R. (1968) The Service Economy. New York and London: Colombia University Press.

Höhenberger, N. / Schmiedeberg, C. (2008) Structural convergence. Center for European, Governance and Economic Development 75, University of Goettingen, Department of Economics.

Janger, J. et al. (2011) Structural Change and the Competitiveness of EU Member States Final Report – CR 2011.

Jorgenson, D. / Timmer, M. (2011) Structural Change in Advanced Nations: A New Set of Stylised Facts, in: Scandinavian Journal of Economics 113(1), pp. 1–29.

Kaldor, N. (1961) Capital Accumulation and Economic Growth, in: F.A. Lutz and D.C. Hague (eds.), Proceedings of a Conference Held by the International Economics Association. London: MacMillan, pp. 177–222.

Kuznets, S. (1971) Economic Growth of Nations: Total Output and Production Structure, Cambridge, MA: Harvard University Press.

Maddison, A. (1980) Economic Growth and Structural Change in Advanced Countries, Chapter 3 in I. Levenson and J. Wheeler (eds.), Western Economies in Transition: Structural Change and Adjustment Policies in Industrial Countries, Boulder, CO: Westview Press.

Melihovs, A. / Kasjanovs, I. (2011) The Convergence Processes in Europe. Discussion Papers 2011/01, Latvijas Banka.

Sepp, J. (2009) Europäische Wirtschaftssysteme durch das Prisma der Branchenstruktur und die Position der Transformationsländer. – Ordnungspolitische Diskurse 2009–11.

Sepp, J. / Paas, T. / Eerma, D. (2009) Sectoral structure of the economy and the position of transition countries in European Union, in G. Prause and T. Muravska (eds.), Baltic Business and Socio-Economic Development 2008, Berliner Wissenschafts-Verlag, pp. 115–129.

Sepp, J. / Varblane, U. (2014) The Decomposition of Productivity Gap between Estonia and Korea. – Ordnungspolitische Diskurse 2014–3.

Wacziarg, R. (2001) Structural Convergence. Stanford University, May, 32 p.

Wacziarg, R. / Imbs, J. (2000) Stages of Diversification. Research Papers 1653, Stanford University, Graduate School of Business.

Bernhard J. Seliger

Lessons of Korea for Emerging Economies: An unexpected journey from rags to riches, from crisis to recovery[1]

In the 1960s the Republic of Korea's (South Korea) president Park Chung-Hee, among other things influenced by a visit to Germany in 1964, embarked on the building of the first national motorway, from Seoul to Busan, linking the two economic centres of the poor South Korea until now dependent on foreign aid and still devastated by the war. A major international institution (the World Bank) called this plan utopian, calling attention to some basic missing ingredients for such a large project: there was no major construction industry with experience in such large-scale projects, no steel industry, no car industry and, accordingly, even if the project succeeded, no traffic could be expected on the planned highway. Today, Korea is one of the major international contractors for construction projects, with a number of heavyweights in the industry, has a world-leading steel factory and indeed a whole steel city (Posco in Pohang), is one of the leading car manufacturers of the world and among the largest trading nations. A veritable journey from rags to riches.

However, this journey was not smooth and, indeed, in 1997, when the Asian Financial Crisis hit the country, it seemed to have come to an abrupt end. Again, South Korea underwent dramatic change in the last one and a half decades, from being considered a 'tiger in trouble' in the wake of the Asian crisis to a showcase of economic development. Today South Korea is an active donor of development aid, receiving countless delegations from countries interested in the specific Korean way of development and also supporting its trade policy with sending out development officials and engineers. The judgement of 1998 was itself a complete reversal of previous enthusiastic reviews of world record high growth for several decades, from the 1960s to the 1990s. Korea, once considered a shrimp between two mighty whales, Japan and China, as neighbours, veritably made a jump to become a tiger. After the steep decline of 1998, this tiger again showed its claws,

---

1   Reprint from: Lessons of Korea for emerging economies: an unexpected journey from rags to riches, from crisis to recovery, in: Robert Looney (ed.), Handbook of Emerging Economies, London: Routledge (ISBN: 1857436709), pp. 531–538.

a transformation almost as astonishing as its original 'economic miracle', as the following comparison of Korea in 1998 and 2011 shows.

In 1998, South Korea suffered from a severe recession, triggered by the currency crisis it had experienced a year before. After two years of growing macroeconomic imbalance, in particular growing current account deficits, as well as a contagion from the spreading currency crisis in South-East Asia since the summer of 1997, by the end of the year Korea had a record low of usable foreign reserves of barely more than US$7 billion. The South Korean won, previously managed in a narrow band to the US dollar, had to be floated and drastically depreciated, and South Korea's sovereign rating was lowered, which made repaying debt more costly and caused the stock market to crash.

In 2011 the South Korean economy marked for the first time a trade volume of more than $1 trillion. The nominal per capita gross domestic product (GDP) reached a record $24,000. South Korea's economy, though hurt by the subsequent financial crisis in 2008 and the lingering woes over the world economy, grew throughout this period. In July 2011, the free trade agreement between South Korea and the European Union (EU) took effect, and in late 2011 the free trade agreement (FTA) with the USA was approved in a tumultuous session of the Korean Parliament. From 2012, South Korea enjoyed free trade with an area representing two thirds of the world's GDP. Also, South Korea's national success has become increasingly a benchmark for other countries as South Korea transforms into a leading world economy. From being a receiver of development aid it has become a major donor, hosting an Organisation for Economic Co-operation and Development (OECD) Development Assistance Committee (representing the most important donors of development aid) forum in November 2011 in Busan. It also took a leading role in the G20 during the financial crisis of 2008 and 2009, hosted a G20 summit in 2010, and is leading efforts to implement a new vision of green growth at the regional and international levels.

What triggered this remarkable resurgence of South Korea? While international aid under the umbrella of the International Monetary Fund (IMF), a steep depreciation of the Korean won and improving macroeconomic factors certainly helped to overcome the immediate crisis, it does not explain Korea's post-crisis development. Other countries working under the same external environment had much less success. To understand Korea's outperformance, one needs to look at institutional change after the crisis. While the popular explanation of the Korean crisis made it macroeconomic, and even an 'IMF crisis', blaming international forces for the downfall, nevertheless, the Korean government and companies understood that unresolved structural issues were at the heart of the crisis and started to embrace change, beginning with the unprecedented election of an opposition candidate and peaceful democratic power transfer in 1997 and 1998, and then implementing change in the public sector, the labour market, the private sector, monetary and financial policy, the foreign direct investment (FDI) regime, trade relations and other areas. In this sense, recent South Korean economic history is also a story from crisis to recovery.

Let us first look back at the origins of the 'miracle at the Han river', as South Koreans like to call their rapid economic development since the early 1960s. For centuries Korea had been a feudal agrarian society in which economic well-being was less a question of industriousness, and mostly dependent on the harvest, largely determined by the weather, and sometimes on political events, like wars, local turmoil, extortionist landlords, etc. Trade (for example, export of porcelain to Japan) was marginal, and traders belonged to the lowest class of society (sang) in the strict hierarchy formed according to a Confucian model of in the period of the Chosun kingdom (1392–1910). Accordingly, the monetization and commercialization of society were extremely low. The invasions by Japan in 1592 and the Manchu in 1637 lowered trade to a minimum. The decline of the Chinese Empire after the opium wars (1839–42 and 1856–60) was understood in Korea as a warning, with the lesson being to withdraw into almost complete isolation, which brought Korea the reputation of being a 'hermit kingdom'. After successfully fighting off various French and American trade and military missions and persecuting foreign missionaries, the newly rising Japan forced Korea to open up with the so-called Gangwha treaty of 1876. This was a prelude to 30 years of fighting between China, the old though mostly nominal tributary overlord Japan, and Russia over domination of Korea, which ended with Korea becoming a protectorate of Japan in 1905 and an outright colony in 1910. The opening of Korea brought foreign trade missions, more trade, and new ideas and innovations into the country. In 1900 the railway between Seoul and Incheon was opened. Treaties with a number of states were concluded. Nevertheless, trade remained marginal and is estimated to have been not more than 5% of GDP before colonization.

This changed dramatically with the modernization forced upon the Korean economy after Japanese colonization. The share of export goods in total production rose until the World War II to more than 25% of GDP, the share of import goods to almost 35%. Foreign trade was clearly focused on Japan and dependent on Japan; for example, rice exports from the early colonial period to the beginning of the Pacific war in 1937 rose seven-fold. After the end of the colonial era, which brought many painful memories to Koreans, among them the attempt to erase the Korean cultural identity, many scholars focused on Korea's dependence on Japan and negated any positive impact of its colonization on the economy. However, from a purely economic point of view, modernization by Japan brought many advantages and laid some foundations for the later economic development: Japan paid prices for Korean rice and raw materials like iron that were higher than world market prices; in the northern part of Korea an industrial base developed and began to open up new markets abroad (obviously, mainly in the Japanese-dominated area); modern education in schools and universities, which barely began in the pre-colonial period, brought new educational opportunities to Korea's middle class; but most important of all, Korea for the first time was thoroughly integrated into an Asian production network. Some of the predecessors of the later large Korean conglomerates originated in this period, like Samsung in 1938.

The independence of Korea in 1945 and the subsequent division into South and North brought new problems for South Korea. The industrial base of Korea was mostly in the raw material-rich North of the country, and at the same time Japan as a destination for Korean rice exports ceased to exist. Anyway, the turmoil after independence brought a massive decline in production and in 1948 Korea, a traditional rice exporter, even had to import large quantities of its main staple food. The Korean War from 1950 to 1953 torpedoed the attempts to rebuild the economy and led to a new strong dependence, this time on its main ally, the USA. From 1952 to 1961 the South Korean government budget was almost half financed by foreign aid. Exports, later the drivers of economic success, almost completely ceased, accounting for 1% of GDP in 1954 and 2% in 1962. Among the main export goods were women's hair (to make wigs), pig bristle, octopus and other sea food, and some raw materials.

South Korea's first post-independence president, Rhee Syngman tried, in accordance with the prevailing development theories of the time, to develop domestic industries like cement and steel by protecting them from foreign competition and substituting, thereby, foreign with domestic production. This policy of import substitution, unfortunately, did not work, since the lack of competition domestically as well as internationally worked as a disincentive for the growth of competitive industries. A fixed and overvalued exchange rate for the Korean currency, paired with high inflation rates, did not help economic development either. The reduction of military aid led to bottlenecks in urgently needed imports. In 1960, after mass protests due to election fraud and corruption, Rhee Syngman had to resign and leave the country. His successor, President Chang Myon, had no luck in governing the country, seeing a time of growing anarchy. Only when Park Chung-Hee, a relatively young officer educated in a Japanese military academy, led a coup d'état and afterwards reigned the country with iron fist, did South Korea's rise as a trading nation, a developmental state and dictatorship, begin.

After his coup, Park Chung-Hee faced the following challenges: the economy, having grown after the end of the Korean War, already in 1956 was again in recession and in the crisis year of Lessons of Korea for emerging economies 1960 barely grew by 1.2%. Widespread corruption had been the reason for the ousting of President Rhee, but it could not effectively be stopped by President Chang. Frequent strikes and demonstrations substituted for political debate and crippled the economy. Much more serious, in the competition of systems in the global Cold War, Korea was particularly exposed and South Korea compared unfavourably to the North. There, the introduction of a centrally planned economy and forced accumulation led initially to high growth rates, Also, politically, systemic competition was tough. Kim Il-sung, after successfully getting rid of rivalling factions, became an important representative of socialism in Asia, with good relations, too, with the USSR and the People's Republic of China. South Korea was dependent in political, military and economic matters on its main ally, the USA, but after the coup it drastically reduced aid, leading to severe current account problems.

In this situation the reform of economic policy had the highest priority. The introduction of an efficient and corruption-free economic administration was the precondition for the strategy of indicative planning chosen by the new president to develop the economy. Indicative planning, which in contrast to central planning does not force companies to comply with plans, but relies on developing broad government guidelines and targets for economic development, had been used with varying success in a number of countries, in particular developed countries, after the World War II, including France and the Netherlands. In Korea it became an outright success. The Economic Planning Board from 1961 to 1996 designed a series of seven five-year plans, and guided companies with selective incentives to realize these plans. In particular, politically guided credit allocation was important, since due to uncertainty about market and political conditions for most companies, medium- or long-term financing of projects without state support was impossible. Successful economic development was achieved with the help of three new policies.

The most important element was the change from a strategy of import substitution to a strategy of export orientation in foreign trade. This was officially done in only the second document of the first five-year plan of 1966. Besides infrastructure development and a few other industries, where import substitution remained in place as a goal, the government focused all efforts on direct export promotion. This included advantages for exporting companies in the tax system, subsidies, priority in credit allocation and foreign currency availability, as well as administrative support for export-oriented companies. Selective liberalization of trade meant that imports of raw materials, intermediate products and investment goods were free, while imports of consumption goods and for production for the domestic market were restricted. The former positive list of imports was changed to a negative list (all not explicitly restricted imports were allowed). Administrative support meant, for example, faster administrative procedures, but most of all less corruption. From 1963 to 1971 mainly industrial exports were supported, e.g. in textiles and consumer electronics and appliances. In the 1970s a period of support for heavy industry and chemical industry followed. The focus of the 1980s was rather macroeconomic stability, after the second oil price shock and domestic political turmoil (Park Chung-Hee was killed in 1979 and after another unsuccessful democratic interlude a new dictator, Chun Doo-Hwan, governed until 1987). In 1987, political democratization was accompanied by economic liberalization and the decline of the importance of indicative planning.

The second important element of the new policy was collaboration with the emerging conglomerates. Export orientation for the Korean industry meant to comply with quality and prices of the world market, an important advantage compared to import-substitution policies. At the same time it brought the problem that success on world markets could only be achieved through using economies of scale (i.e. lower average costs, when quantities of production are rising). The rise of competitive industries large enough to use economies of scale in the policy of import substitution theoretically should happen through protection of domestic markets. In the new policy of export orientation this was no longer possible. Therefore, the state began to promote the development of large conglomerates, some of which had already started in the Japanese period as small trading companies. These conglomerates, called chaebol and closely resembling their Japanese counterparts, the keiretsu, grew to become a trademark of South Korea's economic success, including such household names as Samsung, Hyundai or LG. Relations between government and chaebol were not free from tension; however, the government actively supported them, in particular in new overseas markets like the Middle East, when the building boom began in this region. At the same time, the government forced the chaebol in times of crisis (like during the oil price shocks) to soften the impact of economic shocks. If a company went bankrupt, healthy chaebol were forced to acquire and restructure it, thereby reducing social problems due to lay-offs in crisis times and having near-zero unemployment. This was an important element of social policy during the military dictatorship. At the same time, this policy led to a widespread attitude among chaebol owners that turnover growth is more important than profit growth, and to a form of unchecked, irrational acquisitions and diversification in often completely unrelated branches. Internal subsidies for unprofitable parts of conglomerates became widespread. Acquisitions were supported by politically allocated credit, and furthered by close collusion of banks and chaebol. Later, this was one of the structural reasons for the economic and financial crisis of 1997 and 1998.

The third new policy, besides the export orientation and collaboration and promotion of conglomerates, was the active development of new trade destinations and also the search for new donors. After the USA reduced military aid due to the coup by President Park, South Korea from 1963 sent more than 20,000 guest workers (miners and nurses) to West Germany, at that time in urgent need of workers, as a guarantee for German credits when normal credit sourcing on international capital markets was impossible. In 1965, even more important for the future development of Korea, relations with Japan were normalized. This was highly unpopular in the Korean population, but not only stabilized the government budget through cheap credit, but also allowed access to Japanese technology, which until today is a main ingredient in many of South Korea's most successful export goods.

The success of these new policies was extraordinary. The average growth rate of GDP from the 1960s to the 1990s was around 8% annually, the average per capita income in 1995 reached $10,000, starting in the 1950s with less than $200. Inflation and unemployment were low, and from 1977 there was even a lack of workers. Exports grew in the 1970s on average more than 45% annually. This also led to the growth of imports, fuelling a growing standard of living of the population and the rise of a large new middle class. The government budget was mostly in balance, which the World Bank in its famous 1993 report on the East Asian miracle sees as an important recipe for macroeconomic stability. Exports not only grew in quantity, but also changed from raw materials to industrial goods and, from the 1990s, high technology. In the mid-1990s South Korea was the world's fifth largest car manufacturer, the second largest ship builder, and a leading producer of semiconductors. These industries, using the low wages of largely uneducated workers, were substituted by capital-intensive production with highly specialized workers earning good wages, though the labour market remains divided between these exportoriented industries and a domestic industry relying mainly on low-paid workers. The success of the Korean export-oriented policies can be seen in its growth in US dollar value, from $0.04 billion in 1961 to $466.38 billion in 2010. By the mid-1980s South Korea was a world trading power. Intra-industrial trade played a growing role in its development, capital-intensive exports increased and

Korean brands (e.g. in electronics or the automotive industry) gradually became more important, while comparative cost advantages due to low wages decreased. While export growth was high, imports even grew faster until 1986, when Korea for the fast time had a trade surplus, which lasted until 1989, furthered by the Seoul Olympic Games of 1988. Then again, until the crisis year of 1997, imports grew faster, spurred by liberalization of formerly restricted imports for consumer goods. Additionally, easier access to capital markets, in particular short-term capital, at the time when the so-called East Asian economic miracle first gained international attention, was recklessly used by chaebol to finance further growth, leading to record debt levels of chaebol—another contributor to the crisis of 1997. For example, Kia Motors had a debt-to-equity level of 520% in 1997, and the 30 largest chaebol had an average level of 330%.

The cost of servicing these debts greatly reduced the profitability of many projects. According to estimates by the Hyundai Economic Research Institute in 1997, the 12 Korean companies ranking among the world's 500 largest had some of the lowest profitability indicators among the 500 companies. Chaebol had the biggest share in Korean economic growth, and the 30 largest ones produced approximately 80% of Korean GDP. In addition to low profitability, many chaebol diversified without following a coherent strategy. For example, the fur maker Jindo, which went bankrupt in 1998, had container, automotive parts, construction, waste management and retail subsidiaries. The five biggest chaebol in 1997 (Hyundai Group, Daewoo, Samsung Group, SK Corporation and LG Corporation) each had more than 100 subsidiaries, but only 10% to 20% of them were profitable. Internal cross-subsidization of a conglomerate's subsidiaries was the norm. This allowed also unprofitable business to stay in the market and reduced the allocative efficiency of the Korean economy. The lack of transparency in their business organization, caused by ties among families, financial institutions and areas of the media, led to allegations of 'crony capitalism'.

South Korea's admission to the OECD in 1996, after being a founding member of the World Trade Organization (WTO) a year earlier, was the visible expression of the success of the developmental model of Korea. Equally impressive was that economic success finally, after many decades of thinly disguised military dictatorship, brought peaceful democratization. However, the policy of high growth through the particular Korean model also was prone to crises. Neo-mercantilist policies focusing on exports and restricting imports led to the development of narrow oligopolies, collusive behaviour and inefficiency on domestic markets. When WTO and OECD membership brought pressure for the opening of markets, not least the capital markets, President Kim Young-Sam, the first civilian president elected by free elections since 1993, initiated a 'globalization' (segewha) programme to prepare to open up the markets, but failed to achieve this due to opposition from conglomerates, which had outgrown political pressure and at the same time had become 'too big to fail'.

When in 1997 the Korean economy was shaken by the downfall of the South-East Asian economies, the Kim Young-Sam government made some mistakes. The government tried to maintain the unrealistic exchange rate of the won against the dollar, thereby aggravating speculation in the currency, which led to its eventual fall. Eager to avoid bad press, the government did not correctly inform the public about the steady depletion of foreign exchange reserves. Consequently, the government's request for IMF assistance came as a shock and humiliation to many Koreans. A few months after he took over office, Kim Dae-Jung and his government developed a reform programme which was publicized by the Ministry of Finance and the Economy as 'DJnomics', named after the initials of President Kim Dae-Jung. Based on strict adherence to IMF conditions (which were relaxed several times due to Korea's worsening economic situation), the core of the reforms was the 'four plus one' policy. This policy involved the simultaneous reform of the labour market, the financial sector, the public sector and the private sector, together with the opening of Korea's markets to foreign competition.

The first project of 'four plus one' was the reform of the labour market, which was formerly characterized by strong antagonism between activist trade unions and powerful employers. In the late 1980s and early 1990s, following their legalization, trade unions frequently resorted to long and sometimes violent strikes to gain wage raises far above productivity levels. Negotiations between employers and trade unions lacked a legal framework and institutional routine. Under the reform programme, tripartite (government-business-labour) negotiations were institutionalized, which allowed for more consensus-oriented negotiations. While strike threats are frequent and the tripartite negotiations often break down in some sectors, labour negotiations after the crisis improved dramatically.

The second part of the reforms concerned the financial sector, which showed its weaknesses in the crisis when numerous banks and financial institutions went bankrupt. Banks, insurance companies and investment trust funds were all riddled with bad loans. As part of the IMF conditions, stakes in Seoul Bank and Korea First Bank were sold to foreign investors to guarantee a freer market and increased competition. However, negotiations with foreign investors were slow and problematic, since the foreign buyers wanted government guarantees on bad debts, while the government wanted to prevent the Korean public from having the impression it was selling off Korean assets cheap, as well as employment guarantees.

Ultimately, only massive state subsidies made the deals possible. Overall, results of financial reforms were mixed, with a considerable success of the Korean Asset Management Company (KAMCO) in buying and restructuring bad debt, but subsequent smaller crises in the investment trust and credit card business costing additional taxpayer money.

The third group of reforms was of the public sector, characterized by a strong bureaucracy in the Confucian tradition, which acted closely with the chaebol. While the meritocratic bureaucracy in Korea's history was held in high esteem, the problems of corruption and favouritism as a result of its dominant position were well known. The last two military rulers, Chun Doo-Hwan and Roh Tae-Woo, have been convicted of corruption involving several hundred million dollars. Also, after democratization corruption flourished, as shown by the 1997 bribes-for-loans scandal at Hanbo Iron & Steel Company, one of the events directly preceding the Korean financial crisis. The government has tried to resolve this problem from two angles. First, deregulation and privatization made corruption pay less: in private companies free from state involvement, only profits count. Second, an anticorruption commission was formed to erase corruption in office. This second part, however, has been inhibited by the frequent cases of corruption in the government itself, most visibly in the corruption cases surrounding practically every presidency, in particular the wider presidential families. Another aspect of public-sector reform was increased transparency and the reduction of red tape. Here again, reforms have been successful, reducing the number of business regulations by half and thereby reducing the necessity and scope for corruption.

The last reform was the reform of the private sector, especially of the debt-ridden, secretive chaebol and their system of maintaining unprofitable businesses by cross-subsidization. Here again, results of the reform were mixed. While cross-subsidies almost disappeared and debt-equity ratios have fallen due to the improved economic situation after 1999, many chaebol have only superficially reformed. For example, even after formal reorganization, the firms' strong old family ties did not disappear. Together with the four major reform programmes, the process of opening the market to foreign competitors began. In some sectors, state regulations that acted as obstacles to trade were abolished. In the tourism industry, for instance, foreign firms previously were not allowed to invest in the Seoul area, and in the alcohol trade, discriminatory taxes against foreign brands were eliminated. In other sectors, such as the wholesale and retail systems, the de facto oligopolistic Korean market structure made market opening necessary. FDI is the field where the reform policy has brought major successful changes. Lessons of Korea for emerging economies where the reform policy has brought major successful changes. For a long time, Korea had been hostile to foreign investment. While the Kim Young-Sam administration gradually lowered barriers to investment, the Kim Dae-Jung administration more boldly opened markets and aggressively wooed FDI. Not only did FDI mean an inflow of capital, it also involved injections of management expertise or technological capability. This was not only seen as instrumental in overcoming the currency and financial crisis, but also in furthering Korean efforts to restructure its ailing corporate and financial sectors. Already in 1999, Korea seemed to be back to the old growth path, with double-digit growth. However, subsequently growth became lower again and it became clear that the non-inflationary growth rate after the crisis was much lower than before. Given that decades of growth had considerably increased the economic basis, this does not seem surprising, and the ability of South Korea to steer through the latest world financial crisis without a recession has been very impressive.

Some 15 years after the onset of the Asian crisis, South Korea is a vibrant economy that has withstood the international financial crisis of 2008 to 2009 in a remarkable manner, exercising international leadership in the field of green growth and rising to the status of a large and respected middle power on an equal footing with Japan, for instance. Though economic debates and fears of the past still resound, as protests against the KORUS FTA in 2011 have shown, Korea underwent major change. It embraced institutional changes, it opened its markets further and overcame some of the old traumata haunting the former Japanese colony and divided nation, in particular the fear of losing its cultural identity by opening up. On the contrary, today Korean culture, in particular popular culture, has made great advances in South-East Asia, in China, in Japan and other parts of the world. South Korea has become a confident (and that does not always mean easier) middle power in world affairs, and a model for many countries searching for a recipe for development. Certainly, the South Korean developmental success cannot be emulated in a simplistic manner. The ingredients of its success were very specific and some of them may not work at all outside Korea. However, the Korean case is certainly a hope for all countries searching for a way to develop their economy, not least South Korea's own dismal brother in the North, that poverty can be overcome, though it is not an easy path and means sacrifices of hard-working generations, and that crises, perhaps unavoidable, can be used to get rid of institutional 'sclerosis' and free the economy to embark anew on a growth path.

Index

List of Authors

Ahrens, Joachim (Prof. Dr.) International Economics, Private University of Applied Sciences, Göttingen, Germany, (E-Mail: ahrens@pfh.de)

Hoen, Herman W. (Prof. Dr.) University of Groningen, Faculty of Arts, Oude Kijk in 't Jatstraat 26, 9712 EK Groningen, Netherlands (E-Mail: h.w.hoen@rug.nl)

Joamets, Jürgen University of Tartu, Faculty of Economics and Business Administration, Narva Rd 4, 51009 Tartu, Estonia

Kaldaru, Helje (Prof. Dr.) University of Tartu, Faculty of Economics and Business Administration, Narva Rd. 4, 51009 Tartu, Estonia (E-Mail: helje.kaldaru@ut.ee)

Kroos, Karmo (Lecturer, PhD) Estonian Business School, A. Lauteri 3, 10114 Tallinn, Estonia (E-Mail: karmo@tlu.ee)

Paltser, Ingra (research assistant) University of Tartu, Faculty of Economics and Business Administration, Narva mnt. 4, 51009 Tartu, Estland, (E-Mail: Ingra.Palster@ut.ee)

Park, Sung-Jo (Prof. em. Dr. Drs. h. c.), Free University Berlin, Bergengruenstr. 4, 14129 Berlin, Germany (E-Mail: oaspark@hotmail.com)

Reiljan, Janno (Prof. Dr.) University of Tartu Faculty of Economics and Business Administration, Narva mnt. 4, 51009 Tartu, Estland, (E-Mail: Janno.Reiljan@ut.ee)

Seliger, Bernhard (PD Dr. habil.) Hanns Seidel Foundation, Seoul Office, 501, Soo Young Bldg., 13 Hannamdaero 20-gil, Yongsan-Gu, Seoul, Republic of Korea (E-Mail: seliger@hss.or.kr)

Sepp, Jüri (Prof. Dr.) University of Tartu, Faculty of Economics and Business Administration, Narva mnt. 4, 51009 Tartu, Estonia (E-Mail: juri.sepp@ut.ee)

Stark, Manuel (Dr.) Research Fellow, Private University of Applied Sciences, Göttingen, Germany, (E-Mail: mail@manuelstark.com)

Terk, Erik (Prof. Dr.) Tallinn University, Institute of Political Science and Governance, Narva mnt 25, 10120 Tallinn, Estonia, (E-Mail: erik.terk@tlu.ee)

Varblane, Uku (Project manager – analyst) University of Tartu, Faculty of Economics and Business Administration, Narva mnt. 4, 51009 Tartu, Estland, (E-Mail: uku.varblane@ut.ee)

Wrobel, Ralph (Prof. Dr.) University of Applied Sciences Zwickau, Faculty of Business Administration and Economics, P.O. Box 2010 37, 08012 Zwickau, (E-Mail: ralph.wobel@fh-zwickau.de)